Craufurd Tait Ramage

Beautiful Thoughts from Latin Authors

Salzwasser

Craufurd Tait Ramage

Beautiful Thoughts from Latin Authors

1. Auflage | ISBN: 978-3-84605-020-0

Erscheinungsort: Frankfurt, Deutschland

Erscheinungsjahr: 2020

Salzwasser Verlag GmbH

Reprint of the original, first published in 1869.

BEAUTIFUL THOUGHTS

FROM

Latin Authors

BY

CRAUFURD TAIT RAMAGE, LL.D.

AUTHOR OF " BOOKS AND BY-WAYS OF ITALY," " BEAUTIFUL THOUGHTS
FROM GREEK AUTHORS," "BEAUTIFUL THOUGHTS FROM FRENCH
AND ITALIAN AUTHORS," " BEAUTIFUL THOUGHTS FROM
GERMAN AND SPANISH AUTHORS," ETC.

Second Edition

"Classical quotation is the parole of literary men all over the world."
—DR JOHNSON.

Liverpool
EDWARD HOWELL
1869

BEAUTIFUL THOUGHTS

FROM

LATIN AUTHORS.

TO

MORRIS CHARLES JONES, ESQ.

OF GUNGROG,

This Volume is Inscribed

AS A MARK OF ESTEEM AND AFFECTION

BY ONE

WHO KNOWS HIS VIRTUES

AND

VALUES HIS FRIENDSHIP.

PETRONIUS ARBITER

FLOURISHED A.D. 60.

CAIUS PETRONIUS, a celebrated voluptuary at the court of Nero, is called by Tacitus (Ann. xvi. 18. 19) *arbiter elegantiæ.* He passed his days in slumbers and his nights in revelry. He was consul A.D. 61, when he is said to have discharged his official duties with energy. He then relapsed to his former habits, and was admitted among the few chosen companions of the prince. Being suspected, however, of being implicated in the conspiracy of Scaevinus, he put himself to death by opening his veins in a warm bath A.D. 66. He is believed to be the author of what bears the title of *Petronii Arbitri Satyricon,* a prose narrative interspersed with numerous pieces of poetry, a kind of comic romance, in which the adventures of certain parties enable him to hold up to ridicule the folly and dishonesty of all classes of the community in the country in which the scene is laid. The coarseness and obscenity of the descriptions are a proof of the pollution of the age in which it was written.

LAUGHTER.

Satyr. c. 24.

Risu dissolvebat ilia sua.

He burst his sides with immoderate laughter.

NOT A MAN BUT A MERE SHADOW.

Satyr. c. 38.

Phantasia, non homo.

A mere phantom, not a man.

This is like what Shakespeare (" Macbeth," act iii. sc. 1) says :—
" *Mur.* We are men, my liege.
Mac. Ay, in the catalogue ye go for men."

A PHYSICIAN.

Satyr. c. 42.

Medicus nihil aliud est quam animi consolati-

A physician is nothing else than a satisfaction to the

NOT A MAN, BUT PEPPER ITSELF.

Satyr. c. 44.

Piper, non homo.

Pungent as pepper and not a human being.

HYPOCRISY WILL BE DETECTED.

Satyr. c. 80.

Vera redit facies, dissimulata perit.

Our natural countenance returns, the assumed one passes away.

POVERTY.

Satyr. c. 84.

Bonœ mentis soror est paupertas.

Poverty is closely allied to a sound mind.

Euripides (Fr. Polyid. 10) says:—

Πενία δὲ σοφίαν ἔλαχε διὰ τὸ δυστυχές.

" Poverty is wont to acquire wisdom through misfortune."

BEAUTY AND WISDOM.

Satyr. c. 94.

Raram facit misturam cum sapientiâ forma.

Beauty and wisdom are rarely conjoined.

Homer (Odyss. xvii. 454) expresses the same idea:—

οὐκ ἄρα σοί γ' ἐπὶ εἴδεϊ καὶ φρένες ἦσαν.

" Thou hast not wisdom with thy fair form."

ANGER.

Satyr. c. 99.

Incultis asperisque regionibus diutius nives hœrent : aat ubi ea aratro domefacto tellus nitet, dum loqueris, levis pruina dilabitur.   Similiter in pectoribus ira considit ; feras quidem mentes obsidet, eruditas prœlabitur.

In rugged and uncultivated countries the snow lies longer on the ground, but, when it has been subject to the plough, it speedily disappears ; whilst thou art speaking, the light hoar-frost vanishes ; in the same way anger affects our breast ; it fixes itself in the un-located, but in the minds that have been under cultivation it

Mind in Sleep.

Satyr. c. 104.

Quum prostrata sopore
Urget membra quies et mens sine pondere ludit.

When repose steals over the limbs, extended in sleep, and the mind disports without restraint.

Lost Opportunities.

Satyr. c. 128.

Animus, quod perdidit, optat,
Atque in præteritâ se totus imagine versat.

The mind longs for what it has lost, and is wholly intent upon the past.

Envy and Luxury.

Frag. p. 671.

Qui vultur jecur intimum pererrat,
Et pectus trahit intimasque fibras,
Non est quem lepidi vocant poetæ,
Sed corlis mala, livor atque luxus.

The vulture, which gnaws the liver and distracts the breast, is not that which the poets imagine, but the diseases of the heart, envy and luxurious habits.

All the World a Stage.

Frag. p. 673.

Fere totus mundus exercet histrionem.

Almost the whole world practises the art of the player.

So Shakespeare ("As You Like It," act ii. sc. 1) says :—

"All the world's a stage
And all the men and women merely players."

See (Fr.) God and Man.

Fear first made Gods.

Frag. p. 676.

Primus in orbe Deos fecit timor.

It was fear that first introduced gods into the world.

Blabbers of Secrets.

Frag. p. 679.

Nam citius flammas mortales ore tenebunt,

Quam secreta tegant. Quidquid dimittis in aulâ,
Effluit et subitis rumoribus oppida pulsat.

Men could more easily hold fire in their mouths than keep secrets.
Whatever you utter at court gets abroad, and excites the world
with sudden reports.

PHÆDRUS

FLOURISHED PROBABLY ABOUT A.D. 20.

PHÆDRUS is the writer of ninety-seven fables in Latin iambic verse,
divided into five books. Little of his personal history is known.
He was originally a slave, being brought up from Thrace or Mace-
donia, and from the title of his work we may infer that he belonged
to Augustus, who bestowed on him his freedom.

THE POWERFUL.
i. 5.

Nunquam est fidelis cum potente societas.

A partnership with men in power is never safe.

BRAINS.
i. 7.

O quanta species, inquit, cerebrum non habet !

Oh, what a rare head-piece if only it had brains !

ADVICE.
i. 9.

Sibi non cavere, et aliis consilium dare,
Stultum est.

Not to attend to our own affairs, but to be employed in giving
advice to our neighbours, is the act of a fool.

A CHEAT.
i. 10.

Quicunque turpi fraude semel innotuit,
Etiam si verum dicit, amittit fidem.

Whoever has once become notorious for deceit, even if he speaks
the truth, gains no belief.

A Braggart.

i. 11.

Virtutis expers verbis jactans gloriam,
Ignotos fallit, notis est derisui.

A coward, who brags of his courage, may deceive strangers, but is the laughing-stock of those who know him.

Repentance.

i. 13.

Qui se laudari gaudent verbis subdolis,
Serâ dant pœnas turpes pœnitentiâ.

He who takes pleasure in flattering words, generally pays for his folly by repentance though it be late.

The Poor.

i. 15.

In principatu commutando civium
Nil præter domini nomen mutant pauperes.

In a change of government, the poor seldom change anything except the name of their master.

Liars.

i. 17.

Solent mendaces lucro pœnas malefici.

Liars are wont to pay the penalty of their guilt.

Smooth Speeches.

i. 19.

Habent insidias hominis blanditiœ mali.

The fair speeches of the wicked are full of treachery.

An Ill-Judged Plan.

i. 20.

Stultum consilium non modo effectu caret,
Sed ad perniciem quoque mortales devocat.

An ill-judged plan is not only profitless but also leads men to destruction.

Lost Dignity.

i. 21.

Quicumque amisit dignitatem pristinam
Ignavis etiam jocus est in casu gravi.

Whoever has fallen from his former high estate is in his calamity the scorn even of the base.

Sudden Liberality.

i. 23.

Repente liberalis stultis gratus est,
Verum peritis irritos tendit dolos.

A man that is generous all at once, may dupe the fool, but it is in vain that he prepares snares for the wise.

The Poor Imitating the Great.

i. 24.

Inops, potentem dum vult imitari, perit.

The poor, when he tries to ape the powerful, comes to ruin.

To Give Bad Advice to the Wise.

i. 25.

Consilia qui dant prava cautis hominibus,
Et perdunt operam et deridentur turpiter.

Those who give bad advice to the prudent, both lose their pains and are laughed to scorn.

Punishment.

i. 26.

Sua quisque exempla debet æquo animo pati.

Every one ought to bear with patience the fruits of his own conduct.

The Exalted.

i. 28.

Quamvis sublimes debent humiles metuere,
Vindicta docili quia patet solertiæ.

Men, however exalted may be their sphere, ought to be on their guard against the lowly, for skill and address may enable them to take revenge.

Fools Raising a Laugh.

i. 29.

Plerumque stulti risum dum captant levem,
Gravi distringunt alios contumelia
Et sibi nocivum concitant periculum.

Fools often, while they try to raise a silly laugh, provoke by their insulting language and bring themselves into serious danger.

Subjects Suffer.
i. 30.

Humiles laborant, ubi potentes dissident.

Men of low degree suffer when the powerful disagree.

The Success of the Wicked.
ii. 3.

Successus improborum plures allicit.

The success of the wicked is a temptation to many.

Busy-bodies.
ii. 5.

Gratis anhelans, multa agendo nihil agens.

Idly bustling here and there, with much ado doing nothing.

Our own Affairs.
ii. 8.

Dominum videre plurimum in rebus suis.

The master (as the tale declares)
Looks sharpest to his own affairs.

Truth.
iii. 9.

Periculosum est credere, et non credere.
Ergo exploranda est veritas multum, prius
Quam stulta prave judicet sententia.

It is dangerous alike to give or withhold assent; therefore we ought to investigate strictly the truth rather than allow an erroneous impression to pervert our judgment.

What is Truly Disgraceful.
iii. 10.

Id demum est homini turpe, quod meruit pati.

That only is really disgraceful to a man which he has deserved to suffer.

Glory.
iii. 16.

Nisi utile est, quod facimus, stulta est gloria.

Unless what we do be useful, vain is our glory.

APPEARANCES.

Prolog. iv.

Non semper ea sunt quæ videntur, decipit
Frons prima multos.

Things are not always what they seem to be, first appearances deceive many.

THE MOTE IN OUR OWN EYE.

iv. 10.

Hâc re videre nostra mala non possumus ;
Alii simul delinquunt, censores sumus.

Hence we are not able to see our own faults : when others transgress, we are lynx-eyed to see theirs.

RICHES.

iv. 12.

Opes invisæ merito sunt forti viro,
Quia dives arca veram laudem intercipit.

Riches are deservedly despised by a man of honour, because a well-stored chest intercepts the truth.

GRIEVANCES.

Epilogue iv.

Palam mutire plebeio periculum est.

It is dangerous for a man of humble birth to grumble in public.

THE LEARNED MAN.

iv. 19. 1.

Homo doctus in se semper divitias habet.

The learned man has always riches within himself.

EACH MAN HAS PECULIARITIES.

Prolog. v.

Sua cuique quum sit animi cogitatio,
Colorque privus.

Since each has a turn of thinking of his own and a tone peculiar to himself.

RASHNESS.

v. 4.

Paucis temeritas est bono, multis malo.

Rashness brings luck to a few, misfortune to many.

PLAUTUS

BORN PROBABLY ABOUT B.C. 254—DIED B.C. 184.

T. MACCIUS PLAUTUS, the most celebrated comic poet of Rome, a native of Sarsina, was of humble origin, being employed at first as a workman in the service of the actors of the stage. In this way he accumulated a small sum of money, but, having lost it in trade, he was obliged to gain a livelihood by working a hand-mill, grinding corn for a baker. He commenced to write plays a few years before the breaking out of the Second Punic War, and continued his literary labours for about forty years. We possess only twenty comedies of Plautus, though in the time of Varro there were 130 plays which bore his name.

THE REASONABLE AND UNREASONABLE.
Amphit. Prolog. 36.

Nam injusta ab justis impetrare non decet :
Justa autem ab injustis petere, insipientia est.

From the reasonable to ask what is unreasonable is not right ; from the unreasonable to ask what is reasonable is mere madness.

MERIT.
Amphit. Prolog. 78.

Virtute ambire oportet, non favitoribus.
Sat habet favitorum semper, qui recte facit.

We should try to succeed by merit not by favour. He who acquits himself well will always have enough of patrons.

TIME STANDS STILL.
Amphit. i. 1. 116.

Credo ego hâc noctu Nocturnum obdormisse ebrium.
Nam neque se septemtriones quoquam in cœlo commovent,
Neque se luna quoquam mutat, atque, uti exorta est, est
    semel.
Nec jugula, neque vesperugo, neque vergiliæ occidunt.
Ita statim stant signa, neque nox quoquam concedit die.

I believe this night the god of Night has gone to bed drunk, for neither do the Seven Stars move in any direction in the sky, nor does the Moon change her position, but is where she rose ; nor does Orion, or the Evening Star, or the Pleiades set. So stock-still are the stars standing, and the night is yield ing to the day.

PLEASURES AND SORROWS OF LIFE.

Amphit. ii. 2. 1.

Satin', parva res est voluptatum in vitâ,
Atque in ætate agunda,
Præ quam quod molestum est, ita quoique comparatum
Est in ætate hominum,
Ita dîs placitum, voluptatem ut mœror comes consequatur;
Quin incommodi plus malique illico adsit, boni si obtigit
    quid.

Are not the pleasures of life and of our existence scanty in comparison with our troubles? Such is the lot of man. Thus it has pleased heaven that Sorrow should tread on the heels of Pleasure and be her companion: for if aught of good befall us, more of trouble and ill forthwith attends us.

Diphilus (Fr. Com. Gr. p. 1089, M.) says:

Οὐκ ἔστι βίος ὃς οὐχὶ κέκτηται κακά,
Λύπας, μερίμνας, ἁρπαγάς, στρέβλας, νόσους·
Τούτων ὁ θάνατος καθάπερ ἰατρὸς φανεὶς
Ἀπέλυσε τοὺς ἔχοντας ἀναπαύσας ὕπνῳ.

"There is no life that does not meet with some evil, grief, sorrows, plundering, torture, diseases: death appearing like a physician releases the afflicted from all these, causing them to cease by sleep."

VALOUR.

Amphit. ii. 2. 16.

            Virtus præmium est optimum,
Virtus omnibus rebus anteit profecto.
Libertas, salus, vita, res, parentes,
Patria, et prognati tutantur, servantur:
Virtus omnia in se habet, omnia adsunt bona quem penes
    est virtus.

Valour is the best reward; it is valour assuredly that surpasses all things else; our liberty, safety, life, estate, parents, country, too, and children are by this preserved and defended: valour comprises everything in itself; all blessings await the man who is possessed of valour.

WOMAN'S DOWRY.

Amphit. ii. 2. 209.

Non ego illam mihi dotem duco esse, quæ dos dicitur:
Sed pudicitiam et pudorem, et sedatum cupidinem,
Deûm metum, parentum amorem, et cognatûm concordiam:
Tibi morigera, atque ut munifica sim bonis, prosim probis.

I do not consider that to be my portion which is called so, but chastity and modesty, subdued desires, reverence of the gods, affection for my parents, and friendship with my kindred—that I should be obedient to you, bounteous to the good, and ever ready to assist the virtuous.

JEST.

Amphit. iii. 2. 39.

Si quid dictum est per jocum,
Non æquum est id te serio prævortier.

If anything is spoken in jest, it is not fair to turn it to earnest.

LIFE OF MAN.

Amphit. iii. 2. 57.

Nam in hominum ætate multa eveniunt hujusmodi,
Capiunt voluptates, capiunt rursum miserias.
Iræ interveniunt, redeunt rursum in gratiam.
Verum iræ si quæ forte eveniunt hujusmodi,
Inter eos rursum si reventum in gratiam est,
Bis tanto amici sunt inter se quam prius.

For in the life of men many things fall out in this wise—men take their fill of pleasure, then again of misery. Quarrels spring up, and again they are reconciled ; but when these kinds of quarrels arise between loving souls, if they are reconciled, they are doubly friends that they were before.

TRUSTING IS GOOD FOR NOUGHT.

Asin. i. 3. 45.

Diem, aquam, solem, lunam, noctem, hæc argento non emo :
Cætera quæque volumus uti, Græcâ mercamur fide.
Quum à pistore panem petimus, vinum ex oenopolio,
Si æs habent, dant mercem : eâdem nos disciplinâ utimur.
Semper oculatæ nostræ sunt manus, credunt quod vident.
Vetus est, nihili cocio est : scis cujus ? non dico amplius.

I do not purchase with money day-light, water, sun, nor moon, nor night ; what else we want, we buy for ready money. If we want bread from the bakers, wine from the vaults, if money be sent, they give the goods. We act in the same way. Our hands are always full of eyes ; they only credit what they see. It is an old saying, "Money down's the thing." Do you understand me? I'll say no more.

GAIN.

Asin. i. 3. 65.

Necesse est facere sumptum, qui quærit lucrum.

He who would seek for gain, must be at some expen

This is our proverb, " Nothing venture, nothing win." This expression is said to have been often in the mouth of Louis the Twelfth of France.

FORTITUDE.
Asin. ii. 2. 57.

Fortiter malum qui patitur, idem post patitur bonum.

He who endures misfortune with firmness, afterwards enjoys good fortune.

THE PET LAMB.
Asin. iii. 1. 60.

Etiam opilio, qui pascit, mater, alienas oves,
Aliquando habet peculiarem, qui spem soletur suam.

The shepherd,. mother, who tends another's sheep, has some few for himself that are his pets.

MODESTY.
Asin. v. 1. 8.

Adolescentem verecundum esse decet.

It well becomes a young man to be modest.

WOMAN.
Aulul. ii. 1. 5.

Nam multum loquaces merito omnes habemur,
Nec mutam profecto repertam ullam esse
Hodie dicunt mulierem ullo in seculo.

I know that we women are all justly accounted praters; they say in the present day that there never was in any age such a wonder to be found as a dumb woman.

Antiphanes (Fr. Com. Gr. p. 568, M.) says :—

Τί φῆς; λαθεῖν ζητῶν τι πρὸς γυναῖκ' ἆρα
'Ερεῖς τὸ πρᾶγμα ; καὶ τί τοῦτο διαφέρει
"Η πᾶσι τοῖς κήρυξιν ἐν ἀγορᾷ φράσαι ;

"What dost thou say? Seeking to conceal a matter, will you really tell it to a woman? Where, pray, is the difference between this and proclaiming it by all the heralds in the market-place?

DAGGERS.
Aulul. ii. 1. 30.

Lapides loqueris.

You speak daggers.

CONTENT.

Aulul. ii. 2. 10.

Si animus est æquus tibi, satis habes, qui bene vitam colas.

If you are but content, you have enough to live upon with comfort.

BREAD.

Aulul. ii. 2. 18.

Alterâ manu fert lapidem, panem ostentat alterâ.

And so he thinks to 'tice me like a dog,
By holding bread in one hand, and a stone,
Ready to knock my brains out, in the other.

KINDNESS TO A POOR MAN.

Aulul. ii. 2. 30.

Nemini credo, qui large blandus est dives pauperi.

I trust no rich man who is officiously kind to a poor one.

UNITE YOURSELF WITH THE VIRTUOUS.

Aulul. ii. 2. 60.

Quám ad probos propinquitate proxime te adjunxeris,
Tam optimum est.

The more closely you can unite yourself with the virtuous, so much the better.

A WOMAN WITH GOOD PRINCIPLES.

Aulul. ii. 2. 63.

Dummodo morata recte veniat, dotata est satis.

Provided a woman be well principled, she has dowry enough.

TO EQUIVOCATE.

Aulul. ii. 2. 81.

At scio, quo vos pacto soleatis perplexarier.
Pactum non pactum est; non pactum pactum est, quod
vobis lubet.

But I understand in what way you, rich people, equivocate; an agreement is no agreement, no agreement is an agreement, just as it suits you.

Feast To-day.
Aulul. ii. 8. 10.

Festo die si quid prodegeris,
Profesto egere liceat nisi peperceris

Feast to-day makes fast to-morrow.

Dress according to your Means.
Aulul. iii. 6. 5.

Pro re nitorem et gloriam pro copiâ
Qui habent, meminerint sese unde oriundi fient.

Those who have display proportioned to their means and splend-
our according to their circumstances, remember whence they are
sprung.

So Shakespeare ("Hamlet," act i. sc. 3) :—

"Costly thy habit as thy purse can buy,
But not express'd in fancy."

Balls.
Capt. Prolog. 22.

Di nos quasi pilas homines habent.

The gods hold us mortal creatures but as balls to band about in
sport.

Unintentional Good.
Capt. Prolog. 44.

Itidemque ut sœpe jam in multis locis
Plus insciens quis fecit quam prudens boni.

And so it happens oft
In many instances; more good is done
Without our knowledge, than by us intended.

Insignificance of Man.
Capt. Prolog. 52.

Homunculi quanti sunt, cum recogito !

When I reflect upon it, what creatures are we men ! how in-
significant !

Good.
Capt. i. 2. 39.

Tum denique homines nostra intelligimus bona,
Cum quæ in potestate habuimus, ea amisimus.

Then at length we come to know our good, when we have lost it.

Great Geniuses.

Capt. i. 2. 62.

Ut sæpe summa ingenia in occulto latent !

How greatest geniuses oft lie conceal'd !

Fortitude.

Capt. ii. 1. 8.

In re malâ animo si bono utare, adjuvat.

Our best support and succour in distress is fortitude of mind.

Stratagem.

Capt. ii. 1. 26.

Doli non doli sunt, nisi astu colas.

A stratagem is no stratagem, if it be not artfully planned.

Deceitfulness of Men.

Capt. ii. 1. 35.

Fere maxima pars morem hunc homines habent : quod sibi
  volunt,
Dum id impetrant, boni sunt : sed id ubi jam penes sese
  habent,
Ex bonis pessumi et fraudulentissimi
Sunt.

This is too oft the way with most men ;—while they are suing
for a favour, they are gracious ; but when once they have got it,
from gracious they become surly and ready to take every advan-
tage over you.

The Cautious are Often Tricked.

Capt. ii. 2. 5.

Qui cavet ne decipiatur, vix cavet, cum etiam cavet.

And the most cautious, even when he thinks
He 's most upon his guard, is often trick'd.

Fortune.

Capt. ii. 2. 54.

Fortuna humana fingit artatque ut lubet.

Fortune moulds and fashions human beings as she choose

GOD.

Capt. ii. 2. 63.

Est profecto Deus, qui, quæ nos gerimus, auditque et videt.

There is indeed a God, that hears and sees whate'er we do.

LOSS AT TIMES TO BE PREFERRED TO GAIN.

Capt. ii. 2. 75.

Non ego omnino lucrum omne esse utile homini existimo.
Scio ego, multos jam lucrum luculentos homines reddidit.
Est etiam, ubi profecto damnum prœstet facere, quam
lucrum.

I do not regard every kind of gain as serviceable to man. I
know that gain has raised many to high eminence. There are
times, however, when loss should be preferred to gain.

HIS OWN DEAR TO EVERY ONE.

Capt. ii. 3. 40.

Meus mihi, suus cuique est carus.

Mine to me is dear:
Dear is his own to every one.

THE POOR.

Capt. iii. 4. 51.

Est miserorum, ut malevolentes sint atque invideant bonis.

'Tis the nature of the poor to hate and envy men of property.

DEATH.

Capt. iii. 5. 24.

Dum ne ob malefacta peream, parvi æstimo.

Death I esteem a trifle, when not merited by evil actions.

VIRTUE.

Capt. iii. 5. 32.

Qui per Virtutem peritat, non interit.

He who dies for virtue's sake, does not perish.

SURE AS DEATH.

Capt. iii. 5. 74.

Non moriri certius est.

To die is not more certain.

DEATH.

Capt. iii. 5. 83.

Post mortem in morte nihil est, quod metuam mali :
Etsi pervivo usque ad summam ætatem, tamen
Breve spatium est perferundi, quæ minitas mihi.

There is no evil I need dread in death when death is over.
Though I were to survive to the utmost age of man, yet the space
of time to bear the hardships with which you threaten me, would
be short.

FATTED LAMB.

Capt. iv. 2. 82.

Atque agnum afferre propere pinguem.
And bid them bring forthwith a fatted lamb.

TOO LATE.

Capt. iv. 2. 90.

Abi, stultus, post tempus venia.
Go, fool, you come too late.

MAN REGARDLESS OF THOSE FROM WHOM NO FAVOUR IS TO BE RECEIVED.

Capt. v. 3. 8.

Mos est oblivisci hominibus,
Neque novisse, cujus nihili sit faciunda gratia.

It is the usual way with men not to remember or know the man
whose favour is worth nothing.

NO RUMOUR IS WITHOUT FOUNDATION.

Curcul. i. 1. 53.

Flamma fumo est proxima.
Flame follows very close on smoke.

The Spaniards say:—"Donde fuego se hace, humo sale." "Where fire
is made, smoke arises."

LABOUR ATTENDS EVERY PURSUIT.

Curcul. i. 1. 55.

Qui e nuce nucleum esse vult, frangat nucem.

LOVE.
Curcul. i. 3. 23.

Bonum est, pauxillum amare sane ; insane non bonum est.

It is good to love in a moderate degree ; to distraction, it is not good.

BLESSINGS.
Curcul. i. 3. 32.

Nulli est homini perpetuum bonum.

No blessing lasts for ever.

A REASONABLE LOVER.
Curcul. i. 3. 45.

Auro contra cedo modestum amatorem.

Find me a reasonable lover against his weight in gold.

THE PROVIDENT.
Curcul. iii. 1. 10.

Qui homo mature quæsivit pecuniam,
Nisi-eam mature parsit, mature esurit.

The man who has got rich speedily, must speedily be provident or speedily will starve.

Gueudeville, in his translation, says that this was a favourite maxim of Louis XII. of France.

ABUSE.
Curcul. iv. 2. 27.

Indignis si male dicitur, maledictum id esse dico :
Verum si dignis dicitur, benedictum'st, meo quidem animo.

If abuse be uttered against those who do not deserve it, that I consider to be abuse ; but if it be uttered against those who are deserving, it is fair censure, in my way of thinking, at least.

AN UNLUCKY DAY.
Menæch. v. 5. 1.

Edepol næ hic dies pervorsus et advorsus mihi obtigit.

Upon my word, this day certainly has turned out both perverse and adverse for me.

A MADMAN.
Menæch. v. 2. 90.

Hei mihi, insanire me ajunt, ultro cum ipsi insaniunt.

The world calls me mad, when they are all mad together.

DEATH.
Casin. ii. 1. 12.
Acheruntis pabulum.
Food for death.

A LOVER INSENSIBLE TO EVERYTHING BUT LOVE.
Casin. iv. 2. 16.
Qui amat, tamen hercle si esurit, nullum esurit.
He that is in love, faith, if he be hungry, is not hungry at all.

LOVE.
Cistell. i. 1. 71.
Amor et melle et felle est fœcundissimus :
Gustu dat dulce, amarum ad satietatem usque oggerit.
Love has both its gall and honey in abundance; it has sweet-
ness to the taste, but it presents bitterness also to satiety.

NO BLISS PERPETUAL.
Cistell. i. 3. 46.
Ut sunt humana, nihil est perpetuum datum.
Such is the state of all things human, that no bliss of man is
perpetual.

SAIL SHIFTED ACCORDING TO THE WIND.
Epid. i. 1. 50.
Utcunque in alto ventus est, exin velum vertitur.
Whichever way the wind blows at sea, in that direction the
sail is shifted.

WISDOM.
Epid. i. 1. 60.
Plus scire satius est, quam loqui.
'Tis better for one to know more than he utters.

A FRIEND IN NEED.
Epid. i. 2. 9.
Nihil agit, qui diffidentem verbis solatus suis.
Is est amicus, qui in re dubiâ te juvat, ubi re est opus.
The man, that comforts a desponding friend
With words alone, does nothing. He's a friend
Indeed, who proves himself a friend in need.

Useless to be Bounteous in Words.
Epid. i. 2. 14.

Quid te igitur retulit
Beneficum esse oratione, si ad rem auxilium emortuum est?

What does it signify your being bounteous in words, if all real aid be dead and gone?

I Have no Interest in the Matter.
Epid. ii. 2. 81.

Mihi istic nec seritur nec metitur.

There is neither sowing nor reaping for me in this matter.

A Good Lawyer.
Epid. ii. 2. 108.

Hic poterit cavere recte, jura qui et leges tenet.

He will be able to take all due precautions, who understands the laws and ordinances.

The Mind.
Epid. iii. 3. 1.

Non oris caussâ modo homines æquum fuit
Sibi habere speculum, ubi os contemplarent suum :
Sed qui perspicere possent cor Sapientiæ,
Igitur perspicere ut possint cordis copiam.

It were right that a man should hold up a mirror not only to his face, but to his mind; that he might see the very heart of his discretion, and judge its power and extent.

Old Men.
Epid. iii. 3. 11.

Profecto deliramus interdum senes.

But truth it is, we old folks sometimes dote.

A Friend in Need.
Epid. iii. 3. 43.

Nihil homini amico est opportuno amicius.

There is nothing more desirable to a man than a friend in need.

MENTAL AGONY.
Epid. iv. 1. 1.

Si quid est homini miseriarum, quod miserescat, miser ex
    animo est.
Id ego experior, cui multa in unum locum confluunt, quæ
    meum
Pectus pulsant simul : multiplex ærumna me exercitam
    habet : paupertas,
Pavor territat mentem animi.

If there be any misery for which a man ought to be pitied, it is
when the malady is in his mind. This I experience when many
shapes of ill assail me : many forms of sorrow, poverty, fear,
alarm my innocent mind.

SMELL.
Epid. iv. 2. 9.

Aliter catuli longe olent, aliter sues.

Puppies have one smell, pigs quite another.

TO REAP EVIL FOR GOOD.
Epid. v. 2. 53.

Ut acerbum est, pro bene factis cum mali messem metas.

How hard it is, when you reap a harvest of evil for good that
you have done.

COAXING IS MERE BIRD-LIME.
Bacchid. i. 1. 16.

Viscus merus vestra est blanditia.

Your coaxing is mere bird-lime.

MAN PROPOSES.
Bacchid. i. 2. 36.

Sperat quidem animus : quo eveniat, diis in manu est.

Man proposes, God disposes.

THE UNGRATEFUL.
Bacchid. iii. 2. 10.

Nam pol quidem, meo animo, ingrato homine nihil im-
    pensiu'st.
Malefactorem amitti satius, quam relinqui beneficum.
Nimio præstat, impendiosum te, quam ingratum dicier.
Illum laudabunt boni ; hoc etiam ipsi culpabunt mali.

For, by Pollux! nothing is, in my opinion, more base than an ungrateful man. It is better that a thief should escape, than that a generous friend should be forsaken. It is better to be extravagant, than to be called ungrateful. Good men will praise that, even bad men will condemn the latter.

MODESTY.
Bacchid. iii. 3. 80.

Nam ego illum periisse duco, cui quidem periit pudor.

For him I reckon lost, who's lost to shame.

Diphilus (Fr. Com. Gr. p. 1093, M.) says:—

Οὐκ ἔστ' ἀναιδοῦς ζῷον εὐθαρσέστερον.

"There is no creature more bold than the shameless."

FALSE FRIENDS.
Bacchid. iii. 6. 10.

Multi more isto atque exemplo vivunt, quos cum censeas
Esse amicos, reperiuntur falsi falsimoniis,
Linguâ factiosi, inertes operâ, sublestâ fide.
Nullus est, quoi non invideant rem secundam obtingere.
Sibi ne invideatur, ipsi ignavi recte cavent.

There are many of such life and manners, who, when you think them friends, are found most false, profuse in promises, sparing in deeds, of infirm faith. There are none of them who do not envy those whom fortune prospers: by their indolence they take good care to escape all envy.

A WORTHLESS MAN.
Bacchid. iii. 6. 29.

Nequam hominis ego parvipendo gratiam.

I set little value on the esteem of a worthless man.

DEATH IN YOUTH.
Bacchid. iv. 7. 18.

Quem di diligunt,
Adolescens moritur, dum valet, sentit, sapit.

He, whom the gods love, dies young, while he is in health, has his senses and his judgment sound.

Theognis (425) says:—

Πάντων μὲν μὴ φῦναι ἐπιχθονίοισιν ἄριστον
μηδ' ἐσιδεῖν αὐγὰς ὀξέος ἠελίου,
φύντα δ' ὅπως ὤκιστα πύλας 'Αΐδαο περῆσαι
καὶ κεῖσθαι πολλὴν γῆν ἐπαμησάμενον.

"It is indeed the best thing of all for mortals not to be born nor to see the rays of the bright sun : but if born to enter as speedily as possible the gates of Pluto, and to lie down with much earth heaped upon him."

TROUBLES.
Mostell. i. 1. 70.

Hoc scito nimio celerius
Venire quod molestum est, quam id quod cupide petas.

Know this, that troubles come on us swifter much than things we wish.

TRUTH.
Mostell. i. 3. 26.

Ego verum amo, verum volo mihi dîci : mendacem odi.

I love truth, and wish to have it always spoken to me : I hate a liar.

THINGS UNHOPED FOR.
Mostell. i. 3. 42.

Insperata accidunt magis sœpe quam quœ speres.

Things we hope not for oftener come to pass than things we wish for.

"TO WHITEN A BLACKAMOOR."
Mostell. i. 3. 102.

Unâ operâ ebur atramento candefacere postules.

It is the same as if you were to try to whiten ivory with ink.

This is applied to those whose design is good but marred in the execution.

WOMAN'S BEST SMELL.
Mostell. i. 3. 141.

Ecastor mulier recte olet, ubi nihil olet.
Nam istœ veteres, quœ se unguentis unctitant, interpoles,
Vetulœ, edentulœ, quœ vitia corporis fuco occulunt,
Ubi sese sudor cum unguentis consociavit, illico
Itidem olent quasi cum una multa jura confundit cocus.

A woman's best smell is to smell of nothing. For these your anointed hags, who still new vamp themselves, and hide their wrinkles with paint, when once the sweat and perfume mix, will stink worse than the greasy compound, when a cook pours all his broths together.

MISCONDUCT.
Mostell. i. 3. 155.

Pulchrum ornatum turpes mores pejus cœno collinunt.

Ill conduct soils the finest ornaments worse than dirt.

PROCRASTINATION IS BAD.
Mostell. ii. 1. 32.

Miserum est opus,
Igitur demum fodere puteum, ubi sitis fauces tenet.

It is a miserable thing to be digging a well at the moment when thirst has seized your throat.

STEADINESS.
Mostell. ii. 1. 64.

Plumâ haud interest, patronus, an cliens probior siet
Homini, cui nulla in pectore est audacia.

It does not matter a feather whether a man be supported by patron or client, if he himself wants steadiness and courage.

GUILTY CONSCIENCE.
Mostell. iii. 1. 13.

Nihil est miserius, quam animus hominis conscius.

Nothing so wretched as a guilty conscience.

A LIE.
Mostell. iii. 1. 134.

Hercle audivi esse optimum mendacium.
Quicquid Dei dicunt, id rectum est dicere.

By Hercules! I have often heard that your piping-hot lie is the best of lies : what the gods dictate, that is right.

MASTERS AND SERVANTS.
Mostell. iv. 1. 16.

Ut servi volunt esse herum, ita solet esse.
Bonis boni sunt : improbi, qui malus fuit.

As servants wish their master to be, such is he wont to be. Masters are good to the good, severe to him who is bad.

DANGEROUS TO GO TO LAW.
Mostell. v. 1. 52.

Nescis tu quam meticulosa res sit ire ad judicem.

You little know what a ticklish thing it is to go to law.

Advice from Sacred Temples.

Mostell. v. 1. 56.

Consilia firmiora sunt de divinis locia.

Counsels are of higher sanction when taken in sacred places.

Woman full of Wiles.

Mil. Glor. ii. 2. 34.

Domi habet animum falsiloquum, falsificum, falsijurium.
Domi dolos, domi delenifica facta, domi fallacias :
Nam mulier olitori nunquam supplicat, si qua est mala.
Domi habet hortum et condimenta ad omnes mores male-
    ficos.

She has a lying tongue, a wit that is ripe for mischief, an un-
daunted assurance ; she has at home within herself a mind fraught
with false words, false actions, and false oaths. For a woman, if
she is bent on ill, never goes begging to the gardener for material :
she has a garden at home and a stock of her own for all mis-
chievous contrivances.

Ignorance is sometimes Best.

Mil. Glor. ii. 6. 80.

Etiam illud quod scies nesciveris :
  Ne videris, quod videris.

Know not what you know, and see not what you see.

Good Counsel.

Mil. Glor. iii. 1. 5.

Nam bonum consilium surripitur sæpissime,
Si minus cum curâ aut cate locus loquendi lectus est :
Quippe si resciverint inimici consilium tuum,
Tuopte tibi consilio occludunt linguam, et constringunt
    manus :
Atque eadem, quæ illis voluisti facere, faciunt tibi.

For a well-divised plan is very often filched away, if the place
for speaking be not chosen with care and caution : for if the enemy
learn your plans, they can tie your tongue and bind your hands
with your own counsel, and do the same to you that you intended
to do to them.

Just and Good.

Mil. Glor. iii. 1. 17.

Facile est imperium in bonos.

The sway is easy o'er the just and good.

Green Old Age.
Mil. Glor. iii. 1. 38.

Si albus capillus hic videtur, neutiquam ingenio est senex.

What though his hair be gray, he is not old in mind.

He who Finds Fault with the Gods.
Mil. Glor. iii. 1. 38.

Qui deorum consilia culpet, stultus inscitusqqe sit.

He who would blame the designs of the gods, must be foolish and ignorant.

A Guest.
Mil. Glor. iii. 1. 146.

Hospes nullus tam in amici hospitium divorti potest,
Quin, ubi triduum continuum fuerit, jam odiosus siet.

No one can be such a welcome guest in the house of a friend, that he will not become a bore when he has stayed three continuous days.

Wisdom.
Mil. Glor. iii. 3. 12.

Nemo solus satis sapit.

Every man, however wise, requires the advice of some sagacious friend in the affairs of life.

Woman.
Mil. Glor. iii. 3. 14.

Si quid faciendum est mulieri male atque malitiose,
Ea sibi immortalis memoria est meminisse et sempiterna.
Sin bene quid aut fideliter faciendum est, eo deveniunt,
Obliviosae extemplo uti fiant, meminisse nequeunt.

If a woman has any malicious mischief to do, in that case her memory is immortal in remembering it for ever; if any good or honourable deed is to be done, it will fall out that those same women become oblivious that instant, and cannot remember.

To Drown his Voice by Talking.
Pseudol. i. 2. 74.

Sermone huic obsonas.

You drown his voice by your talking.

WHAT WE ARE ASHAMED OF.
Pseudol. i. 3. 47.

Nimio id quod pudet facilius fertur, quam illud quod piget.

We bear with more ease what we are ashamed of, than what we are vexed at.

COMPLAIN TO YOUR STEPMOTHER.
Pseudol. i. 3. 79.

Apud novercam querere.

Complain to your step-mother.
This is a hard hit at step-mothers.

LABOUR LOST.
Pseudol. i. 3. 135.

In pertusum ingerimus dicta dolium, operam ludimus.

All we say is just like pouring water into a sieve. Our labour is all in vain.

TALE-BEARERS.
Pseudol. i. 5. 12.

Homines qui gestant, quique auscultant crimina,
Si meo arbitratu liceat, omnes pendeant,
Gestores linguis, auditores auribus.

Your tittle-tattlers, and those who listen to slander, by my good will, should all be hanged—the former by their tongues, the latter by the ears.

COURAGE IN A DANGEROUS CRISIS.
Pseudol. i. 5. 37.

Bonus animus in malâ re, dimidium est mali.

Courage in danger is half of the crisis got over.

TO SEE THROUGH A CLOUD DARKLY.
Pseudol. i. 5. 45.

Sunt quæ te volumus percontari, quæ quasi
Per nebulam nosmet scimus atque audivimus.

There are some things respecting which we wish to question you, which we ourselves know and have heard imperfectly as through a cloud.

THE MOTE IN YOUR OWN EYE.
Pseudol. ii. 2. 18.

Non soles respicere te, cum dicas injuste alteri?

Do you never look back at yourself, when you abuse another person?

FORTUNE.
Pseudol. ii. 3. 12.

Centum doctûm hominum consilia sola hæc devincit dea
Fortuna: atque hoc verum est: proinde ut quisque eâ
    utitur,
Ita præcellet, atque exinde sapere eum omnes dicimus:
Bene ubi quod consilium discimus accidisse, hominem
    catum
Eum esse declaramus: stultum autem illum, cui vertit male.
Stulti haud scimus, frustra aut scimus, cum quid cupienter
    dari
Petimus nobis, quasi quid in rem sit, possimus noscere.
Certa amittimus, dum incerta petimus: atque hoc evenit·
In labore atque in dolore, ut mors obrepat interim.

It is the goddess Fortune alone that gets the better of a hundred wise heads; and there is truth in this, that according as each takes advantage of her, he advances in life, and hence we all declare that such an one is a man of sense: when we hear of a man being successful, that in our eyes is a proof of wisdom; when he fails, he is a fool. Fools that we are, when we pray the gods to grant us what we wish, we know not, or if we do, it is in vain, what will be to our advantage. We lose a certainty and grasp a shadow. What follows, but that in the midst of labours and sorrows, death creeps upon us in the interim.

WINE TRIPS US UP.
Pseudol. v. 1. 5.

Magnum hoc vitium vino est.
Pedes captat primum, luctator dolosu'st.

This is the great fault in wine: it first trips up the feet, it is a cunning wrestler.

WOMAN.
Pœnul. i. 2. 1.

Negotii sibi volet vim parare,
Navem, et mulierem, hæc duo comparato;
Nam nullæ magis res duæ plus negotii
Habent, eas forte si exornare occœperis,
Neque unquam satis hæ duæ res ornantur.

2 D

The man who wants to be fully employed should procure a woman and a ship; for no two things produce more trouble, if perchance you begin to rig them. These two things can never be rigged enough.

GOLDEN MEAN.
Pœnul. i. 2. 29.

Modus omnibus in rebus, soror, optimum est habitu.
Nimia omnia nimium exhibent negocium hominibus ex se.

In everything the golden mean is best: all things in excess are a plague.

A GOOD DISPOSITION.
Pœnul. i. 2. 90.

Bono ingenio me esse ornatam, quam auro multo mavolo.
Aurum fortunâ invenitur, naturâ ingenium bonum.
Bonam ego, quam beatam me esse nimio dici mavolo.

A good disposition I far prefer to gold; for gold is the gift of fortune; goodness of disposition is the gift of nature. I prefer much rather to be called good than fortunate.

GOOD WINE REQUIRES NO BUSH.
Pœnul. i. 2. 128.

Invendibili merci oportet ultro emptorem adducere,
Proba merx facile emptorem reperit, tametsi in abstruso sita est.

To unsaleable wares we must try to entice the buyer; good wares easily find a purchaser, although they be hid in a corner.

YOU ARE AS SLOW AS A SNAIL.
Pœnul. iii. 1. 29.

Vicistis cochleam tarditate.

You have surpassed a snail in slowness.

A GUIDE.
Pœnul. iii. 3. 14.

Viam qui nescit, quâ deveniat ad mare,
Eum oportet amnem quærere comitem sibi.

The man who does not know his way to the sea, should always take a river for his guide.

Rich Men.

Pœnul. iii. 6. 16.

Verum ita sunt isti nostri divites.
Si quid bene facias, levior plumâ est gratia ;
Si quid peccatum'st, plumbeas iras gerunt.

But such is the disposition of all those rich people of ours:
serve them, their thanks are lighter than a feather ; offend them,
their vengeance falls like lead.

Ill Got, ill Spent.

Pœnul. iv. 2. 22.

Male partum, male disperit.

For what is ill got is ill spent.

God.

Pœnul. v. 4. 14.

Juppiter! qui genus colis alisque hominum, per quem
    vivimus vitalem œvum,
Quem penes spes vitœ sunt hominum omnium, da diem
    hunc sospitem quœso.

Great Jove! who dost preserve and guard mankind, by whom
we live and breathe this vital air, on whom depends the hope of
human life, grant this day to be prosperous to my fortunes.

Disgrace added to Poverty.

Pers. iii. 1. 19.

Si ad paupertatem admigrant infamiœ
Gravior paupertas fit, fides sublestior.

If disgrace be added to poverty, poverty must be more unendur-
able, our character more frail.

Disgrace.

Pers. iii. 1. 27.

Hominum immortalis est infamia ;
Etiam tum vivit, cum esse credas mortuam.

Disgrace is immortal, and lives when one would think it dead.

Experience.

Pers. iv. 3.

Te de aliis, quam alios de te suaviu'st.

It is sweeter to gain wisdom from others' woes, than others
should learn from ours.

Register of Good and Evil Deeds.

Rud. Prolog. 9.

Qui est imperator Divûm atque hominum Juppiter,
Is nos per gentes alium alia disparat,
Hominum qui facta, mores, pietatem, et fidem
Noscamus, ut quemque adjuvet opulentia :
Qui falsas lites falsis testimoniis
Petunt, quique in jure abjurant pecuniam,
Eorum referimus nomina, exscripta ad Jovem :
Cotidie ille scit, quis hic quærat malum.

Jove, supreme sovereign of gods and men, scatters us among
nations to mark the people's actions, manners, piety, and faith,
that each may find reward according to his virtues ; those who
suborn false witnesses to gain a villanous suit in law, who shuffle
off due payments by false swearing, their names written down, we
return to Jove : each day he is informed of those that call for
vengeance.

Euripides (Fr. Melan. 12) says :—

α. Δοκεῖτε πηδᾶν τἀδικήματ' εἰς θεοὺς
    Πτεροῖσι, κἄπειτ' ἐν Διὸς δέλτου πτυχαῖς
    Γράφειν τιν' αὐτά, Ζῆνα δ' εἰσορῶντά νιν
    Θνητοῖς δικάζειν ; οὐδ' ὁ πᾶς ἂν οὐρανὸς
    Διὸς γράφοντος τὰς βροτῶν ἁμαρτίας
    Ἐξαρκέσειεν, οὐδ' ἐκεῖνος ἂν σκοπῶν
    Πέμπειν ἑκάστῳ ζημίαν ἀλλ' ἡ Δίκη
    Ἐνταῦθα πού 'στιν ἐγγὺς, εἰ βούλεσθ' ὁρᾶν.

β. Ταύτας μὲν ἀνθρώποισιν, ὦ γύναι, θεοὶ
    Τίσεις διδοῦσιν, οὓς ἂν ἐχθαίρωσ', ἐπεὶ
    Οὔ σφιν πονηρόν ἐστιν.

" A. Do you think that the wicked deeds of men fly on wings up to the
gods, there to be written down in the portfolio of Jove, and that Jove looks
at them assigning punishment for each ? Why, the whole of heaven would
not be able to contain the sins of mankind, so numerous are they, nor
would he be able to read and affix the penalty to each ; but vengeance
dwells very close to us, if we will only look. B. O woman, the gods inflict
punishment on those whom they hate, since wickedness is not agreeable to
them."

Wicked Men.

Rud. Prolog. 22.

Hoc scelesti illi in animum inducunt suum,
Jovem se placare posse donis, hostiis :
Et operam, et sumptum perdunt : id eo sit, quia
Nihil ei acceptum est à perjuris supplicii.
Facilius, si qui pius est à Diis supplicans,
Quam qui scelestus est, inveniet veniam sibi.

Wicked men fondly imagine that they can appease Jove with gifts and sacrifice, losing both their labour and their money : this is so, because no petition of the perjured is acceptable to him. The good will sooner find pardon from above, in praying to the gods, than he that is wicked.

OTHERS' MISFORTUNES.
Rud. i. 3. 1.

Nimio hominum fortunæ minus miseræ memorantur,
Quam reapse experiundo iis datur acerbum.

> The storied miseries of men's mishaps,
> (How sad soe'er relation sets them forth,)
> Are far less sharp than those we know and feel
> Ourselves from sore experience.

UNEXPECTED GOOD.
Rud. ii. 3. 69.

Nam multa præter spem, scio, multis bona evenisse,
At ego etiam qui speraverint, spem decepisse multos.

For I know good oft befalls us when we least expect it : and true it is, that when we trust in hope, we are often disappointed.

EQUANIMITY.
Rud. ii. 3. 74.

Animus æquus optimum est ærumnæ condimentum.

A well-balanced mind is the best remedy against affliction.

THE GODS MAKE SPORT OF MEN.
Rud. iii. 1. 7.

Miris modis dii ludos faciunt hominibus,
Mirisque exemplis somnia in somnis danunt.

In wondrous ways the gods make sport of men, and in wondrous fashions they send dreams in sleep.

WHEN A WOMAN'S GOOD DISPOSITIONS ARE DISCOVERED.
Stich. i. 2. 60.

Ubi facillime spectatur mulier, quæ ingenio est bono ?
Cum malefaciundi est potestas, quæ ne faciat, id temperat.

When is it best discerned a woman has good dispositions ?
When she, who has the power of doing ill, refrains from doing it.

THE BUSY-BODY.

Stich. i. 3. 55.

Nam curiosus nemo est, quin sit malevolus.

For the busy-body is ever ill-natured.

PRIDE.

Stich. ii. 1. 27.

Secundas fortunas decent superbiæ.

High airs befit prosperous fortune.

PROSPERITY.

Stich. iv. 1. 16.

Ut cuique homini res parata est, firmi amici sunt : si res labat,
Itidem amici collabascunt. Res amicos invenit.

According as men thrive, their friends are true; if their affairs go to wreck, their friends sink with them. Fortune finds friends.

EVIL MANNERS.

Trinum. i. 1. 8.

Mores mali,
Quasi herbâ irriguâ succrêrunt uberrime.

Evil manners, like well watered plants, have shot up in abundance.

EVIL KNOWN IS BEST.

Trinum. i. 2. 25.

Habeas ut nactus : nota mala res optima'st.

Keep what you've got : the evil that we know is best.

[Euripides (Fr. Antiop. 7) says :—

Φρονῶ δ' ἃ πάσχω· καὶ τόδ' οὐ σμικρὸν κακόν·
Τὸ μὴ εἰδέναι γὰρ ἡδονὴν ἔχει τινὰ
Νοσοῦντα· κέρδος δ' ἐν κακοῖς ἀγνωσία.

"I feel what I suffer, and that is no small evil : for not to feel that you are ill has some pleasure : ignorance of misfortunes has some advantage."

THE GOOD OUGHT TO KEEP SUSPICION FROM THEMSELVES.

Trinum. i. 2. 41.

Omnes bonos bonasque accurare addecet,
Suspicionem, et culpam, ut ab se segregent.

It becomes all good men and women to be on their guard, and keep even the suspicion of guilt away.

FRIENDS.

Trinum. i. 2. 54.

Sunt, quos scio esse amicos, sunt, quos suspicor :
Sunt quorum ingenia, atque animos, non possum noscere,
Ad amici partem, an ad inimici perveniant.
Sed tu ex amicis certis mihi es certissimus.

There are, I know, are friends ; there are, I think so ; there are,
whose dispositions and minds I cannot know, or whether to enrol
them among my friends or foes. But you I hold of all my fast
friends the most steadfast.

BUSY-BODIES.

Trinum. i. 3. 1.

Nihil est profecto stultius, neque stolidius,
Neque mendaciloquius, neque argutum magis,
Neque confidentiloquius, neque perjurius,
'Quam urbani assidui cives, quos scurras vocant.
Atque egomet me adeo cum illis una ibidem traho,
Qui illorum verbis falsis acceptor fui,
Qui omnia se simulant scire nec quicquam sciunt.
Quod quisque in animo habet aut habiturus est, sciunt.
Quod in aurem rex reginæ dixit id sciunt.
Quæ neque futura, neque facta sunt, tamen ii sciunt.

In truth there is nothing more foolish or more stupid, nothing
more lying, or indeed more tattling, more self-conceited, or more
forsworn, than those men of the city everlastingly gossiping about,
whom they call busy-bodies. And I too should rank with them, who
have been the swallower of the false tales of those who pretend
that they know everything, and yet know nothing. They know,
forsooth, your thoughts present and future. They know what the
king whispered in the ear of the queen : that which neither is,
nor is likely to be, do these fellows know.

LOVE.

Trinum. ii. 1. 27.

Amor amara dat tibi satis, quod ægre sit ; fugit forum,
    fugat tuos
Cognatos, fugat ipse se à suo contuitu ;
Neque enim cum sibi amicum volunt dici ; mille modis
    amor ignorandu'st,
Procul adhibendus est, atque abstinendus : nam qui in
    amorem
Præcipitavit, pejus perit, quam si saxo saliat ; apage sis
    amor.

Tuas res tibi habe. Amor, mihi amicus ne fuas unquam ;
    sunt tamen
Quos miseros maleque habeas, quos tibi obnoxios fecisti.
Certum'st ad frugem applicare animum : quanquam ibi
    animo
Labos grandis capitur. Boni sibi hæc expetunt, rem, fidem,
    honorem,
Gloriam, et gratiam ; hoc probis pretium'st : eo mihi magis
    lubet
Cum probis potius, quam cum improbis vivere vanidicis.

Love gives bitters enough to create disgust : love shuns the
bustle of the bar, drives off relations, and drives himself away
from his own contemplation. There is no man who would woo
him as his friend : in a thousand ways is love to be held a stranger,
to be kept at a distance, and wholly abstained from. For he,
who plunges into love, perishes more dreadfully than if he leapt
from a rock. Love, get thou gone, then : I divorce thee from me,
and utterly repudiate thee. Love, never be thou friend of mine.
Go, torture those that are bound to thee. I am determined hence-
forth to apply my mind to my advancement in life, though in that
the toil be great. Good men wish these things for themselves,
gain, credit, honour, glory, and esteem : these are the rewards of
the upright. It is my choice, then, to herd with the upright
rather than with the deceitful spreader of lies.

Shakespeare has a somewhat similar passage in " Romeo and Juliet " (act
i. sc. 1) :—

    " But all so soon as the all-cheering sun
    Should in the farther East begin to draw
    The shady curtains from Aurora's bed,
    Away from light steals home my heavy son,
    And private in his chamber pens himself ;
    Shuts up his windows, locks fair daylight out,
    And makes himself an artificial night."

BAD AND ENVIOUS MEN.
Trinum. ii. 2. 6.

Novi ego hoc seculum moribus quibus sit : malus bonum
    malum
Esse volt, ut sit sui similis : turbant, miscent mores mali ;
    rapax,
Avarus, invidus, sacrum profanum, publicum privatum
    habent.

I know what the manners of this age are. The bad would fain
corrupt the good and make them like themselves : our evil man-
ners confound, disorder everything. The greedy, the envious,
turn what is sacred to profane, the public good to private
interest.

PASSIONS.
Trinum. ii. 2. 29.

Tu si animum vicisti, potius quam animus te, est quod
gaudeas.

If you have vanquished your inclination and not been van-
quished by it, you have reason to rejoice.

THE UPRIGHT.
Trinum. ii. 2. 39.

Is probus est, quem non pœnitet, quam probus sit, et frugi
bonæ,
Qui ipsus sibi satis placet, nec probus est, nec frugi bonæ.
Qui ipsus se contemnit, in eo est indoles industriæ.

He is upright who does not repent that he is upright : he who
seeks only self-gratification is not the upright man, nor is he
really honest : the man who thinks but meanly of himself, shows
that there is a just and honest nature in him.

WHAT IS YOURS IS MINE.
Trinum. ii. 2. 47.

Quod tuum'st, meum'st : omne meum est autem tuum.

For what is yours is mine, and mine is yours.

BE NOT OVER-GENEROUS.
Trinum. ii. 2. 61.

Præmonstro tibi
Ut ita te aliorum miserescat, ne tui alios misereat.

I warn you before hand, that you have compassion on others in
such a way that others may not have cause to have compassion on
you.

THE WISE MAN.
Trinum. ii. 2. 82.

Sapiens quidem pol ipse fingit fortunam sibi.
Eo ne multa, quæ nevolt, eveniunt, nisi fictor malu'st.

A wise man, in truth, is the maker of his own fortune, and,
unless he be a bungling workman, little can befall him which he
would wish to change.

Euripides (Fr. Incert. 72) says :—

Μισῶ σοφιστὴν ὅστις οὐχ αὑτῷ σοφός·

" I hate the wise man who is not wise for himself."

EAT ONE'S CAKE AND HAVE IT.
Trinum. ii. 4. 12.

Non tibi illud apparere, si sumas, potest,
Nisi tu immortale rere esse argentum tibi.
Sero atque stulte, prius quod cautum oportuit,
Postquam comedit rem, post rationem putat.

You cannot eat your cake and have it too, unless you think
your money is immortal. Too late and unwisely—a caution that
should have been used before—after he has eaten up his sub-
stance, he reckons the cost.

BEST WISHES.
Trinum. ii. 4. 38.

Nequam illud verbum'st, Bene vult, nisi qui benefacit.

Best wishes! What avails that phrase, unless
Best services attend them.

NO ONE OUGHT TO BE BASHFUL AT TABLE.
Trinum. ii. 4. 77.

Verecundari neminem apud mensam decet.

At table no one should be bashful.

WILD OATS.
Trinum. ii. 4. 128.

Post id, frumenti quum alibi messis maxima'st,
Tribus tantis illi minus reddit, quam obseveris.
Hem! istic oportet obseri mores malos,
Si in obserendo possint interficeri.

Besides that, when elsewhere the harvest of wheat is most
abundant, there it comes up less by one-fourth than what you
have sowed. There methinks it were a proper place for men to
sow their wild oats where they would not spring up.

LOVE.
Trinum. iii. 2. 42.

Ita est amor, balista ut jacitur : nihil sic celer est, neque
    volat.
Atque is mores hominum moros et morosos efficit.
Minus placet, magis quod suadetur : quod dissuadetur
    placet.
Cum inopia'st, cupias : quando ejus copia'st, tum non velis.

Ille qui aspellit, is compellit : ille qui consuadet, vetat.
Insanum est malum in hospitium devorti ad Cupidinem.

It is with love as with a stone whirled from a balista ; nothing
is so swift or that flies so directly : it makes the manners of men
both foolish and froward. What you would persuade him to, he
likes not, and embraces that from which you would dissuade him.
What there is lack of, that will he covet ; when it is in his power,
he will have none of it. Whoso bids him to avoid a thing, invites
him to it ; he interdicts, who recommends it. It is the height of
madness ever to take up your abode with love.

RELATIONS.
Trinum. iii. 2. 58.

Numquam erit alienis gravis, qui suis se concinnat levem.

Never will he be respected by others who makes himself despised
by his own relatives.

THE POOR.
Trinum. iv. 1. 11.

Hoc diis dignum'st, semper mendicis modesti sint.

'Tis worthy of the gods to have respect
Unto the poor.

ABSENT FRIEND.
Trinum. iv. 2. 81.

Ne male loquare absenti amico.

You should not speak ill of an absent friend.

THE BELL.
Trinum. iv. 2. 162.

Nunquam ædepol temere tinnit tintiunabulum :
Nisi quis illud tractat, aut movet, mutum est, tacet.

The bell doth never clink of itself: unless it is handled and
moved, it is dumb.

LENDERS.
Trinum. iv. 3. 43.

Si quis mutuum quid dederit, sit pro proprio perditum.
Cum repetas, inimicum amicum beneficio invenis tuo.
Si mage exigere cupias, duarum rerum exoritur optio :
Vel illud, quod credideris, perdas, vel illum amicum ami-
scris.

What you lend is lost ; when you ask for it back, you may find
a friend made an enemy by your kindness. If you begin to press

him further, you have the choice of two things—either to lose your loan or lose your friend.

Axienious (Fr. Com. Gr. p. 772, M.) says :—

> Ὅταν δανείσῃ τις πονηρῷ χρήματα
> Ἀνὴρ δικαίως τὸν τόκον λύπας ἔχει.

" When a good man lends money to the wicked, he receives grief for interest."

Coat nearer than Cloak.

Trinum. v. 2. 30.

Tunica propior pallio est.

My coat,
Dear sir, is nearer to me than my cloak.

Mote in our own Eye.

Trucul. i. 2. 58.

Quia, qui alterum incusat probri, eum ipsum se intueri
   oportet.

Because those, who twit others with their faults, should look at home.

The Heart.

Trucul. i. 2. 76.

In melle sunt linguæ sitæ vostræ, atque orationes,
Lacteque ; corda felle sunt lita, atque acerbo aceto.
Linguis dicta dulcia datis.

Your tongues and talk are steeped in honey and milk ; your hearts are steeped in gall and sour vinegar.   You give us sugared words.

Woman.

Trucul. ii. 5. 12.

Male quod mulier facere incepit, nisi id efficere perpetrat,
Id illi morbo, id illi senio est, et illi miseræ miseria'st.
Si bene facere incepit, ejus eam cito odium percipit.
Nimis quam paucæ sunt defessæ, male quæ facere occœ-
   perunt :
Nimis quam paucæ efficiunt, si quid occœperint bene facere.
Mulieri nimio male facere melius est onus, quam bene.

Whenever a woman once begins a fraud, unless she perfects it, she will find pain and grief and misery. If she begins to do what is right, how soon will she be weary. How few are tired with acting wrong ; how very few carry it out, if they have commenced to do anything aright. A woman finds it a much easier task to do an evil than a virtuous deed.

Seeing is Believing.
Trucul. ii. 6. 8.

Pluris est oculatus testis unus, quam auriti decem,
Qui audiunt, audita dicunt : qui vident, plane sciunt.

One eye-witness weighs more than ten hear-says. Those who hear, speak of what they have heard ; those who see, know beyond mistake.

Valour.
Trucul. ii. 6. 12.

Strenui nimio plus prosunt populo quam arguti, et cati.
Facile sibi facunditatem virtus argutam invenit.

The valiant profit more their country than the finest, cleverest speakers. Valour once known will soon find eloquence to trumpet forth her praise.

Eloquence without Valour.
Trucul. ii. 6. 14.

Sine virtute argutum civem mihi habeam pro præfica,
Quæ alios collaudare eapse se vero non potest.

Without valour an eloquent citizen is like a hired mourner, who praises other people for that which she cannot do herself.

Envy.
Trucul. iv. 2. 31.

Invidere alii bene esse, tibi male esse, miseria est.
Qui invident, egent : illi quibus invidetur, rem habent.

For to envy because it goes well with another and goes badly with yourself, is misery. Those who envy, pine in poverty ; they who are envied, abound in wealth.

To Kick against the Pricks.
Trucul. iv. 2. 54.

Si stimulos pugnis cædis, manibus plus dolet.
De nihilo illi est irasci, quæ te non flocci facit.

If you thump a goad with your fist, your hands are hurt the most. To vent your rage against her, who does not care a straw, is folly.

The Weakest goes to the Wall.
Trucul. iv. 3. 30.

Plus potest, qui plus valet.

Why, the weakest always goes to the wall.

THE MOUSE.

Trucul. iv. 4. 15.

Cogitato, mus pusillus quam sit sapiens bestia,
Ætatem qui uni cubili nunquam committit suam:
Quia si unum ostium obsideatur, aliud perfugium gerit.

Consider the little mouse, how wise a creature it is, which never
intrusts its life to one hole only; for when it finds one entrance
blocked up, it has some other outlet.

NO GOOD UNMIXED.

Merc. i. 2. 34.

Dic mihi, an boni quid usquam est, quod quisquam uti
    possiet
Sine malo omni, aut ne laborem capias, cum illo uti voles?

Tell me, was ever good without some little ill? or where you
must not endure labour when you wish to enjoy it?

OLD AGE IS SECOND CHILDHOOD.

Merc. ii. 2. 24.

Senex cum extemplo est, jam nec sentit, nec sapit;
Ajunt solere eum rursum repuerascere.

When a man reaches the last stage of life,—"Sans sense, sans
taste, sans eyes, sans everything,"—they say that he has grown a
child again.

EVERYTHING AWRY.

Merc. ii. 3. 1.

Homo me miserior nullus est æque, opinor,
Neque adversa cui sint plura sempiterna.
Satin' quicquid est, ut, quam rem agere occœpi,
Proprium nequit mihi cvenire quod cupio?
Ita mihi mala res objicitur aliqua,
Bonum quæ meum comprimit consilium.

Never, I verily believe, was man so miserable as myself, nor one
who had more everlasting crosses. Is it not the fact, that what-
ever thing I have commenced falls not out as I desire? Some evil
fortune comes across me still, destroying my best laid plans.

TO BEAT ABOUT THE BUSH.

Merc. iii. 4. 23.

Odiosa est oratio, cum rem agas, longinquum loqui.

It is a tiresome way of speaking, when you should despatch the
business, to beat about the bush.

A Deformed Man.

Merc. iii. 4. 53.

Canum, varum, ventriosum, bucculentum, breviculum,
Subnigris oculis, oblongis malis, pansam aliquantulum.

 ust this : bald-pated, bandy-legged, pot-bellied,
Wide-mouth'd, short, blear-eyed, lanthorn-jaw'd, splay-footed.

Bad Neighbours.

Merc. iv. 4. 33.

Aliquid mali esse propter vicinum malum.

A bad neighbour brings bad fortune with him.

Learn Experience from Others.

Merc. iv. 7. 40.

Feliciter sapit, qui alieno periculo sapit.

He gets wisdom in a fortunate way, who gets wisdom at another's
 ponse.

This is the Scotch proverb :—" Better learn frae your neebor's scathe than
 e your ain." This passage is from the interpolated scene in the
 Mercator," supposed to have been written by Hermolaüs Barbarus.

Opposite Paths.

Merc. v. 2. 32.

 i hunc item properes, ut istuc properas, facias rectius.
 uc secundus ventus nunc est, cape modo vorsoriam.
 [ic Favonius serenus est, istic auster imbricus :
 [ic facit tranquillitatem, iste omnes fluctûs conciet.
 espice huc ad dextram, Charine, nonne ex adverso vides ?
 Tubes atra, imberque instat ; aspice nunc ad sinisteram,
 œlum ut splendore est plenum, ex adverso vides.

If you would hasten in this direction, as you are hastening in
 hat, you would be wiser ; this way the wind is prosperous, only
 ok about. Here is a fair western breeze, and there the south
 eavy with rain. This spreads a peaceful calm, the other stirs up
 ll the waves. Make towards the land, Charinus ! Don't you see
 ight opposite ? Black clouds and showers are coming on. Look
 ow to the left, how full the heaven is of brightness. Don't you
 se right opposite ?

No Tricks on Travellers.

Merc. v. 2. 90.

Erras, me decipere haud potes.

No, no ; no tricks on travellers.

MEN OF RANK.
Merc. v. 4. 8.

Qui bono sunt genere nati, si sunt ingenio malo,
Suopte culpam genere capiunt : genus ingenio improbant.

Whene'er men of rank are ill disposed, their evil disposition stains that rank.

PLINIUS MAJOR

BORN A.D. 23—DIED A.D. 79.

CAIUS PLINIUS SECUNDUS was born at Comum, or, as others think, at Verona, A.D. 23. After being educated at Rome, he went to Germany A.D. 46, where he served under L. Pomponius Secundus, being appointed to the command of a troop of cavalry. Towards the end of the reign of Nero he was procurator in Spain, where he was A.D. 71, when his brother-in-law died, leaving his son, the younger Pliny, to his guardianship. He returned to Rome in the reign of Vespasian A.D. 72, when he adopted his nephew. He became the friend of the emperor, and was appointed admiral of the fleet. The circumstances of his death are graphically described in a letter of the younger Pliny to Tacitus, (Ep. vi. 16.) He was overwhelmed and suffocated by the sulphureous exhalations from the eruption of Vesuvius A.D. 79, whither he had gone to examine the extraordinary phenomenon.

TO ASSIST MAN IS TO BE A GOD.
H. N. ii. 5. 4.

Deus est mortali juvare mortalem et hæc ad æternam gloriam via.

For man to assist man, is to be a god; this is the path to eternal glory.

Hence the proverb :—" Homo homini Deus."

WHAT GODS CANNOT DO ACCORDING TO THE IDEA OF THE ANCIENTS.
H. N. ii. 5. 10.

Imperfectæ vero in homine naturæ præcipua solatia, ne Deum quidem posse omnia. Namque nec sibi potest mor-

tem consciscere, si velit, quod homini dedit optimum in
tantis vitæ pœnis : nec mortales æternitate donare, aut
revocare defunctos : nec facere, ut qui vixit, non vixerit ;
qui honores gessit, non gesserit : nullunque habere in
præterita jus, præterquam oblivionis.

One of the chief comforts to man for the imperfection of his
nature is, that God cannot do all things. For He cannot give
death to Himself, even if He wished, the best thing He has be-
stowed upon man amidst the many calamities of life ; nor yet can
He give immortality to man, or recal them to life ; nor bring it
about that he who has lived, should not have lived, or he who has
borne honours, should not have borne them ; nor has He any
power over the past except that of oblivion.

GOOD FOR MAN THAT THERE IS A BELIEF IN GOD.
H. N. ii. 5. 10.

Deos agere curam rerum humanarum credi, ex usu vitæ
est : pœnasque maleficiis, aliquando seras, nunquam autem
irritas esse.

It is advantageous that the gods should be believed to attend to
the affairs of man, and the punishment for evil deeds, though some-
times late, is never fruitless.

NATURE A PARENT OR STEPMOTHER TO MAN.
H. N. vii. 1. 1.

Non sit ut satis æstimare, parens melior homini an
tristior noverca fuerit.

So that it is not possible to determine whether (Nature) is a
kind parent or harsh stepmother to man.

MAN PRONE TO TEARS.
H. N. vii. 1. 2.

Nullum tot animalium aliud ad lacrymas (pronius.)

No other of so many animals is more prone to tears.

A Greek proverb quoted by Eustathius (Il. i. 349) says :—

ἀγαθοὶ δ'ἀριδάκρυες ἀνδρες·

"The good are prone to tears."

Shakespeare ("Much Ado About Nothing," act i. sc. 1) says :—

"*Leonato.* Did he break out into tears ?

Messenger. In great measure.

Leonato. A kind overflow of kindness: there are no faces truer than
those that are so washed."

2 E

Man is the only Animal that Fights with his Like.
H. N. vii. 1. 6.

Cætera animantia in suo genere probè degunt ; congregari videmus, et stare contra dissimilia : Leonum feritas inter se non dimicat : serpentum morsus non petit serpentes ; ne maris quidem bellum nisi in diversa genera sæviunt. At Hercule, homini plurima ex homini sunt mala.

Other animals live affectionately with their like ; we see them crowd together and stand against those that are dissimilar ; fierce lions do not fight with each other ; serpents do not attack serpents, nor do the wild monsters of the deep rage against their like. But, by Hercules, very many calamities arise to man from his fellow-man.

Boileau (Sat. viii. 125) says :—

> " Voit-on les loups brigands comme nous inhumains,
> Pour détrousser les loups courir les grands chemins ?
> Jamais pour s'agrandir vit on en sa manie
> Un tigre en factions partager l'Hyrcanie ?
> L'ours a-t-il dans les bois la guerre avec les ours ?
> Le vautour dans les airs fond-il sur les vautours ?
>
> L'animal le plus fier qu'enfante la nature
> Dans un autre animal respecte sa figure."

The Mighty Power of Nature.
H. N. vii. 1. 7.

Naturæ vero rerum vis atque majestas in omnibus momentis fide caret, si quis modo partes ejus, ac non totam complectatur animo.

The power and majesty of the nature of things fail to receive credit at all times, if one merely looks at its parts and do not embrace the vast whole in our conceptions.

No One is Wise at All Times.
H. N. vii. 41. 2.

Nemo mortalium omnibus horis sapit.

No one is wise at all times.

Blessings of Life not Equal to its Ills.
H. N. vii. 41. 3.

Bona malis paria non sunt, etiam pari numero : nec lætitia ulla minimo mœrore pensanda.

The blessings of life are not equal to its ills, though the number of the two may be equal ; nor can any pleasure compensate for the least pain.

NOTHING BETTER THAN A SHORT LIFE.
H. N. vii. 51. 3.

Natura vero nihil hominibus brevitate vitæ præstitit melius.

Nature has given to man nothing of more value than shortness of life.

AN OLD HEAD ON YOUNG SHOULDERS.
H. N. vii. 52. 2.

Senilem juventam prematuræ mortis esse signum.

That an old head on young shoulders was the sign of premature death.

We find the same idea in Seneca (Cont. lib. ii. 1) when speaking of Alfius Flavus :—

" Tam mature magnum ingenium non esse vitale :" and Apuleius quotes a passage from some poet, " Odi puerulos præcoci sapientiâ."

MAN IS NOT IMMORTAL.
H. N. vii. 56. 1.

Omnibus a supremâ die eadem, quæ ante primum : nec magis a morte sensus ullus aut corpori aut animæ quam ante natalem.

His last day places man in the same state as he was before he was born : nor after death has the body or soul any more feeling than they had before birth.

See (Gr.) The soul.

THE BRAIN.
H. N. xi. 49. 2.

Habet cerebrum sensus arcem : hic mentis est regimen.

Men have the brains as a kind of citadel of the senses : here is what guides the thinking principle.

MAN DESIROUS OF NOVELTY.
H. N. xii. 5. 3.

Est natura hominum novitatis avida.

Man is by nature fond of novelty.

CHANCE IS A SECOND MASTER.
H. N. xvii. 24. 1.

Casus magister alius.

Chance is a second master.

A MASTER'S EYE.
H. N. xviii. 8. 4.

Majores fertilissimum in agro oculum domini esse dixerunt.

Our ancestors used to say that the eye of the master was the best manure for the field.

See (Gr.) Master, the eye of the house.

WISDOM OVERSHADOWED BY WINE.
H. N. xxiii. 23. 1.

In proverbium cessit, sapientiam vino obumbrari.

It has passed into a proverb, that wisdom is overshadowed by wine.

PLINIUS MINOR
BORN A.D. 61.

C. PLINIUS CÆCILIUS SECUNDUS was the son of C. Cæcilius and Plinia, the sister of C. Plinius, the author of the "Natural History." He was born at Comum on Lake Larius, and was educated at Rome under the care of his uncle, who adopted him after the death of his father. He filled many offices in succession, was quæstor A.D. 93, and consul A.D. 100. During the reign of Trajan he was proconsul of Asia, and it was then that he consulted the emperor respecting the punishment of the Christians. It is found in the tenth book (Ep. 97), with the emperor's answer, (Ep. 98.) Nothing is known as to the time of his death.

LITERARY STUDIES.
Ep. i. 3.

Ipse te in alto isto pinguique secessu studiis adseris? Hoc sit negotium tuum, hoc otium ; hic labor, hæc quies : in his vigiliis, in his etiam somnus reponatur. Effinge aliquid et excude, quod sit perpetuo tuum : nam reliqua

rerum tuarum post te alium atque alium dominum sortien-
tur ; hoc numquam desinet esse, si semel cœperit, tuum.

Are you enjoying the pleasures of literary study in that calm
and rich retreat of yours? That should be the employment of
your idle as well as serious moments ; that should be at once your
business and amusement ; on that should be bestowed your wak-
ing as well as sleeping thoughts. Create and bring forth some-
thing which shall be really and forever your own : all your other
possessions will pass from you to some other heir ; this alone, if
once yours, will remain yours forever.

Thomas Hood says:—"Experience enables me to depose to the comfort
and blessing that literature can prove in seasons of sickness and sorrow ;—
how powerfully intellectual pursuits can help in keeping the head from
crazing and the heart from breaking."

Fear of Stronger Effect than Love.
i. 5.

Timetur a pluribus, quod plerumque fortius amore est.

He is feared by many, a feeling which is generally stronger than
love.

Popularity of the Bad.
i. 5.

Gratia malorum tam infida est quam ipsi.

The popularity of the bad is as little to be depended upon as he
is himself.

Reward of Virtue.
i. 8.

Præterea meminimus quanto majore animo honestatis
fructus in conscientiâ, quam in famâ, reponatur. Sequi
enim gloria, non appeti, debet : nec, si casu aliquo non
sequatur, idcirco, quod gloriam meruit, minus pulchrum
est.

Besides I am convinced how much more noble it is to place the
reward of good conduct in the silent approbation of one's own
breast, than in the applause of the world. Fame ought to be the
consequence, not the motive of our actions ; and though it should
not attend the worthy deed, yet it is by no means the less meri-
torious for not having received the applause it deserved.

Gay (Epist. iv.) says :—

    " Why to true merit should they have regard ?
    They know that virtue is its own reward."

CENSORIOUSNESS.

i. 8.

Homines enim, quum rem destruere non possunt, jacta-
tionem ejus incessunt. Ita si silenda feceris, factum ipsum ;
si laudanda, quod non sileas ipse, culpatur.

For the disposition of men is that, if they are not able to ob-
literate an action, they find fault with its vanity. Thus, whether
you perform what might be passed over without notice, or draw
attention to your own praiseworthy deeds, in either way you
incur blame.

Addison says :—"Censure, says an ingenious author, is the tax a man
pays to the public for being eminent. It is a folly for an eminent man to
think of escaping it and a weakness to be affected by it. All the illustrious
persons of antiquity, and indeed, of every age of the world, have passed
through this fiery persecution. There is no defence against reproach but
obscurity ; it is a kind of concomitant to greatness, as satires and invectives
were an essential part of a Roman triumph."

SOLITUDE.

i. 9.

Mecum tantum et cum libellis loquor. O rectam sincer-
amque vitam ! o dulce otium, honestumque, ac pœne omni
negotio pulchrius ! o mare ! o littus, verum secretumque
Μουσεῖον ! quam multa invenitis ! quam multa dictatis !

I converse only with myself and books. Honest and guileless
life ! sweet and honourable repose, more perhaps to be desired
than any kind of employment. Thou sea and shore, solemn and
solitary scene for contemplation, with how many noble thoughts
hast thou inspired me !

Milton ("Paradise Lost," ix. l. 250) says :—

"Solitude sometimes is best society
And short retirement urges sweet return."

Byron ("Childe Harold," cant. iv. st. 178) says :—

"There is a pleasure in the pathless woods,
There is a rapture on the lonely shore,
There is society, where none intrudes,
By the deep sea, and music in its roar."

DOUBT.

i. 18.

Si tutius putas illud cautissimi cujusque præceptum,
quod dubitas, ne feceris.

Though you may think it more safe to pursue this maxim, to
which every prudent man attends ; never do anything concerning
the wisdom of which you are in doubt.

CONSCIENCE.

i. 22.

Ornat hæc magnitudo animi, quæ nihil ad ostentationem, omnia ad conscientiam refert : recteque facti non ex populi sermone mercedem, sed ex facto, petit.

Such is his greatness of mind that he placed no part of his happiness in vain-glory, but referred everything to the secret approbation of his conscience, seeking the reward of his good conduct not from popular applause, but from the simple feeling of having acted virtuously.

Antiphanes (Fr. Com. Gr. p. 566, M.) says :—

Τὸ μὴ συνειδέναι γὰρ αὐτοῦ τῷ βίῳ
Ἀδίκημα μηδὲν ἡδονὴν πολλὴν ἔχει.

" For to be conscious of no crime during one's life is a great pleasure."

Shakespeare (" Henry VIII.," act iii. sc. 2) says :—

" I feel within me
A peace above all earthly dignities,
A still and quiet conscience."

See (Fr.) Conscience.

A DEAR BARGAIN.

i. 24.

Nam mala emptio semper ingrata est, eo maxime, quod exprobrare stultitiam domino videtur.

For a dear bargain is always annoying, particularly on this account, that it is a reflection on the judgment of the buyer.

DEATH.

ii. 1.

Et ille quidem plenus annis abiit, plenus honoribus, illis etiam quos recusavit.

He died full of years and of honours, equally illustrious by those he refused as by those he accepted.

THE LIVING VOICE.

ii. 3.

Præterea multo magis, ut vulgo dicitur, viva vox afficit : nam licet acriora sint, quæ legas, altius tamen in animo sedent, quæ pronuntiatio, vultus, habitus, gestus etiam dicentis adfigit.

Besides, as is usually the case, we are much more affected by the words which we hear, for though what you read in books may be more pointed, yet there is something in the voice, the look, the carriage, and even the gesture of the speaker, that makes a deeper impression upon the mind.

INVITATIONS TO DINNER.

ii. 6.

Eadem omnibus pono. Ad cœnam enim, non ad notam, invito: cunctisque rebus exœquo, quos mensâ et toro æquavi.

I receive all my guests with equal honour. For they are invited to supper, and not to be labelled according to rank. I make every man on a level with myself whom I admit to my table.

PUBLIC STATUES MEMORIALS OF GLORY.

ii. 7.

Etenim si defunctorum imagines domi positæ dolorem nostrum levant, quanto magis hæc, quibus in celeberrimo loco non modo species et vultus illorum, sed honor etiam et gloria refertur?

For if our grief is alleviated by gazing on the pictures of departed friends in our houses, how much more pleasure is there in looking on those public representations of them, which are memorials not only of their air and countenance, but of the honour and esteem with which they were regarded by their fellow-citizens.

FRAILTY OF HUMAN MONUMENTS.

ii. 10.

Habe ante oculos mortalitatem, a quâ asserere te hoc uno monumento potes: nam cœtera, fragilia et caduca, non minus quam ipsi homines, occidunt, desinuntque.

Recollect how fleeting are all human things, and that there is nothing so likely to hand down your name as a poem; all other monuments are frail and fading, passing away as quickly as the men whose memory they pretend to perpetuate.

THE RIGHT OF A QUESTION CANNOT BE DISCERNED IN A CROWDED MEETING.

ii. 11.

Patescit enim, quum separaris a turbâ, contemplatio rerum quæ turbâ teguntur.

The real gist of the question can only be clearly seen when you are separated from the clamours of a confused meeting.

VOTES.
ii. 12.

Sed hoc pluribus visum est; numerantur enim sententiæ, non ponderantur : nec aliud in publico consilio potest fieri, in quo nihil est tam inæquale, quam æqualitas ipsa ; nam, quum sit impar prudentia, par omnium jus est.

The majority were swayed the other way; for votes go by numbers and not weight, nor can it be otherwise in such public assemblies, where nothing is more unequal than that equality which prevails in them ; for, though every individual has the same right of suffrage, every individual has not the same strength of judgment to direct it.

See (Fr.) Votes.

AN OBJECT IN POSSESSION.
ii. 15.

Nihil enim æque gratum est adeptis, quam concupiscentibus.

An object in possession seldom retains the same charms which it had when it was longed for.

A STORY.
ii. 20.

Assem para, et accipe auream fabulam.

Give me a penny, and I will tell you a story worth gold.

LIFE OF MAN.
iii. 3.

Vita hominum altos recessûs magnasque latebras habet.

The life of man contains mysterious depths and skeleton closets.

Dickens says :—" There are chords in the human heart—strange varying strings—which are only struck by accident ; which will remain mute and senseless to appeals the most passionate and earnest, and respond at last to the slightest casual touch. In the most insensible or childish minds, there is some train of reflection, which art can seldom lead, or skill assist, but which will reveal itself, as great truths have done by chance, and when the discoverer has the plainest and simplest end in view."

See (Fr.) Smouldering fires.

FAVOUR REFUSED CANCELS ALL YOU HAVE CONFERRED.
iii. 4.

Nam quamlibet sæpe obligati, si quid unum neges, hoc solum meminerunt, quod negatum est.

For however often a man may receive an obligation from you, if you refuse a request, all former favours are effaced by this one denial.

SENSE OF INJURY.

iii. 9.

Plerumque dolor etiam venustos facit.

A strong sense of injury often gives point to the expression of our feelings.

PARTIALITY.

iii. 9.

Etenim tum maxime favor et ambitio dominatur, quum sub aliquâ specie severitatis delitescere potest.

For then more particularly partiality and the desire of currying favour with the great prevail, when they are able to be concealed under the specious appearance of severity.

THE BALLOT.

iii. 20.

Quæ nunc immodico favore corrupta, ad tacita suffragia, quasi ad remedium, decucurrerunt; quod interim plane remedium fuit; erat enim novum et subitum. Sed vereor ne procedente tempore ex ipso remedio vitia nascantur: est enim periculum ne tacitis suffragiis impudentia irrepat. Nam quotocuique eadem honestatis cura secreto, quæ palam ! Multi famam, conscientiam pauci verentur.

The elections have been lately carried on with excessive corruption, they have had recourse to the ballot, no doubt in the meanwhile a remedy, for it was new and suddenly adopted. Still I am afraid lest in process of time it should introduce new inconveniences; for there is danger lest shameless conduct should creep in under the cover of secret voting. For how few are there who preserve the same delicacy of conduct in secret as when exposed to the view of the world? The truth is that many more men pay regard to the opinion of the world than to conscience.

See (Fr.) Votes.

MODESTY.

iv. 7.

Recta ingenia debilitat verecundia, perversa confirmat audacia.

Modesty weakens the exertions of genius, while effrontery gives strength to the wrong-headed.

Johnson says:—" Modesty in a man is never to be allowed as a good quality, but a weakness, if it suppresses his virtue, and hides it from the world when he has at the same time a mind to exert himself."

Genius the Gift of Heaven.
iv. 8.

Sed nimirum quæ sunt in manu hominum, ea et mihi
et multis contigerunt : illud vero ut adipisci arduum, sic
etiam sperare nimium est, quod dari non nisi a diis potest.

But it is no doubt true that honours bestowed by man may be
conferred on me and many others, whereas genius, which is the
gift alone of heaven, is both difficult to attain and even too much
to hope for.

Dryden (" To Congreve on the Double Dealer ") says :—

" Time, Place, and Action may with pains be wrought,
But genius must be born ; and never can be taught."

See (Gr.) Genius, man of.

Men Fond of Praise even from Inferiors.
iv. 12.

Omnes enim, qui gloriâ famâque ducuntur, mirum in
modum assensio et laus, a minoribus etiam profecta, de-
lectat.

Those who are excited by a desire of fame, are fond of praise
and flattery, though it comes from their inferiors.

See (Gr. Fr.) Praise.

A wide-spread Reputation.
iv. 12.

Etenim nescio quo pacto vel magis homines juvat gloria
lata, quam magna.

For I know not how it is but men are generally more pleased
with a wide-spread than a great reputation.

Diseases in the State.
iv. 22.

Utque in corporibus, sic in imperio, gravissimus est mor-
bus, qui a capite diffunditur.

It is in the body politic, as in the natural, those disorders are
most dangerous that flow from the head.

To Name the Man.
iv. 22.

Dixi omnia, quum hominem nominavi.

After I have named the man, I need say no more.

TIME.

iv. 24.

Si computes annos, exiguum tempus; si vices rerum, ævum putes. Quod potest esse documento, nihil desperare, nulli rei fidere, quum videamus tot varietates tam volubili orbe circumagi.

If you compute the time in which these revolutions have happened, it is but a few years; if you number the incidents, it seems an age; and it is a lesson that will teach us to check both our despair and our presumption, when we observe such a variety of events rapidly revolving in so narrow a circle.

Shakespeare ("As You Like It," act iii. sc. 2) says:—

"Time travels in divers paces with divers persons. He ambles with a priest that lacks Latin, and a rich man that hath not the gout: for the one sleeps easily, because he cannot study; and the other lives merrily, because he feels no pain: the one lacking the burden of lean and wasteful learning; the other knowing no burden of heavy, tedious penury. These Time ambles withal. He trots hard with a young maid, between the contract of her marriage and the day it is solemnised; if the interim be but a se'nnight, Time's pace is so hard that it seems the length of seven years. He gallops with a thief to the gallows: for though he goes as softly as foot can fall, he thinks himself too soon there. He stays still with lawyers in the vacation: for they sleep between term and term, and then they perceive not how Time moves."

Euripides (Fr. Antiop. 41) says:—

Φεῦ φεῦ, βρότειαι πημάτων ὅσαι τύχαι
Ὅσαι τε μορφαί· τέρμα δ' οὐκ εἴποι τις ἄν.

"Alas, alas, how many are the varieties and forms of the miseries of mankind: one could not reach the end of them."

DEATH.

v. 5.

Mihi autem videtur acerba semper et immatura mors eorum, qui immortale aliquid parant. Nam qui voluptatibus dediti quasi in diem vivunt, vivendi causas quotidie finiunt: qui vero posteros cogitant, et memoriam sui operibus extendunt, his nulla mors non repentina est, ut quæ semper inchoatum aliquid abrumpat.

Death is ever, in my opinion, bitter and premature to those who are engaged on some immortal work. For those who live from day to day immersed in pleasure, finish with each day the whole purpose of their existence; while those who look forward to posterity, and endeavour by their exertions to hand down their name to future generations, to such death is always premature, as it ever carries them off from the midst of some unfinished design.

Epictetus (iii. 10) speaks in a different strain:—

"At what employment would you have death find you? For my

would have it in some humane, beneficent, public-spirited, noble action.
But if I cannot be found doing any such great things, yet at least I would
be doing what I cannot be restrained from, what is given me to do—correct-
ing myself, improving that faculty which makes use of the phenomena of
existence to produce tranquillity, and render to the several relations of life
their due ; and if I am so fortunate, advancing still further in the security
of judging right. If death overtakes me in such a situation, it is enough
for me if I can stretch out my hands to God and say, 'The opportunities I
have received from Thee of comprehending and obeying Thy administration
I have not neglected. As far as in me lay, I have not dishonoured Thee.
See how I have used my perceptions ; how my convictions. Have I at any
time found fault with Thee? Have I been discontented with Thy dispen-
sations, or wished them otherwise? Have I transgressed the relations of
life? I thank Thee that Thou hast brought me into being. I am satisfied
with the time I have enjoyed the things Thou hast given me. Receive
them back again, and distribute them as Thou wilt. For they were all
Thine and Thou gavest them me.'"

THE LIVING VOICE.

v. 7.

Nam sermonem vultus, gestus, vox ipsa moderatur ;
epistola, omnibus commendationibus destituta, malignitati
interpretantium exponitur.

For the sense of the speaker is determined by the countenance,
the gesture, and even the tone of the voice ; whereas a letter,
being destitute of these advantages, is more liable to the malig-
nant construction of those who are inclined to misinterpret its
meaning.

Shakespeare (" Coriolanus," act iii. sc. 2) says :—

"For in such business
Action is eloquence, and the eyes of the ignorant
More learned than their ears."

See (Gr.) Oratory, power of.

HISTORY.

v. 8.

Mihi pulchrum imprimis videtur, non pati occidere,
quibus æternitas debeatur, aliorumque famam cum suâ
extendere.

It appears to me a noble employment to rescue from oblivion
those who deserve to be eternally remembered, and by extending
the reputation of others, to advance at the same time our own.

See (Gr. Fr.) History.

LOVE OF FAME.

v. 8.

Me autem nihil æque ac diuturnitatis amor et cupido
sollicitat : res homine dignissimæ, præsertim qui nullius
sibi conscius culpæ, posteritatis memoriam non reformidet.

Nothing, I allow, excites me so much as the desire of having my name handed down to posterity; a passion highly worthy of the human breast, especially of his who, not being conscious of any crime, fears not to be known to future generations.

So Milton ("Lycidas," l. 70):—

"Fame is the spur that the clear spirit doth raise."

ORATORY AND POETRY.

v. 8.

Orationi et carmini est parva gratia, nisi eloquentia sit summa. Historia quoquo modo scripta delectat.

Oratory and poetry are of little value, unless they reach the highest perfection; but history, in whatever way it may be executed, is a source of pleasure.

LIBERALITY.

v. 12.

Nescit enim semel incitata liberalitas stare, cujus pulchritudinem usus ipse commendat.

Generosity, when once she is set forward, knows not how to stop, and the more familiar we are with the lovely form, the more enamoured we become of her charms.

Shakespeare ("Antony and Cleopatra," act v. sc. 2) says:—

"For his bounty,
There was no winter in 't; an autumn 'twas,
That grew the more by reaping."

See (Fr.) Liberality.

GRIEF.

v. 16.

Ut enim crudum adhuc vulnus medentium manus reformidat, deinde patitur, atque ultro requirit: sic recens animi dolor consolationes rejicit ac refugit, mox desiderat, et clementer admotis acquiescit.

For a fresh wound shrinks from the hand of the surgeon, then gradually submits to and even calls for it; so a mind under the first impression of a misfortune shuns and rejects all comfort, but at length, if touched with tenderness, calmly and willingly resigns itself.

ELOQUENCE AND LOQUACITY.

v. 20.

Nam eloquentia vix uni aut alteri; hæc vero, quam Candidus loquentiam appellat, multis atque etiam impudentissimo cuique maxime contingit.

Eloquence is indeed the talent of very few, but that faculty which Candidus calls loquacity is common to numbers, and generally attends impudence.

ACTION RIGHT OR WRONG ACCORDING TO SUCCESS.

v. 21.

Est omnino iniquum, sed usu receptum, quod honesta consilia vel turpia, prout male aut prospere cedunt, ita vel probantur vel reprehenduntur. Inde plerumque eadem facta, modo diligentiæ, modo vanitatis, modo libertatis, modo furoris nomen accipiunt.

It is the usual custom of the world (though a very unequitable rule of estimation) to pronounce an action to be either right or wrong, as it is attended with good or ill success; and accordingly you shall hear the very same conduct attributed to zeal or folly, to liberty or licentiousness, as the event happens to prove.

OPPORTUNITY AND FRIENDS REQUIRED FOR RISING IN THE WORLD.

vi. 23.

Neque enim cuiquam tam clarum statim ingenium est, ut possit emergere, nisi illi materia, occasio, fautor etiam commendatorque contingat.

For no man possesses so commanding a genius as to be able at once to emerge from obscurity unless some subject present itself, and an opportunity when he can display his talents, with a friend to promote his advancement.

HUMAN ACTIONS.

vi. 24.

Quam multum interest, quid a quo fiat! Eadem enim facta claritate vel obscuritate facientium, aut tolluntur altissime, aut humillime deprimuntur.

How much does the reputation of human actions depend upon the position of those who perform them! For the very same acts, according as they proceed from a person of high or low rank, are either much extolled or left unnoticed.

THE OPINION OF THE MULTITUDE.

vii. 17.

Opinor, quia in numero ipso est quoddam magnum collatumque consilium; quibusque singulis judicii parum, omnibus plurimum.

The reason, I believe, is that there is a large collective wisdom in a multitude ; though individually their judgment may be of little weight, united it becomes of great importance.

See (Gr. Fr.) Multitude.

PUBLIC INTEREST.
vii. 18.

Sed oportet privatis utilitatibus publicas,. mortalibus æternas anteferre ; multoque diligentius muneri suo consulere, quam facultatibus.

But the interest of the public ought always to supersede every private consideration, as what is eternal is to be preferred to what is mortal ; and a man of true generosity will study in what manner to render his benefaction most advantageous, rather than how he may bestow it with least expense.

MODESTY.
vii. 25.

O quantum eruditorum aut modestia ipsorum, aut quies operit ac subtrahit famæ ! At nos eos tantum dicturi aliquid aut lecturi timemus, qui studia sua proferunt ; quum illi qui tacent, hoc amplius præstent, quod maximum opus silentio reverentur.

How many of the learned are concealed from view by modesty, or an unwillingness to have their name brought before the public. Yet, when we are going to speak or recite our works in crowded assemblies, it is the judgment only of those who possess ostentatious talents of whom we stand in awe: whereas we ought rather to revere the decisions of those who form their opinions of works of genius in their closets, undisturbed by the noise of public assemblies.

See (Gr. Fr.) Modesty.

COUNTRY GENTLEMEN.
vii. 25.

Auxit sollicitudinem meam, effecitque, ut illis, quos doctissimos novi, non minus hos seductos et quasi rusticos verear. Idem suadeo tibi. Sunt enim, ut in castris, sic etiam in litteris nostris plures cultu pagano, quos cinctos et armatos, et quidem ardentissimo ingenio, diligenter scrutatus invenies.

In short, his conversation has increased my solicitude concerning my works, and taught me to revere the judgment of these studious country gentlemen, as much as that of more known and distinguished literati. Let me persuade you to consider them in the same light; for, believe me, upon a careful observation you will often find in the literary as well as military world, most powerful abilities concealed under a rustic garb.

SICKNESS.
vii. 26.

Dum homo est infirmus, tunc deos, tunc hominem esse se meminit : invidet nemini, neminem miratur, neminem despicit, ac ne sermonibus quidem malignis aut attendit, aut alitur.

When a man is labouring under the pain of any distemper, it is then that he recollects there are gods, and that he himself is but a man : no mortal is then the object of his envy, his admiration, or his contempt, and having no malice to gratify, the tales of slander excite not his attention.

HISTORY.
vii. 33.

Nam nec historia debet egredi veritatem, et honeste factis veritas sufficit.

History ought to be guided by truth ; and worthy actions require nothing more.

See (Gr.) History.

EQUITY.
viii. 2.

Mihi autem egregium imprimis videtur, ut foris, ita domi, ut in magnis, ita in parvis, ut in alienis, ita in suis, agitare justitiam. Nam si paria peccata, pares etiam laudes.

I hold it particularly worthy of a man of honour to be governed by the principles of strict equity in his domestic as well as public conduct; in small, as in great affairs; in his own concerns, as well as in those of others : and if every deviation from rectitude is equally criminal, every approach to it must be equally laudable.

FOREBODING OF EVIL.
viii. 17.

Nam parvulum differt, patiaris adversa, an expectes ; nisi quod tamen est dolendi modus, non est timendi. Doleas enim, quantum scias accidisse ; timeas, quantum possit accidere.

For there is very little difference between the enduring and fearing a danger, except this much, indeed, that there are some bounds to the feeling but none to the apprehending of it. For you can suffer only as much as you have actually suffered, but you may apprehend all that may possibly happen.

A WILL.
viii. 18.

Falsum est nimirum, quod creditur vulgo, testamenta hominum speculum esse morum.

It is a mistaken maxim too generally advanced, that a man's will is a kind of mirror wherein one may clearly discern his genuine character.

THINGS NEAR AT HAND OVERLOOKED.
viii. 20.

Ad quæ noscenda iter ingredi, transmittere mare solemus, ea sub oculis posita negligimus : seu quia ita naturâ comparatum, ut proximorum incuriosi, longinqua sectemur : seu quod omnium rerum cupido languescit, quum facilis occasio est : seu quod differimus tanquam sæpe visuri, quod datur videre, quoties velis cernere.

Those works of art or nature which are usually the motives of our travels, are often overlooked and neglected if they happen to lie within our reach ; whether it be that we are naturally less inquisitive concerning those things which are near us, while our curiosity is excited by remote objects ; or because the easiness of gratifying a desire is always sure to damp it ; or, perhaps, that we defer from time to time viewing, whilst we have an opportunity of seeing whatever we please.

FORGIVENESS.
viii. 22.

Optimum et emendatissimum existimo, qui ceteris ita ignoscit, tanquam ipse quotidie peccet ; ita peccatis abstinet, tanquam nemini ignoscat.

The highest of characters, in my estimation, is his, who is as ready to pardon the moral errors of mankind, as if he were every day guilty of some himself ; and at the same time as cautious of committing a fault, as if he never forgave one.

AFFECTION.
viii. 24.

Male vim suam potestas aliorum contumeliis experitur : male terrore veneratio adquiritur ; longeque valentior

amor ad obtinendum, quod velis, quam timor. Nam timor
abit, si recedas ; manet amor : ac sicut ille in odium, hic
in reverentiam vertitur.

Ill, believe me, is power proved by insult ; ill can terror com-
mand veneration, and far more efficacious is affection in obtaining
one's purpose than fear. For terror operates no longer than its
object is present, but love produces its effects when the object is
at a distance, and as absence changes the former into hatred, it
raises the latter into respect.

Milton ("Paradise Lost," l. 523) says to the same effect :—

> " Who overcomes
> By force, hath overcome but half his foe."

LIBERTY AND GOVERNMENT.
viii. 24.

Nam quid ordinatione civilius? quid libertate pretiosius?
Porro quam turpe, si ordinatio eversione, libertas servitute
mutetur ?

For, what is more becoming our social nature than well regulated
government, or more valuable than liberty? How ignominious,
then, must his conduct be, who turns the first into anarchy and
the last into slavery?

HAPPINESS.
ix. 3.

Alius alium, ego beatissimum existimo, qui bonæ man-
suræque famæ præsumptione perfruitur, certusque posteri-
tatis cum futurâ gloriâ vivit.

Mankind differ in their notions of supreme happiness; but in
my opinion he truly possesses it, who lives in the conscious antici-
pation of honest fame, and the glorious figure he shall make in the
eyes of posterity.

EQUALITY.
ix. 5.

Temperare mihi non possum, quominus laudem, similis
monenti, quod eum modum tenes, ut discrimina ordinum
dignitatumque custodias : quæ si confusa, turbata, permista
sunt, nihil est ipsâ æqualitate inæqualius.

However, I cannot forbear adding a caution to my praise and
recommending it to you, to conduct yourself in such a manner as
to preserve the proper distinction of rank and dignity. For to
level and confound the different orders of society is far from pro-
ducing an equality among mankind ; it is, in fact, the most un-
equal thing imaginable.

See (Gr. Fr.) Equality.

SUMMER FRIENDS.
ix. 9.

Non ut plerique, qui tantum viventes amant, seu potius amare se simulant, ac ne simulant quidem, nisi quos florentes vident. Nam miserorum, non secus ac defunctorum, obliviscuntur.

Far different from those who love, or rather, I should more properly say, who counterfeit love to none but the living. Nor indeed even that any longer than they are the favourites of fortune; for the unhappy are no more the object of their remembrance than the dead.

G. Herbert ("The Answer"):—

"Like summer friends,
Flies of estates and summershine."

DELIBERATION.
ix. 13.

Expertus usu, de eo quod destinaveris, non esse consulendos, quibus consultis obsequi debeas.

Experience having taught me never to advise with a person concerning that which we have already determined, where he has a right to expect that one shall be decided by his judgment.

INQUISITIVENESS.
ix. 27.

Incitantur enim homines ad agnoscenda, quæ differuntur.

Nothing raises the inquisitive disposition of mankind so much as to defer its gratification.

MEDIOCRITY.
ix. 29.

Ut satius est unum aliquid insigniter facere, quam plurima mediocriter, ita plurima mediocriter, si non possis unum insigniter.

As it is better to excel in any single art than to arrive only at mediocrity in several, so a moderate skill in several is to be preferred where one cannot attain to perfection in any.

TRUE BENEFICENCE.
ix. 30.

Primum est autem suo esse contentum: deinde, quos præcipue scias indigere, sustentantem foventemque, orbe quodam societatis ambire.

The first and fundamental principle of genuine beneficence is to be contented with one's own ; and after that to cherish and embrace all the most indigent of every kind in one comprehensive circle of general benevolence.

AVARICE.

ix. 30.

Ea invasit homines, habendi cupido, ut possideri magis, quam possidere videantur.

The lust of avarice has so totally seized upon mankind, that their wealth seems rather to possess them, than they to possess their wealth.

THE LONGEST DAY COMES TO AN END.

ix. 36.

Longissimus dies cito conditur.

The longest day soon comes to an end.

THE LIFE OF A PRINCE.

Panegyr. 2.

Vita principis censura est.

The life of a prince is a calling of other men's lives to an account.

INNOCENCE.

Panegyr. 3.

Animadverto enim, etiam deos ipsos, non tam accuratis adorantium precibus, quam innocentiâ et sanctitate lætari : gratioremque existimari, qui delubris eorum puram castamque mentem, quam qui meditatum carmen intulerit.

I observe that the gods themselves are propitiated not so much by prayers as by innocence and sanctity of life ; and that those are regarded with more favour who bring into their temples a pure and chaste mind, than the man who repeats a prepared prayer.

VICISSITUDES.

Panegyr. 5.

Habet has vices conditio mortalium, ut adversa ex secundis, ex adversis secunda nascantur. Occultat utrorumque semina Deus, et plerumque bonorum malorumque causæ sub diversâ specie latent.

Such is the changeful condition of mankind, that adversity is known from prosperity, and prosperity from adversity. God hides in obscurity the causes of both, and frequently the reasons of the good and evil that befals man lies concealed under both.

Simonides of Coos (Fr. 29, S.) thus speaks of life :—

οὐκ ἐστὶν κακὸν
ἀνεπίδόκητον ἀνθρώποις· ὀλίγῳ δὲ χρόνῳ
πάντα μεταρρίπτει θεός.

"There is no evil that may not be expected by men : in a short time God turns all things upside down."

PROSPERITY AND ADVERSITY.
Panegyr. 31.
Secunda felices, adversa magnos probant.

Prosperity tries the fortunate, adversity the great.

Antiphanes (Fr. Com. Gr. p. 569, M.) says :—

Πλοῦτος δὲ βάσανός ἐστιν ἀνθρώπου τρόπων.

"Riches are what test a man's character."

POWER OF DECEIVING.
Panegyr. 62.
Nemo omnes, neminem omnes fefellerunt.

No one has been able to deceive the whole world, nor has the whole world ever deceived any one.

PROPERTIUS

BORN PROBABLY ABOUT B.C. 51—DIED ABOUT B.C. 15.

SEXTUS AURELIUS PROPERTIUS was born, it is supposed, at Hispellum or Assisium, but there are no satisfactory materials for his personal history. He is believed to have been deprived of his paternal property during the civil wars, and then was thrown upon his wits for a livelihood, becoming "the man of wit and pleasure about town." He was patronised by Mæcenas, and this is probably all that can be said with certainty respecting him.

WHAT IS EFFECTIVE IN LOVE.
i. 1. 16.
Tantum in amore preces et benefacta valent.

So much do prayers and generous deeds avail in love.

GRIEF IS THE CAUSE OF LOVE ELEGIES.
i. 7. 7.

Nec tantum ingenio, quantum servire dolori
Cogor, et ætatis tempora dura queri.

I do not write so much from the impulse of genius as to soothe
the cares of love, and to bewail life's unabating woe.

Petrarch seems to have had this passage in view (Sonn. 262) :—

" E certo ogni mio studio in quel temp'era
Pur di sfogare il doloroso core
In qualche modo, non d'acquistar fama,
Pianger cercai, non del pianto onore."

" Assuredly all my desire at that time was to relieve my heart in some
way, not to acquire fame. I sought to weep, not honour from my grief."

LOVE ENJOYS THE TEAR.
i. 12. 16.

Nonnihil adspersis gaudet amor lacrymis.

Love enjoys the falling tear.

Thus Tasso, in his " Amyntas," (l. 2,) says beautifully :—

" Pasce l'agna l'herbetto, il lupo l'agno ;
Mà il crudo Amor di lagrime si pasce,
Nè se ne mostra mai satollo."

" The lamb feeds on the herbage, the wolf on the lamb ; but sad love feeds
on tears, nor is ever satisfied."

CYNTHIA, MY FIRST AND LAST LOVE.
i. 12. 19.

Mi neque amare aliam, neque ab hac discedere fas est :
Cynthia prima fuit, Cynthia finis erit.

I can neither love another nor depart from her : Cynthia first
charmed, and last shall claim my heart.

So Ovid (Met. xiv. 682) says :—

" Tu primus et ultimus illi
Ardor eris."

TIME SPENT WITH OUR LOVE NEVER APPEARS LONG.
i. 19. 25.

Dum licet, inter nos igitur lætemur amantes.
Non satis est ullo tempore longus amor.

Then let us enjoy short-lived pleasures while we may : an age
of passion seems but as a day.

Business.

ii. 1. 46.

Quâ pote quisque, in eâ conterat arte diem.

Let every man employ himself in the business with which he is
best acquainted.

Woman easily Counterfeits Words and Actions.

ii. 9. 31.

Sed vobis facile est verba et componere fraudes :
  Hoc unum didicit fœmina semper opus.
Non sic incerto mutantur flamine Syrtes,
  Nec folia hiberno tam tremefacta Noto ;
Quam cito fœmineâ non constat fœdus in irâ,
  Sive ea causa gravis, sive ea causa levis.

It is easy for you to counterfeit words and actions ; every woman
is adapted for such work. The quicksands are not more easily
changed by the wind, nor are the leaves more readily whirled by
the winter's blast, than woman veers in her wrath, whether the
cause of her excitement be serious or trivial.

Boldness.

ii. 10. 5.

Quod si deficiant vires, audacia certe
Laus erit : in magnis et voluisse sat est.

But if strength fail, boldness at least will be deserving of praise ;
in great enterprises to have even attempted is enough.

Love.

ii. 14. 18.

Scilicet insano nemo in amore videt.

Love blinds mankind.

Futurity.

ii. 27. 1.

At vos incertam, mortales, funeris horam
  Quæritis, et quâ sit Mors aditura viâ ;
Quæritis et cœlo Phœnicum inventa sereno,
  Quæ sit stella homini commoda, quæque mala.

But you, O men, are anxious to know the hidden hour of death
and in what way you shall die,—what star is propitious and
fatal to man.

DEATH.

ii. 28. 57.

Nec forma æternum, aut cuiquam est fortuna perennis.
Longius, aut propius, mors sua quemque manet.

Beauty is fading, nor is fortune stable ; sooner or later death comes to all.

Euripides (Fr. Hypsip. 6) says :—

Ἔφυ μὲν οὐδεὶς ὅστις οὐ πονεῖ βροτῶν·
Θάπτει τε τέκνα χἄτερ' ἂν κτᾶται νέα,
Αὐτός τε θνήσκει, καὶ τάδ' ἄχθονται βροτοὶ
Εἰς γῆν φέροντες γῆν· ἀναγκαίως δ' ἔχει
Βίον θερίζειν ὥστε κάρπιμον στάχυν,
Καὶ τὸν μὲν εἶναι, τὸν δὲ μή· τό ταῦτα δεῖ
Στένειν ἅπερ δεῖ κατὰ φύσιν διεκπερᾶν ;
Δεινὸν γὰρ οὐδὲν τῶν ἀναγκαίων βροτοῖς.

" There is no one of mortals not subject to grief; he buries his children and begets others ; he himself dies and men grieve over him, bearing dust to dust ; the life of all must be reaped like the ears of corn: this man lives and this man dies. Why grieve about things which take place according to the laws of nature ? For there is nothing to which men must submit by necessity that ought to be regarded grievous."

Aristophanes (Fr. Com. Gr. I. p. 309. M.) says :—

Τὸ γὰρ φοβεῖσθαι τὸν θάνατον λῆρος πολύς·
Πᾶσιν γὰρ ἡμῖν τοῦτ' ὀφείλεται παθεῖν.

" For to fear death is great folly ; since it is fated to all of us to die."

THE POET IMMORTAL.

iii. 2. 23.

At non ingenio quæsitum nomen ab ævo
Excidet : ingenio stat sine morte decus.

Fame obtained from the endowments of the mind will never perish ; eternal honour awaits the noble.

RICHES.

iii. 5. 13.

Haud ullas portabis opes Acherontis ad undas ;
Nudus ab infernâ, stulte, vehere rate.

O fool, thou shalt carry no riches beyond the grave ;
Thou shalt be ferried over naked in Charon's boat.

MONEY.

iii. 7. 1.

Ergo sollicitæ tu causa, pecunia, vitæ es,
Per te immaturum mortis adimus iter.

Tu vitiis hominum crudelia pabula præbes ;
Semina curarum de capite orta tuo.

O money, thou art the fruitful source of cares ; thou leadest us
to a premature grave ; thou affordest support to the vices of men ;
the seeds of evil spring up from thee.

ALL THINGS.
iii. 9. 7.

Omnia non pariter rerum sunt omnibus apta.

All things are not equally suited to all.

GOLD.
iii. 13. 48.

Aurum omnes victâ jam pietate colunt ;
Auro pulsa fides ; auro venalia jura ;
Aurum lex sequitur, mox sine lege pudor.

All now worship gold to the neglect of the gods ; by gold good
faith is banished ; justice is sold for gold, the law follows gold,
and soon the modest woman will be without the protection of the
laws.

A ROAD DIFFICULT BUT GLORIOUS.
iv. 10. 3.

Magnum iter adscendo ; sed dat mihi gloria vires.

I am climbing a difficult road, but the glory that attends suc-
cess, gives me strength for the labour.

PUBLIUS SYRUS

FLOURISHED B.C. 45.

PUBLIUS SYRUS, a slave brought to Rome some years before the
downfall of the republic, was designated Syrus from the country
of his birth. Of his personal history nothing is known except
that at the games exhibited by Cæsar, B.C. 45, he challenged all
the dramatists of the day to contend with him in improvising
upon any given theme, and carried off the palm from every com-
petitor. A compilation of pithy sayings under the title of "Publii
Syri Sententiæ," extending to upwards of a thousand lines in
Iambic and Trochaic measures, is now extant. The following are
a selection from these sayings.

A Drunk Man.

Absentem lædit, cum ebrio qui litigat.

He, who contends with the drunken, injures the absent.

A Hasty Decision.

Ad pænitendum properat, cito qui judicat.

He, who decides hastily, will soon repent of his decision.

Suspicion.

Ad tristem partem strenua est suspicio.

The losing side is full of suspicion.

Debts.

Æs debitorem leve ; grave inimicum facit.

A slight debt produces a debtor; a heavy one an enemy.

Property.

Aliena nobis, nostra plus aliis placent.

That which belongs to another pleases us most; while that, which is ours, is more pleasing to others.

Debt.

Alienum æs homini ingenuo acerba est servitus.

Debt is grievous slavery to the free born.

Love.

Amare et sapere vix Deo conceditur.

To love, and at the same time to be wise, is scarcely granted even to a god.

A Friend.

Amicum lædere ne joco quidem licet.

It is not allowable, even in jest, to injure a friend.

A Friend.

Amicum perdere est damnorum maximum.

To lose a friend is the greatest of all losses.

Love.

Amor animi arbitrio sumitur, non ponitur.

To love is in our power, but not to lay it aside.

PASSIONS.

Animo imperabit sapiens, stultus serviet.
The wise man is the master of his passions, the fool is their slave.

THE OLD WOMAN.

Anus cum ludit, morte delicias facit.
When the old crone frolics, she flirts with death.

RELAXATION.

Arcum intensio frangit, animum remissio.
Straining breaks the bow, and relaxation the mind.

A WOMAN.

Aut amat aut odit mulier, nihil est tertium.
A woman either loves or hates ; she knows no medium.

UNION.

Auxilia humilia firma consensus facit.
Union gives strength and firmness to the humblest aids.

A KINDNESS.

Beneficium accipere, libertatem est vendere.
Accept a favour and you sell your freedom.

THE BENEVOLENT.

Benignus etiam dandi causam cogitat.
The beneficent even looks out for a reason to confer favours.
See Senec. Benef. II. c. 2.

TO DIE.

Bis emori est alterius arbitrio mori.
It is to die twice to die at the will of another.

KINDNESS.

Bis gratum est, quod dato opus est, ultro si offeras.
Spontaneous kindness is always most acceptable.

A CONQUEROR.

Bis vincit, qui se vincit in victoriâ.
He conquers twice who conquers himself in victory.

Good Things.

Bonarum rerum consuetudo est pessima.

The continuance of prosperity is prejudicial.

The Good.

Bonis nocet, quisquis pepercerit malis.

He hurts the good who spares the bad.

Misfortunes of Others.

Bonum est fugienda adspicere in alieno malo.

It is good to see in the misfortunes of others what we should avoid.

Danger.

Caret periculo, qui etiam tutus cavet.

He is most safe from danger who, even when safe, is on his guard.

Repentance.

Cave ne quidquam incipias, quod post pœniteat.

Take care not to begin anything of which you may repent.

Danger.

Citius venit periculum, cum contemnitur.

Danger arrives the sooner when it is despised.

Lover.

Cogas amantem irasci, amare si velis.

You should force a lover to be angry, if you wish her to love.

Companion.

Comes jucundus in viâ pro vehiculo est.

A pleasant companion causes you not to perceive the length of the journey.

Relationship.

Conjunctio animi maxima est cognatio.

Unity of feelings and affections is the strongest relationship.

Prudence.

Consilio melius vincas quam iracundiâ.

You conquer better by prudence than by passion.

THE FORTUNATE.

Contra felicem vix Deus vires habet.

Even God can scarcely get the better of the fortunate.

REPUTATION.

Damnum appellandum est cum malâ fumâ lucrum.

The gain which is made at the expense of reputation should be set down as a loss.

OPPORTUNITY.

Deliberando sæpe perit occasio.

While we are deliberating, the opportunity is often lost.

DELIBERATION.

Deliberandum est diu, quod statuendum est semel.

That should be considered long which can be decided but once.

ACCUSATIONS.

Difficilem oportet aurem habere ad crimina.

We should not lend an easy ear to accusations.

DAYS.

Discipulus est priori posterior dies.

Each succeeding day is the scholar of that which preceded.

WAR.

Diu apparandum est bellum, ut vincas celerius.

Preparations for war are to be made for a long time before, that you may more quickly conquer.

PAIN.

Dolor animo gravior est, quam corporis dolor.

The pain of the mind is worse than the pain of the body.

TO FORGET.

Etiam oblivisci, quod scis, interdum expedit.

It is sometimes expedient to forget what we know.

A WOUND.

Etiam sanato vulnere cicatrix manet.

Even after a wound is healed the scar remains.

DIGNITY.

Facilius crescit quam inchoatur dignitas.

It is more easy to obtain an accession of dignity, than to acquire in the first instance.

TRIAL.

Fatetur facinus is, qui judicium fugit.

He who flies from trial confesses his crime.

PROSPERITY.

Felicitas nutrix est iracundiæ.

Prosperity is the nurse of passion.

FAITH.

Fides, ut anima, unde abiit, eo nunquam redit.

Trust, like the soul, never returns when it has once gone.

COUNTENANCE.

Formosa facies muta commendatio est.

A pleasing countenance is a silent commendation.

FORTUNE.

Fortuna nimium quem fovet, stultum facit.

Fortune, when she caresses a man too much, makes him a fool.

FORTUNE.

Fortuna vitrea est, tum, cum splendet, frangitur.

Fortune is brittle as glass; at the very time she shines, she is broken.

There is a German proverb, which expresses this very graphically:—
"Glück und Glas, wie bald bricht das!"

PATIENCE.

Furor fit læsa sœpius patientia.

Patience, when too often outraged, is converted into madness.

REMEDIES.

Graviora quædam sunt remedia periculis.

Some remedies are worse than the disease.

Seneca (Med. 435) expresses this idea thus:—
"Remedia toties invenit nobis Deus
Periculis pejora."

"God has often found for us remedies worse than the dangers in which we are involved."

HABIT.

Gravissimum est imperium consuetudinis.
The power of habit is very strong.

HEIR.

Hæredis fletus sub personâ risus est.
The weeping of an heir is laughter under a mask.

GLORY.

Heu! quam difficilis gloriæ custodia est!
How difficult, alas! is it to maintain the glory we have in!

PASSION.

Homo extra corpus est suum, cum irascitur.
A man is beside himself when he is in a passion.

MAN.

Homo vitæ commodatus, non donatus est.
Man has been lent to life, not given over to it.
This is well expressed in a German translation :—
" Dem leben ist der Mensch geliehen, nicht geschenkt."

THE TIMES.

Honeste servit, qui succumbit tempori.
He, who yields to the exigencies of the times, acts wis

HATE.

Id agas, tuo te merito ne quis oderit.
Take care that no one hate you justly.

FORGIVE.

Ignoscito sæpe alteri, nunquam tibi.
Forgive others many things, yourself nothing.

UNGRATEFUL.

Ingratus unus omnibus miseris nocet.
One ungrateful man does an injury to all who are wret

INJURIES.

Injuriarum remedium est oblivio.
The best remedies for injuries is to forget them.

KINDNESS.

Inopi beneficium bis dat, qui dat celeriter.

He confers a kindness twice on a poor man who gives quickly.

MADMAN.

Insanus omnis furere credit cæteros.

Every madman thinks all other men mad.

FAULT.

Invitat culpam, qui delictum præterit.

He who overlooks one fault, invites the commission of another.
Thus in German :—

"Das Ubergehn der Schuld reist Andre zum Verbrechen."

THE JUDGE.

Judex damnatur, cum nocens absolvitur.

The judge is condemned when the guilty is acquitted.

MAGNANIMITY.

Magnam fortunam magnus etiam animus docet.

Magnanimity becomes a great fortune.

MISCHIEF.

Malefacere qui vult, nunquam non causam invenit.

He who wishes to do mischief, is never without a reason.

EMPIRE.

Male imperando summum imperium amittitur.

The greatest empire may be lost by the misrule of its governors.
Thus Euripides (Suppl. 190) says :—

Ἔχει σὲ ποιμέν᾽ ἐσθλὸν· ὃυ χρείᾳ πόλεις
Πολλαὶ διώλοντ᾽ ἐνδεεῖς στρατηλάτου.

"For it possesses thee as an able ruler, through want of which many cities have perished from lack of a general."

MALEVOLENT.

Malevolus animus abditos dentes habet.

The malevolent have secret teeth.

MASTER.

Minor est quam servus, dominus qui servos timet.

The master is lower than a servant who dreads his servants.

2 G

FORTUNE.

Miserrima est fortuna, quæ inimico caret.

That fortune is most wretched which is without an enemy.

TO CONCEAL.

Miserum est tacere cogi, quod cupias loqui.

It is miserable to be compelled to conceal what you wish to proclaim.

DELAY.

Mora omnis odio est, sed facit sapientiam.

Every delay is hateful, but it gives wisdom.

DEATH.

Mori est felicis antequam mortem invocèt.

It is fortunate to die before you call upon death.

FEAR.

Necesse est multos timeat, quem multi timent.

He who is feared by many must fear many.

NECESSITY.

Necessitas dat legem, non ipsa accipit.

Necessity imposes law, does not herself receive it.

Simonides of Ceos (Fr. 4. 23, 8.) says:—

'Ανάγκᾳ δ' ουδὲ θεοὶ μάχονται.

"Not even the gods contend with necessity."

HIGH STATION.

Nemo timendo ad summum pervenit locum.

No one has arrived at high station without undergoing some hazard.

WICKEDNESS.

Nequitia pœna maxima ipsamet sui est.

Wickedness is its own punishment.

TRUTH.

Nimium altercando veritas amittitur.

In excessive altercation truth is lost.

This is well translated in German :—

" Durch zuviel und stark
Disputieren Thut man die
Wahrheit auch verlieren."

To Please.

Non quam multis placeas, sed qualibus, stude.
Do not care how many, but whom, you please.

Gain.

Nullus tantus quæstus, quam, quod habes, parcere.
There is no gain so certain as that which arises from sparing what you have.

Opportunity.

Occasio ægre offertur, facile amittitur.
A good opportunity is seldom presented, and is easily lost.

Life.

O vita misero longa, felici brevis !
O life ! long to the miserable, short to the happy !

Apollodorus (Fr. Com. Gr. p. 1106, M.) says :—

Τοῖς γὰρ μεριμνῶσιν τε καὶ λυπουμένοις
Ἅπασα νὺξ ἔοικε φαίνεσθαι μακρά.

" For to the care-worn and those in grief, every night appears to be long."

Wickedness.

Paucorum improbitas universis calamitas.
The wickedness of a few brings calamity on all.

God.

Puras Deus, non plenas adspicit manus.
God looks to pure and not to full hands.

Good Man.

Repente dives nemo factus est bonus.
No good man ever became suddenly rich.

Friends.

Secreto amicos admone, lauda palam.
Admonish your friends secretly, praise them openly.

To Perish.

Solatium grande est cum universo una rapi.
It is a great consolation to perish with all the world.

To Fear.

Stultum est timere, quod vitare non potes.

It is foolish to fear what you cannot avoid.

Miser.

Tam deëst avaro quod habet, quam quod non habet.

The miser is in as much want of that which he has as of that which he has not.

Hasty Counsels.

Velox consilium sequitur pœnitentia.

Hasty counsels are quickly followed by repentance.

To be Known.

Vis omnibus esse notus, nóris neminem.

You wish to be known to all ; you will know no one.

Flattery.

Vitium fuit, nunc mos est assentatio.

Flattery, which was formerly a vice, is now a custom.

Shipwreck.

Improbe Neptunum accusat, qui iterum naufragium facit.

That man foolishly blames the sea, who is a second time shipwrecked.

Ranks.

Ni gradus servetur, nulli tutus est summus locus.

Unless ranks are observed, the highest place is safe to no one.

To Live.

Non aliter vives in solitudine, aliter in foro.

You should not live one way in private and another in public.

Silence.

Sæpius locutum, nunquam me tacuisse pœnitet.

I regret often that I have spoken, never that I have been silent.

Amphis (Fr. Com. Gr. 655, M.) says :—

Οὐκ ἔστι κρεῖττον τοῦ σιωπᾶν οὐδὲ ἕν.

" There is nothing better than silence."

CONVERSATION.

Sermo animi est imago ; qualis vir, talis et oratio est.

The conversation is the image of the mind. As the man, so is his mode of talking.

HIGHEST.

Si vis ad summum progredi, ab infimo ordire.

If you wish to arrive at the highest, begin from the lowest.

QUINTILIANUS

BORN A.D. 40—DIED ABOUT A.D. 118.

MARCUS FABIUS QUINTILIANUS, the most celebrated of Roman rhetoricians, was a native of Calagurris (Calahorra) in the upper valley of the Ebro. Though educated at Rome, he seems to have returned to Spain, as we find him accompanying Galba to Rome, A.D. 68. He acquired some reputation at the bar, though he was chiefly distinguished as a teacher of eloquence. Among his pupils were Pliny the younger, and the two grand-nephews of Domitian. By this emperor he was adorned with the insignia of the consulship, and was the first public instructor who received a regular salary from the imperial exchequer. The great work of Quintilian is a complete system of rhetoric, in twelve books, entitled, "De Institutione Oratoris," Libri xii., dedicated to his friend Marcellus Victorius.

ORATOR.

Proœmium i. 2.

Oratorem autem instituimus illum perfectum, qui esse nisi vir bonus non potest.

Now, according to my definition, no man can be a complete orator unless he is a good man.

GENIUS.

Proœmium i. 4.

Illud tamen in primis testandum est, nihil praecepta atque artes valere nisi adjuvante naturâ.

One thing, however, I must premise, that without the assistance of natural capacity, rules and precepts are of no efficacy.

DIVINE ORIGIN OF THE MIND.
Lib. i. 1.

Sicut aves ad volatum, equi ad cursum, ad sævitiam feræ gignuntur; ita nobis propria est mentis agitatio atque solertia, unde origo animi cælestis creditur.

As birds are provided by nature with a propensity to fly, horses to run, and wild beasts to be savage, so the working and the sagacity of the brain is peculiar to man; and hence it is that his mind is supposed to be of divine original.

THE DULL.
i. 1.

Hebetes vero et indociles non magis secundum naturam homines eduntur, quam prodigiosa corpora et monstris insignia; sed hi pauci admodum.

The dull and the indocile are in no other sense the productions of nature than are monstrous shapes and extraordinary objects, which are very rare.

YOUTH TENACIOUS OF WHAT IT IMBIBES.
i. 2.

Naturâ tenacissimi sumus eorum quæ rudibus annis percipimus; ut sapor, quo nova imbuas, durat: nec lanarum colores, quibus simplex ille candor mutatus est, elui possunt.

By nature we are very tenacious of what we imbibe in the dawn of life, in the same manner as new vessels retain the flavour which they first drink in. There is no recovering wool to its native whiteness after it is dyed.

SMATTERERS.
i. 2.

Nihil enim pejus est iis qui, paulum aliquid ultra primas literas progressi, falsam sibi scientiæ persuasionem induerunt.

For nothing is more nauseous than men who, having just got a smattering in learning, vainly persuade themselves that they are men of knowledge.

HANDWRITING.
i. 5.

Non est aliena res, quæ fere ab honestis negligi solet, cura bene ac velociter scribendi.

Men of quality are in the wrong to undervalue, as they often do, the practice of a fair and quick hand in writing; for it is no immaterial accomplishment.

THE SCHOOLMASTER.
i. 2. 1.

Nec sane quisquam literis saltem leviter imbutus, eum in quo studium ingeniumque perspexerit, non in suam quoque gloriam peculiariter fovebit.

A master, let him have but a moderate tincture of learning, will not, merely for his own credit, cherish application and genius, wherever he finds them.

AMBITION.
i. 2. 2.

Licet ipsa vitium sit ambitio, frequenter tamen causa virtutum est.

Though ambition in itself is a vice, yet it is often the parent of virtues.

MIMICRY.
i. 3. 1.

Non dabit mihi spem bonæ indolis, qui hoc imitandi studio petit, ut rideatur.

I have no great opinion of any boy's capacity, whose whole aim is to raise a laugh by his talent of mimicry.

PREMATURITY OF GENIUS.
i. 3. 1.

Illud ingeniorum velut præcox genus, non temere unquam pervenit ad frugem.

It seldom happens that a premature shoot of genius ever arrives at maturity.

A BOY OF GENIUS.
i. 3. 2.

Mihi ille detur puer, quem laus excitet, quem gloria juvet, qui victus fleat. Hic erit alendus ambitu, hunc mordebit objurgatio, hunc honor excitabit: in hoc desidiam nunquam verebor.

Give me the boy who rouses when he is praised, who profits when he is encouraged, and who cries when he is defeated. Such a boy will be fired by ambition; he will be stung by reproach, and animated by preference: never shall I apprehend any bad consequences from idleness in such a boy.

EVIL HABITS.

i. 3. 3.

Frangas enim citius quam corrigas quæ in pravum indur-
uerunt.

For evil habits, when they once settle, are more easily broken
than mended.

CUSTOM.

i. 4. 3.

Consuetudo vero, certissima loquendi magistra : uten-
dumque plane sermone, ut nummo, cui publica forma est.

The common usage of learned men, however, is the surest
director of speaking ; and language, like money, when it receives
the public stamp, ought to have currency.

USAGE OF LANGUAGE.

i. 4. 3.

Ergo consuetudinem sermonis, vocabo consensum erudi-
torum ; sicut vivendi, consensum bonorum.

I therefore look upon the general practice of the learned to be
the usage of language, in like manner as the general practice of the
virtuous is to be considered as the usage of life.

MUSIC.

i. 8. 1.

Etiam singulorum fatigatio quamlibet se rudi modula-
tione solatur.

For every man, when at work, even by himself, has his own song,
however rude it may be, that softens his labour.

R. Gifford "Contemplation:"—

"Verse sweetens toil, however rude the sound ;
All at her work the village maiden sings,
Nor, while she turns the giddy wheel around,
Revolves the sad vicissitudes of things."

THE ILLITERATE.

i. 8. 1.

Denique in proverbium usque Græcorum celebratum est,
indoctos a musis atque gratiis abesse.

In short, it has become a proverb amongst the Greeks, that the
illiterate has no acquaintance with the muses and the graces

THE MIND.

i. 11. 1.

Mens mutatione recreabitur : sicut in cibis, quorum
liversitate reficitur stomachus, et pluribus minore fastidio
ilitur.

Our minds are like our stomachs ; they are whetted by the change
f their food, and variety supplies both with fresh appetite.

ELOQUENCE.

i. 11. 3.

Qui vero imaginem ipsam eloquentiæ divinâ quâdam
nente conceperit, quique illam (ut ait non ignobilis tragi-
:us) reginam rerum orationem ponet ante oculos, fructum-
jue non ex stipe advocationum, sed ex animo suo et con-
emplatione ac scientiâ petet, perpetuum illum nec fortunæ
ubjectum.

But give me the reader who figures in his mind the idea of elo-
juence, all divine as she is, who, with Euripides, gazes upon her
ll-subduing charms ; who seeks not his reward from the venal fee
or his voice, but from that reflection, that imagination, that per-
ection of mind, which time cannot destroy, nor fortune affect.

EXPERIENCE.

ii. 5. 5.

Nam in omnibus fere minus valent præcepta quam ex-
erimenta.

For in almost every art experience is more serviceable than
recepts.

TO MAKE THE WORSE APPEAR THE BETTER REASON.

ii. 17. 1.

Nam et Socrati objiciunt comici, docere eum quomodo
ejorem causam meliorem faciat.

For comic writers charge Socrates with making the worse appear
he better reason.

Milton ("Paradise Lost," ii. 113) says :—

> " Though his tongue
> Dropt manna, and could make the worse
> Appear the better reason."

SPEECH.
ii. 17. 2.

Deus ille princeps, parens rerum fabricatorque mund
nullo magis hominem separavit a ceteris, quæ quidem mor
talia sunt, animalibus, quam dicendi facultate.

God, that all powerful Creator of nature, and Architect of th
world, has impressed man with no character so proper to distin
guish him from other animals, as by the faculty of speech.

WHAT ART CAN EFFECT.
ii. 20. 1.

Denique natura materiæ, ars doctrinæ est. Hæc fingi
illa fingitur. Nihil ars sine materiâ; materiæ etiam sii
arte pretium est. Ars summa, materiâ optimâ melior.

In short, nature supplies the material, art works upon it. A
can effect nothing without material, yet there is an inherent valu
in the material though untouched by the art of man. Perfectic
of art is superior to the best material.

RIDICULING THE MISERABLE.
vi. 3. 5.

Nam adversus miseros inhumanus est jocus.

For it is unfeeling to ridicule the wretched.

A JEST.
vi. 3. 5.

Ludere nunquam velimus, longeque absit propositul
illud: potius amicum quam dictum perdidi.

Let all malice be removed, and let us never adopt that maxin
Rather to lose our friend than our jest.

A LAUGH.
vi. 3. 5.

Nimium risus pretium est, si probitatis impendio consta

A laugh is too dearly bought when purchased at the expense
virtue.

WHAT MAKES A MAN ELOQUENT.
vii. 7. 2.

Pectus est quod disertos facit et vis mentis.

It is the heart and mental energy that inspires elo

Brilliant Thoughts in Oratory.

viii. 5. 2.

Ego vero hæc lumina orationis, velut oculos quosdam esse eloquentiæ credo. Sed neque oculos esse toto corpore velim, ne cætera membra suum officium perdant.

Brilliant thoughts are, I consider, as it were the eyes of eloquence; but I would not that the body were all eyes, lest the other members should lose their proper functions.

To Destroy One's Neighbour.

xii. 1. 1.

Mutos enim nasci, et egere omni rationc satius fuisset, quam Providentiæ munera in mutuam pernicicm convertere.

For it would have been better that man should have been born dumb, nay, void of all reason, rather than that he should employ the gifts of Providence to the destruction of his neighbour.

A Wicked Conscience.

xii. 1. 1.

Nihil est enim tam occupatum, tam multiforme, tot ac tam variis affectibus concisum atque laceratum, quam mala mens. Nam et cum insidiatur, spe, curis, labore distringitur: et jam cum sceleris compos fuerit, solicitudine, pœnitentiâ, pœnarum omnium expectatione torquetur.

For there is nothing so distracted, of such different forms, so cut up and tortured by many and various apprehensions, as a wicked conscience. For while it is contriving the ruin of another, itself is under the torture of uncertainty, anxiety, and dread. Nay, even when it is successful in iniquity, it is tormented with disquiet, remorse, and the expectation of the most dreadful punishments.

Virtue must Receive a Finishing Stroke from Learning.

xii. 2. 1.

Virtus etiamsi quosdam impetûs a naturâ sumit, tamen perficienda doctrinâ est.

Virtue, though she in some measure receives her beginning from nature, yet she gets her finishing excellences from learning.

EASY TO BE VIRTUOUS.
xii. 11. 2.

Natura enim nos ad mentem optimam genuit : adeoque discere meliora volentibus promptum est, ut vere intuenti mirum sit illud magis, malos esse tam multos.

Nature has formed us with honest inclinations, and, when we are so inclined, it is so very easy to be virtuous, that, if we seriously reflect, nothing is more astonishing than to see so many wicked.

SALLUSTIUS

BORN B.C. 86—DIED B.C. 34.

C. SALLUSTIUS CRISPUS was born, B.C. 86, at Amiternum, in the country of the Sabines. In B.C. 52 we find him tribunus plebis, and two years afterwards he was ejected from the senate by the censors on account of immoral conduct. However, he seems to have been restored to his rank, as he was prætor in B.C. 47. Next year he accompanied Cæsar in his African war, and was there left governor of Numidia. Here he is accused of having amassed immense riches by the oppression of the people, and many scandalous tales are told respecting him. On returning from Africa he retired into private life, and passed quietly through the troublesome period after Cæsar's death, dying B.C. 34.

MIND AND BODY.
Cat. 1.

Nostra omnis vis in animo et corpore sita : animi imperio, corporis servitio magis utimur : alterum nobis cum dis, alterum cum belluis commune est.

Our whole strength resides in the powers of the mind and body ; while we are willing to submit to the directions of the former, we are anxious to render the body subservient to our will. The one is common to us with the gods ; the other, with the lower animals.

MIND.
Cat. 1.

Divitiarum et formæ gloria fluxa atque fragilis ; virtus clara æternaque habetur.

The glory derived from riches and beauty is fleeting and frail: the endowments of the mind form the only illustrious and lasting possession.

Antiphanes (Fr. Com. Gr. p. 570, M.) says:—

Ψυχὴν ἔχειν δεῖ πλουσίαν· τὰ δὲ χρήματα
Ταῦτ' ἐστιν ὄψις, παραπέτασμα τοῦ βίου.

"We must have our mind rich: the riches of the world are merely outward show, that veil the real character."

FORETHOUGHT.
Cat. 1.

Et prius, quam incipias, consulto; et, ubi consulueris, mature facto opus est.

Before one begins, there is need of forethought, and after we have carefully considered, there is need of speedy execution.

MIND.
Cat. 2.

Quæ homines arant, navigant, ædificant, virtuti omnia parent.

All the operations of agriculture, navigation, and architecture depend for their success on the endowments of the mind.

ACTIVE LIFE.
Cat. 2.

Is demum mihi vivere atque frui animâ videtur, qui aliquo negotio intentus, præclari facinoris aut artis bonæ famam quærit. Sed, in magnâ copiâ rerum, aliud alii natura iter ostendit.

He, and he alone, seems to me to have the full enjoyment of his existence, who, in whatever employment he may be engaged, seeks for the reputation arising from some praiseworthy deed or the exercise of some useful talent. But in the great variety of employments, nature points out different paths to different individuals.

CATILINE.
Cat. 5.

Alieni appetens, sui profusus, ardens in cupiditatibus: satis loquentiæ, sapientiæ parum.

Greedy of the possessions of others, lavish of his own, eager in his pursuits, fluent enough in language, but possessed of little common sense.

FORTUNE.
Cat. 8.

Sed profecto Fortuna in omni re dominatur: ea res cunctas ex lubidine magis, quam ex vero, celebrat, obscuratque.

But assuredly Fortune rules in all things; she raises to eminence or buries in oblivion everything from caprice rather than from well-regulated principle.

AMBITION.
Cat. 10.

Ambitio multos mortales falsos fieri subegit; aliud clausum in pectore, aliud in linguâ promptum habere; amicitias inimicitiasque, non ex re, sed ex commodo, æstumare; magisque vultum, quam ingenium, bonum habere.

Ambition hath made many men hypocrites; to have one thing concealed in the breast, and another ready on the tongue; to estimate friendships and enmities, not from their real worth, but from motives of private advantage; and to have a fair outside rather than an honest heart.

THE GOOD AND THE BAD.
Cat. 11.

Gloriam, honorem, imperium, bonus, ignavus æque sibi exoptant: sed ille verâ viâ nititur; huic quia bonæ artes desunt, dolis atque fallaciis contendit.

The virtuous and unprincipled are equally anxious for glory, honour, and command; but the one strives to attain them by honourable means, the other aims at the attainment of his object by knavery and deceit, because good arts fail him.

PROSPERITY.
Cat. 11.

Quippe secundæ res sapientium animos fatigant; ne illi, corruptis moribus, victoriæ temperarent.

The truth is, prosperity unhinges the minds of the wise; much less could they, with their corrupt habits, be expected to refrain from abusing their victory.

THE MALEVOLENT.
Cat. 16.

Scilicet ne per otium torpescerent manus, gratuito potius malus atque crudelis erat.

He was malevolent and cruel, without any views of private advantage, lest his hands should get stiff through want of practice.

FRIENDSHIP.
Cat. 20.

Nam idem velle atque nolle, ea demum firma amicitia est.

For to have the same predilections and the same aversions, that and that alone is the surest bond of friendship.

FORTUNE.
Cat. 20.

En illa, illa, quam sæpe optâstis, libertas, præterea divitiæ, decus, gloria, in oculis sita sunt! Fortuna omnia victoribus præmia posuit.

Behold that, that liberty, for which you have so often panted; besides, riches, honour, glory, are placed before your eyes. Fortune hath given every reward to the conquerors.

THE POOR.
Cat. 37.

Nam semper in civitate, quîs opes nullæ sunt, bonis invident, malos extollunt; vetera odêre, nova exoptant; odio suarum rerum, mutari omnia student; turbâ atque seditionibus sine curâ aluntur; quoniam egestas facile habetur sine damno.

For always in a state, those who have no resources of their own look with an evil eye on the higher classes of their fellow-citizens; elevate to office those who are of the same stamp with themselves; hate old things and desire new; are anxious for change from dislike of their own; are supported by public disturbance without any apprehension for themselves, since poverty is upheld easily without loss.

MATTERS OF IMPORTANCE.
Cat. 51.

Omnes homines, qui de rebus dubiis consultant, ab odio, amicitiâ, irâ, atque misericordiâ, vacuos esse decet.

All who deliberate on matters of importance, ought to be uninfluenced with feelings of hatred, friendship, anger, or compassion.

THE LOW AND THE HIGH.
Cat. 51.

Qui demissi in obscuro vitam habent, si quid iracundiâ deliquêre, pauci sciunt; famâ atque fortunâ pares sunt:

qui, magno imperio præditi, in excelso ætatem agunt,
eorum facta cuncti mortales novêre. Ita in maxumâ for-
tunâ minuma licentia est : neque studere neque odisse, sed
minume irasci, decet. Quæ apud alios iracundia dicitur,
in imperio superbia atque crudelitas appellatur.

Those who pass their lives sunk in obscurity, if they have com-
mitted any offence through the impulse of passion, few know of it;
their reputation and fortune are alike : those who are in great
command and in an exalted station, have their deeds known to all
men. Thus, in the highest condition of life there is the least free-
dom of action. They ought to show neither partiality nor hatred,
but least of all resentment ; what in others is called hastiness of
temper, is in those invested with power styled haughtiness and
cruelty.

DEATH.
Cat. 51.

De pœnâ possumus equidem dicere id, quod res habet :
in luctu atque miseriis mortem ærumnarum requiem, non
cruciatum esse ; eam cuncta mortalium mala dissolvere ;
ultra neque curæ neque gaudio locum esse.

Respecting punishment, we may surely say that which the case
warrants ; in grief and misery death is a reprieve from the sor-
rows of life, not a punishment ; it puts a termination to all the
ills of mankind : beyond the grave there is room for neither care
nor joy.

Euripides (Fr. Antig. 17) says :—

Θάνατος γὰρ ἀνθρώποισι νεικέων τέλος
Ἔχει· τί γὰρ τοῦδ᾽ ἐστὶ μεῖζον ἐν βροτοῖς ;
Τίς γὰρ πετραῖον σκόπελον οὐτάζων δορὶ
Ὀδύναισι δώσει ; τίς δ᾽ ἀτιμάζων νέκυν,
Εἰ μηδὲν αἰσθάνοιτο τῶν παθημάτων.

" For death is the end of troubles to men, for what is better to men than
this? For who wounding a rocky cliff with a spear will cause it pain ? Who
can dishonour the dead if they feel nothing ? "

Æschylus (Fr. Philoct.) says :—

Ὦ θάνατε παιάν, μή μ᾽ ἀτιμάσῃς μολεῖν·
Μόνος γὰρ εἶ σὺ τῶν ἀνηκέστων κακῶν
Ἰατρός· ἄλγος δ᾽ οὐδὲν ἅπτεται νεκρῶν.

" O death, thou deliverer, do not slight me coming to thee : for thou alone
art the physician of incurable ills : no grief reaches the dead."

THE GODS.
Cat. 52.

Non votis neque suppliciis muliebribus auxilia deorum
parantur : vigilando, agendo, bene consulendo, prospera

omnia cedunt : ubi secordiæ te atque ignaviæ tradideris, nequidquam deos implores ; irati infestique sunt.

The aid of the gods is procured not by vows and womanish supplications ; all things turn out well by watching, activity, and good counsel. When you have given yourself up to sloth and idleness, it is in vain to implore the gods ; they are angry and hostile to you.

GOODNESS.

Cat. 54.

Esse, quam videri, bonus malebat.

He preferred to be good in reality, rather than to seem so.

THE SLOTHFUL.

Cat. 58.

Quem neque gloria neque pericula excitant, nequidquam hortere : timor animi auribus officit.

The man who is roused neither by glory nor by danger, it is in vain to exhort ; terror closes the ears of the mind.

Euripides (Fr. Archel. 8) says :—

Νεανίαν γὰρ ἄνδρα χρὴ τολμᾶν ἀεί·
Οὐδεὶς γὰρ ὢν ῥᾴθυμος εὐκλεὴς ἀνήρ,
'Αλλ' οἱ πόνοι τίκτουσι τὴν εὐδοξίαν.

"For a young man ought always to be daring : for no slothful man becomes famous, but it is labour that procures glory."

COWARDS.

Cat. 58.

In fugâ salutem sperare, cum arma, quîs corpus tegitur, ab hostibus averteris, ea vero dementia est. Semper in prœlio maxumum est periculum, qui maxume timent : audacia pro muro habetur.

For to hope for safety in flight when you have turned your arms, with which the body is protected, from the enemy, that indeed is folly. In battle the greatest cowards are in greatest danger ; boldness is the best defence.

MIND.

Jug. 1.

Dux atque imperator vitæ mortalium animus est ; qui ubi ad gloriam virtutis viâ grassatur, abunde pollens potensque et clarus est, neque fortunæ eget : quippe probitatem, industriam, alias artes bonas, neque dare, neque eripere potest.

The mind is the leader and director of mankind; when it aims
at glory by a virtuous life, it is sufficiently powerful, efficient, and
noble; it stands in no need of the assistance of Fortune, since it
can neither give nor take away integrity, industry, nor other praise-
worthy qualities.

THE MIND.
Jug. 2.

Præclara facies, magnæ divitiæ, ad hoc vis corporis, alia
hujuscemodi omnia, brevi dilabuntur; at ingenii egregia
facinora, sicuti anima, immortalia sunt. Postremo, corporis
et fortunæ bonorum ut initium, finis est: omnia orta occi-
dunt, et aucta senescunt; animus incorruptus, æternus,
rector humani generis, agit atque habet cuncta, neque ipse
habetur.

Personal beauty, great riches, strength of body, and all other
things of this kind, pass away in a short time; but the noble pro-
ductions of the mind, like the soul itself, are immortal. In fine,
as there is a beginning, so there is an end of the advantages of per-
son and fortune; all things that rise must set, and those that have
grown must fade away: the mind is incorruptible,[1] eternal, the
governor of the human race, directs and overrules all things, nor
is itself under the power of any.[2]

OPPORTUNITY.
Jug. 6.

Opportunitas etiam mediocres viros spe prædæ trans-
versos agit.

Opportunity leads even moderate men astray from the path of
duty by the hope of self-aggrandisement.

CONCORD.
Jug. 10.

Non exercitus neque thesauri præsidia regni sunt, verum
amici, quos neque armis cogere, neque auro parare queas:
officio et fide pariuntur. Quis autem amicior, quam frater
fratri? aut quem alienum fidum invenies, si tuis hostis
fueris? Equidem ego vobis regnum trado firmum, si boni
eritis; sin mali, imbecillum. Nam concordiâ parvæ res
crescunt, discordiâ maxumæ dilabuntur.

Neither armies nor treasures are the bulwarks of a kingdom; but
friends, whom you can neither command by force, nor purchase by
gold: they are gained by kind offices, and by the exercise of fidelity.
Who ought to be more friendly than a brother to a brother? or

what stranger will you find to be faithful, if you be an enemy to your own connexions? I indeed deliver to you a kingdom, which is strong, if you are good; weak, if you are bad. For a small state increases by concord; the greatest state falls gradually to ruin by dissension.

ROME.

Jug. 35.

Sed postquam Româ egressus est, fertur, sæpe eo tacitus respiciens, postremo dixisse, Urbem venalem, et mature perituram, si emtorem invenerit.

But after he had left Rome, he is said, often looking back in silence, to have exclaimed, "Ah, venal city! destined soon to perish, could it but find a purchaser."

A GOOD MAN.

Jug. 42.

Bono vinci satius est, quam malo more injuriam vincere.

It is better for a good man to be overcome by his opponents than to conquer injustice by unconstitutional means.

A BOASTER.

Jug. 44.

Neque periculi neque laboris patiens, linguâ quam manu promptior.

Impatient of labour and of danger, more ready to boast of their valour than to display it.

ANCESTORS.

Jug. 85.

Majorum gloria posteris lumen est, neque bona neque mala in occulto patitur.

The glory of ancestors sheds a light around posterity; it allows neither their good nor bad qualities to remain in obscurity.

ANCESTORS.

Jug. 85.

Cæterum homines superbissumi procul errant. Majores eorum omnia, quæ licebat, illis, reliquére, divitias, imagines, memoriam sui præclaram: virtutem non reliquére; neque poterant: ea sola neque datur dono, neque accipitur.

But proud men are very much mistaken. Their ancestors have
left all things which are in their power to them—riches, images,
the noble recollection of them ; they have not left their virtue,
nor were they able : it alone can neither be presented as a gift,
nor received.

CHILDREN.
Jug. 85.

Ignaviâ nemo immortalis factus : neque quisquam parens
liberis, uti æterni forent, optavit ; magis, uti boni honesti-
que vitam exigerent.

No one has become immortal by sloth, nor has any parent prayed
that their children should live for ever; but rather that they
should lead an honourable and upright life.

KINGS.
Jug. 113.

Plerumque regiæ voluntates, ut vehementes, sic mobiles,
sæpe ipsæ sibi advorsæ.

In general the desires of kings, though impetuous, are unstable
and often inconsistent.

EVERY ONE THE ARTIFICER OF HIS OWN FORTUNE.
Orat. De Republ. Ordinand.

Fabrum esse sua quemque fortunæ.

Every one is the artificer of his own fortune.

Shakespeare (" Julius Cæsar," act i. sc. 2):—

> " Men at some time are masters of their fates ;
> The fault, dear Brutus, is not in our stars,
> But in ourselves, that we are underlings."

SENECA

BORN ABOUT A.D. 1—DIED A.D. 65.

L. ANNÆUS SENECA, son of M. Annæus Seneca, was born at Cor-
duba, and brought to Rome by his parents when he was a child.
He was educated at Rome, and acquired distinction at an early
age as a pleader of causes, exciting the hatred of Caligula from the
ability he displayed in conducting a cause before him. In the first
year of the reign of Claudius, A.D. 41, he was ordered to retire in
exile to Corsica, where he resided for eight years, being

by the influence of Agrippina, A.D. 49. He then obtained the
prætorship, and became tutor to the emperor Nero. His pupil did
him no credit, but it would be unjust to blame him for the sub-
sequent conduct of Nero. He did not, indeed, make him a good
or a wise man; his natural disposition, however, was probably
irreclaimable. For some years he was the chief minister of Nero,
but, falling into disgrace, he received notice to die, and suffocated
himself in a vapour bath, A.D. 65.

NONE BUT HIMSELF EQUAL TO HIMSELF.

Her. Fur. 84.

Quæris Alcidæ parem ?
Nemo est nisi ipse.

Do you seek a match for the son of Atreus? There is no one
but himself.

Louis Theobald "The Double Falsehood :"—
"None but himself can be his parallel."

ENJOY THE PRESENT.

Her. Fur. 174.

Novit paucos
Secura quies, qui velocis
Memores ævi, tempora nunquam
Reditura tenent. Dum fata sinunt,
Vivite læti : properat cursu
Vita citato, volucrique Die
Rota præcipitis vertitur anni.

Few enjoy the pleasures of peaceful repose, who consider how
swiftly time passes that is never to return. While the fates allow,
eat, drink, and be merry. Life hurries forward with rapid step,
and the wheel of time rolls on in its ceaseless round.

MIGHT MAKES RIGHT.

Her. Fur. 251.

Prosperum ac felix scelus
Virtus vocatur ; sontibus parent boni ;
Jus est in armis, opprimit leges timor.

Successful crime is dignified with the name of virtue ; the good
become the slaves of the impious ; might makes right ; fear silences
the power of the law.

Wordsworth (" Rob Roy's Grave," st. 9) :—
"Because the good old rule
Sufficeth them, the simple plan,

> That they should take who have the power,
> And they should keep who can."

See (Gr.) Might.

The Miserable easily give Credit to Fear.

Her. Fur. 313.

Quod nimis miseri volunt,
Hoc facile credunt.   Imo quod metuunt nimis,
Nunquam moveri posse nec tolli putant :
Prona est timori semper in pejus fides.

The miserable easily give credit to that which they wish.   Nay, they are apt to believe that what they fear can never be got rid of. Fear is ever credulous of evil.

The Pitcher goes once too often to the Well.

Her. Fur. 325.

Iniqua raro maximis virtutibus
Fortuna parcit.   Nemo se tuto diu
Periculis offerre tam crebris potest.
Quem sæpe transit casus, aliquando invenit.

Adverse fortune seldom spares men of the noblest virtues.   No one can with safety expose himself often to dangers.   The man who has often escaped, is at last caught.

To Boast of one's Pedigree.

Her. Fur. 340.

Qui genus jactat suum,
Aliena laudat.

He, who boasts of his descent, praises what belongs to another.

Sovereignty.

Her. Fur. 344.

Alieno in loco
Haud stabile regnum est.

When you occupy the throne of another, your power is insecure.

Envy of those in Power.

Her. Fur. 353.

Ars prima regni posse te invidiam pati.

To be able to endure odium is the first art to be learned by those who aspire to power.

The Proud.
Her. Fur. 385.

Sequitur superbos ultor a tergo Deus.

The avenging God follows close on the haughty.

Die rather than Act against the Will.
Her. Fur. 426.

Cogi qui potest, nescit mori.

The man, who can be forced to act against his will, knows not how to die.

The Ascent to Heaven is not Easy.
Her. Fur. 437.

Non est ad astra mollis e terris via.

The ascent to heaven from this earth is not easy.

Misery the Lot of Humanity.
Her. Fur. 463.

Quemcunque miserum videris, hominem scias.

Whenever you see a fellow-creature in distress, know that you see a human being.

Remembrance of what was Difficult is Pleasant.
Her. Fur. 656.

Quæ fuit durum pati, Meminisse dulce est.

What was difficult to endure is pleasant to call to remembrance.

See (Gr.) Past labours.

The Guilty Overwhelmed by his own Acts.
Her. Fur. 735.

Quod quisque fecit, patitur : auctorem scelus
Repetit, suoque premitur exemplo nocens.

Man suffers for his deeds : crime finds out its author, and the guilty is overwhelmed by his own acts.

We are Dying from the First Moment of our Birth.
Her. Fur. 874.

Prima quæ vitam dedit hora, carpit.

The first moment which gave us birth, begins to take life from us.

The Heavy-Laden.

Her. Fur. 925.

> Detur aliquando otium
> Quiesque fessis.

Let the weary and heavy-laden at length enjoy repose.

The Humble often Receive great Praise.

Thyest. 211.

> Laus vera et humili sæpe contingit viro.

The humble and lowly-born often receive true praise.

Despotism.

Thyest. 214.

> ATR. Ubicunque tantum honesta dominanti licent,
> Precario regnatur. SAT. Ubi non est pudor,
> Nec cura juris, sanctitas, pietas, fides :
> Instabile regnum est. ATR. Sanctitas, pietas, fides,
> Privata bona sunt ; qua juvat, reges eant.

ATR. Wherever a ruler is subject to the law, his power is of precarious tenure. SAT. Nay, rather where neither modesty nor respect for the law or gods, piety nor faith, hold sway, there power is unstable. ATR. My opinion is, that respect for the gods, piety, and faith are merely virtues of men in private stations. Let kings be unshackled in their authority.

A Bad Brother not to be Injured.

Thyest. 219.

> Nefas nocere vel malo fratri puta.

Consider it impious to injure even a bad brother.

The Young easily Perverted.

Thyest. 309.

> Pejora juvenes facile præcepta audiunt ;
> In patre facient, quidquid in patruo doces.
> Sæpe in magistrum scelera redierunt sua.

The young readily listens to evil counsels; they will practise against you, their father, what you have taught them against their uncle. Crimes have often recoiled on those who gave the first lesson.

GREAT COUNSELS BETRAYED BY THE COUNTENANCE.

Thyest. 332.

Magna nolentem quoque
Consilia produnt.

Great counsels betray even the man who is unwilling that his plans should be discovered.

IT IS THE MIND THAT GIVES A KINGDOM.

Thyest. 380.

Mens regnum bona possidet.

An honest heart possesses a kingdom.

Percy's "Reliques of English Poetry," (vol. i. p. 307) :—

"My mind to me a kingdom is
Such perfect joy therein I find,
As far exceeds all earthly bliss,
That God and nature hath assign'd.
Though much I want that most would have,
Yet still my mind forbids to crave."

RETIREMENT TO BE PREFERRED.

Thyest. 388.

Rex est, qui metuit nihil.
Rex est, qui cupiet nihil.
Hoc regnum sibi quisque dat.
Stet, quiqunque volet, potens
Aulæ culmine lubrico :
Me dulcis saturet quies ;
Obscuro positus loco,
Leni perfruar otio.

He is a king who is subject to neither fears nor desires. Every one can confer this on himself. Let whosoever chooses walk along the slippery paths of the court, I prefer peaceful repose, and, resigned to the obscurity of a humble life, shall enjoy the pleasures of retirement.

WHO LIVES FOR OTHERS, NOT FOR HIMSELF.

Thyest. 401.

Illi mors gravis incubat,
Qui notus nimis omnibus
Ignotus moritur sibi.

Death broods heavily over the man who dies more known to others than to himself.

Hénault, (Œuvres diverses,) the author of the celebrated son:
"Averten," says :—

> "Heureux est l'inconnu qui s'est bien su connoître,
> Il ne voit pas de mal à mourir plus qu'à naître.
> Il s'en va comme il est venu."

And again, Maynard says, perhaps still more beautifully :—

> "Las d'espérer et de me plaindre
> Des Muses, des Grands et du Sort,
> C'est ici que j'attends la mort
> Sans la désirer ni la craindre."

THE GIVER TO BE LOOKED AT.
Thyest. 416.

Cum quod datur spectabis, et dantem adspice !

While you look at what is given, look also at the giver.

THE POOR ENJOY A SECURE REPAST.
Thyest. 450.

O quantum bonum est,
Obstare nulli, capere securas dapes
Humi jacentem !   Scelera non intrant casas,
Tutusque mensâ capitur augustâ cibus ;
Venenum in auro bibitur.   Expertus loquor :
Malam bonæ præferre fortunam licet.

What pleasure it is to stand in the way of no one, to be able
enjoy a secure repast ! Crimes do not enter into the cottages
the poor ; we may eat our food with safety on a humble tabl
poison is quaffed from golden cups. I speak from experience :
obscure life is preferable to one spent in a high station.

Diphilus (Fr. Com. Gr. p. 1092, M.) says :—

> Πένητος ἀνδρὸς οὐδὲν εὐτυχέστερον·
> Τὴν ἐπὶ τὸ χεῖρον μεταβολὴν οὐ προσδοκᾷ.

"No one is more fortunate than the poor man : he has no change for
worse to look for."

CAUTION.
Thyest. 487.

Serum est cavendi tempus in mediis malis.

It is too late to be on our guard when we are in the midst
misfortunes.

TO-MORROW.
Thyest. 619.

Nemo tam divos habuit faventes,
Crastinum ut possit sibi polliceri.

Nobody has ever found the gods so much his friend that he can promise himself another day.

See (Gr.) To-morrow.

LOVE OF LIFE.

Thyest. 882.

Vitæ est avidus, quisquis non vult,
Mundo secum moriente, mori.

That man must be enamoured of life, who is not willing to die when the world reaches its last day.

THE MISERABLE.

Thyest. 938.

Proprium hoc miseros sequitur vitium,
Nunquam rebus credere lætis.
Redeat felix Fortuna licet,
Tamen afflictos gaudere piget.

This is the peculiarity of the wretched, that they can never believe that happiness will last. Even though good fortune returns, yet they rejoice in fear and trembling.

PASSIONS ENCOURAGED BY YIELDING.

Hipp. 134.

Qui blandiendo dulce nutrivit malum,
Sero recusat ferre, quod subiit, jugum.

He, who has fostered the sweet poison of love by fondling it, finds it too late to refuse the yoke which he has of his own accord assumed.

PANGS OF A GUILTY CONSCIENCE ARE NEVER AT REST.

Hipp. 163.

Quid pœna præsens, consciæ mentis pavor,
Animusque culpâ plenus et semet timens?
Scelus aliqua tutum, nulla securum tulit.

What never-ending pain are the pangs of a guilty conscience, a mind o'erburdened with crimes, and fearful of itself? Some may sin without suffering from man, none may do so and feel secure.

Shakespeare ("Henry VI.," Pt. III., act v. sc. 6):—

> "Suspicion always haunts the guilty mind;
> The thief doth fear each bush an officer."

THE GREAT IN POWER.
Hipp. 215.

Quod non potest, vult posse, qui nimium potest.
The high in power are often desirous of impossibilities.

A REMEDY.
Hipp. 249.

Pars sanitatis velle sanari fuit.
It is some part of a cure to feel a desire to be cured.

MODES OF DEATH.
Hipp. 475.

Quam varia leti genera mortalem trahunt
Carpuntque turbam, pontus, et ferrum, et doli !
Sed fata credas deesse : sic atram Styga
Jam petimus ultro.

How many kinds of death hurry off and gradually destroy mankind—the sea, the sword, and treachery ! But say we were not subject to these laws of fate, yet of ourselves we hasten to our life's end, to the dark shades of Styx.

A TIMID BEGGAR COURTS A DENIAL.
Hipp. 594.

Qui timide rogat,
Docet negare.
He who begs timorously, courts a refusal.

SUCCESSFUL CRIMES.
Hipp. 598.

Honesta quædam scelera successus facit.
Success gilds some crimes with an honourable title.

See (Gr., Fr.) Success.

LIGHT GRIEFS.
Hipp. 607.

Curæ leves loquuntur, ingentes stupent.

Trifling annoyances find utterance ; deeply-felt pangs are dumb.
Spenser in his " Faerie Queen " (l. 7. 41) thus expresses the same idea :—

" ' Oh ! but,' quoth she, ' great grief will not be told,
And can more easily be thought than said.' "

And Byron (" The Corsair," cant. iii. st. 22) :—

" No words suffice the secret soul to show,
For truth denies all eloquence to woe."

CRIME.

Hipp. 721.

Scelere velandum est scelus.

One crime has to be concealed by another.

BEAUTY.

Hipp. 761.

Anceps forma bonum mortalibus,
Exigui donum breve temporis,
Ut velox celeri pede laberis !
Non sic prata novo vere decentia
Æstatis calidæ despoliat vapor ;
Sævit solstitio cum medius dies,
Et noctes brevibus præcipitat rotis,
Languescunt folio lilia pallido,
Et gratæ capiti deficiunt rosæ,
Ut fulgor, teneris qui radiat genis,
Momento rapitur, nullaque non dies
Formosi spolium corporis abstulit.
Res est forma fugax : quis sapiens bono
Confidat fragili ? Dum licet, utere.
Tempus te tacitum subruet, horaque
Semper præterita deterior subit.

Beauty, a doubtful good to man, the fleeting gift of a short
lived hour, how swiftly dost thou flit away ! Not so quickly do
the hot rays of summer despoil the fresh meadows of the green
with which the late spring has clothed them, when the meridian
sun rages at the solstice, and short nights wheel rapidly past, when
the pale lilies languish and the sweet rose droops, not so quickly,
I say, as beauty, which beams from tender cheeks, vanishes, from
which every day steals some spoil away. Beauty is a fleeting
joy ; what wise man would place his trust in such a frail toy ?
Whilst thou mayst, enjoy it. Time, with silent march, will under-
mine thee, and each succeeding hour is worse than what is past.

Shakespeare in his poem entitled " **The Passionate Pilgrim** " (st. 11) thus
speaks of Beauty :—

" Beauty is but a vain and doubtful good,
  A shining gloss that vadeth suddenly,
A flower that dies, when first it 'gins to bud,
  A brittle glass that 's broken presently.
A doubtful good, a gloss, a glass, a flower,
Lost, vaded, broken, dead, within an hour."

See (Gr.) Beauty.

SECRECY.
Hipp. 876.

Alium silere quod voles, primus sile.

If you would wish another to keep your secret, first keep
yourself.

THE HUMBLE.
Hipp. 1124.

Minor in parvis Fortuna furit,
Leviusque ferit leviora deus.

Fortune rages less against the lowly, and heaven strikes wit
gentle hand the humble.

DEATH AND LIFE.
Phœnis. 152.

Eripere vitam nemo non homini potest ;
At nemo mortem : mille ad hanc aditus patent.

Any one may take life from man, but no one death : a thousan
gates stand open to it.

ENDURE RATHER THAN COMMIT WICKEDNESS.
Phœnis. 494.

Quoties necesse est fallere aut falli a suis,
Patiare potius ipse, quam facias, scelus.

When it is necessary to deceive or to be deceived by our friend
we should endure rather than commit wickedness.

SLAVERY.
Phœnis. 598.

In servitutem cadere de regno grave est.

To sink from a throne into slavery is misery.

WAR.
Phœnis. 629.

·Fortuna belli semper ancipiti in loco est.

The fortune of war is always doubtful.

A GOVERNMENT HATED.
Phœnis. 660.

Invisa nunquam imperia retinentur diu.

A government that is hated seldom lasts.

FORTUNE.
Œdip. 86.

Haud est virile terga Fortunæ dare.

It is not manly to turn our back on Fortune.

THE AFFLICTED.
Œdip. 213.

Dubiam salutem qui dat adflictis, negat.

He who offers doubtful safety to the afflicted refuses it.

MODERATION TO BE SHOWN BY THOSE WHO ASPIRE TO SUPREME POWER.
Œdip. 682.

Certissima est regnare cupienti via,
Laudare modica, et otium ac somnum loqui.
Ab inquieto sæpe simulatur quies.

To the man who aspires to supreme power, it is the wisest policy to show himself enamoured of moderation, and to speak of nothing but the pleasure of quiet retirement. Rest is often assumed by the restless.

TERROR IS THE PROPER GUARD OF A KINGDOM.
Œdip. 703.

Odia qui nimium timet,
Regnare nescit : regna custodit metus.

He who dreads hatred too much, knows not how to reign. Terror is the proper guard of a kingdom.

LET BYGONES BE BYGONES.
Œdip. 826.

Latere semper patere, quod latuit diu.

Leave in concealment what has long been concealed.

EXCESS HAS AN UNSTABLE FOUNDATION.
Œdip. 910.

Quidquid excessit modum,
Pendet instabili loco.

Everything that exceeds the bounds of moderation has an unstable foundation.

See (Gr., Fr.) Excess.

SUFFERINGS OF MANKIND FROM ON HIGH.

Œdip. 983.

Quidquid patimur mortale genus,
Quidquid facimus, venit ex alto.

Whatever mankind suffers or does, comes from on high.

MODERATION MAKES A THRONE STAND SURE.

Troad. 256.

Noscere hoc primum decet,
Quid facere victor debeat, victus pati.
Violenta nemo imperia continuit diu ;
Moderata durant ; quoque Fortuna altius
Evexit ac levavit humanas opes,
Hoc se magis supprimere felicem decet,
Variosque casus tremere, metuentem deos
Nimium faventes. Magna momento obrui
Vincendo didici.

We must first learn that whatever the conqueror chooses to do
to that the conquered must submit. No one has long maintaine
power, if exercised with violence ; moderation insures its co
tinuance ; and the higher Fortune has lifted and placed the pow
of man, the more ought he to conceal his happiness, to dread th
turns of chance, ever fearing that heaven may be too propitiou
I have learnt that in a moment the greatest state may be brough
low by conquest.

CRIME.

Troad. 291.

Qui non vetat peccare, cum possit, jubet.

He, who does not prevent a crime, when it is in his power, e
courages it.

MERCY SOMETIMES IN GIVING DEATH.

Troad. 329.

Mortem misericors saepe pro vitâ dabit.

Mercy is often shown in inflicting death.

A KING.

Troad. 332.

Præferre patriam liberis regem decet.

A king ought to prefer the good of his country to that of h
children.

MORAL FEELINGS.

Troad. 334.

Quod non vetat lex, hoc vetat fieri pudor.

Man is restrained by moral feelings from doing that against which there may be no legal enactment.

How GREAT POWER OUGHT TO BE USED.

Troad. 336.

Minimum decet libere, cui multum licet.

One who possesses great power, ought to use it with gentle hand.

DOES THE SOUL PERISH WITH THE BODY.

Troad. 371.

Verum est? an timidos fabula decipit,
Umbras corporibus vivere conditis?
Cum conjux oculis imposuit manum,
Supremusque dies solibus obstitit,
Et tristis cineres urna coërcuit :
Non prodest animam tradere funeri :
Sed restat miseris vivere longius?
An toti morimur? nullaque pars manet
Nostri ; cum profugo spiritus halitu
Immistus nebulis cessit in aëra,
Et nudum tetigit subdita fax latus?
        Ut calidis fumus ab ignibus
Vanescit spatium per breve sordidus ;
Ut nubes gravidas, quas modo vidimus,
Arctoi Boreæ disjicit impetus ;
Sic hic, quo regimur, spiritus effluet.
Post mortem nihil est, ipsaque mors nihil,
Velocis spatii meta novissima.
Spem ponant avidi ; solliciti metum.
Quæris, quo jaceas post obitum loco?
Quo non nata jacent.
Tempus nos avidum devorat et chaos.
Mors individua est noxia corpori,
Nec parcens animæ.   Tœnara et aspero
Regnum sub domino, limen et obsidens
Custos non facili Cerberus ostio,

Rumores vacui, verbaque inania,
Et par sollicito fabula somnio.

Is it a truth? or fiction binds
  Our fearful mind?
That when to earth we bodies give,
  Souls yet do live?
That when the wife hath closed with cries
  The husband's eyes,
When the last fatal day of light
  Hath spoil'd our sight,
And when, to dust and ashes turn'd,
  Our bones are urn'd—
Souls stand yet in no need at all
  Of funeral,
But that a longer life with pain
  They still retain?
Or die we quite? nor aught we have
  Survives the grave?
When like to smoke unmix'd with skies
  The spirit flies;
And funeral tapers are applied
  To the naked side.
As smoke, which springs from fire, is soon
  Dispersed and gone;
Or clouds which we but now beheld,
  By winds dispell'd;
The spirit, which informs this clay,
  So fleets away.
Nothing is after death; and this,
  Too, nothing is:
The gaol or the extremest space
  Of a swift race.
The covetous their hopes forbear;
  The sad, their fear.
Ask'st thou, whene'er thou com'st to die,
  Where thou shalt lie?
Where lie the unborn? Away time rakes us,
  Then chaos takes us.
Death's individual: like kind
  To body or mind.
Whate'er of Tænarus they sing,
  And hell's fierce king,
How Cerberus still guards the port
  O' th' Stygian court;
All are but idle rumours found,
  And empty sound;
Like the vain fears of melancholy,
  Dreams and fabulous folly.

To Fear.

Troad. 425.

Miserrimum est timere, cum speres nihil.

It is the worst of ills still to fear, when hope has left us.

Nobility.

Troad. 491.

Grave pondus illum, magna nobilitas, premit.

High rank, a heavy burden, weighs him down.

The First Charge.

Troad. 495.

Victor feroces impetus primos habet.

The first charge of the victor's fury is the worst.

Necessity.

Troad. 581.

Necessitas plus posse quam pietas, solet.

Necessity has greater power than affection.

Impressions once Made are not Easily Erased.

Troad. 633.

Dediscit animus sero, quod didicit diu.

The mind is slow to unlearn what it has been long in learning.

To Extend our Charity to the Miserable.

Troad. 697.

Misero datur quodcunque, fortunæ datur.

Whatever we give to the wretched, we lend to fortune.

To Die Without Fear of Death is Desirable.

Troad. 869.

Optanda mors est, sine metu mortis mori.

To die without fear of death is to be desired.

To be Compelled to Commit a Crime.

Troad. 870.

Ad auctores redit

Sceleris coacti culpa.

The guilt of enforced crimes lies on those who impose them.

SLAVERY.

Troad. 989.

Domini pudet, non servitutis.

I am ashamed of the master, not of servitude.

NONE MISERABLE BUT BY COMPARISON.

Troad. 1016.

Ferre, quam sortem patiuntur omnes,
Nemo recusat ;
Nemo se credit miserum, licet sit.
Tolle felices ; removeto multo
Divites auro ; removeto centum
Rura qui scindunt opulenta bubus :
Pauperi surgent animi jacentes.
Est miser nemo, nisi comparatus.
Dulce in immensis posito ruinis,
Neminem lætos habuisse vultus.

Nobody refuses to submit to the fate to which all are subject.
In a common woe no one thinks himself unfortunate, though he be
so. Take hence the happy, lay the rich aside, remove those who
plough wide fields with a hundred oxen, the poor will raise their
drooping heads. There is no one miserable except by comparison.
To those who are seated amidst the ruins of their fortune, it is
pleasant to see none wearing a cheerful look.

THE MOB.

Troad. 1128.

Magna pars vulgi levis
Odit scelus spectatque.

Most of the giddy vulgar hate the act they come to see.

THE MOB.

Troad. 1143.

Stupet omne vulgus ; et fere cuncti magis
Peritura laudant.

The vulgar stand in stupid amazement, and almost all praise
most those things they are going to lose.

ANGER CONCEALED IS DANGEROUS.

Med. 153.

Ira, quæ tegitur, nocet ;
Professa perdunt odia vindictæ locum.

Resentment concealed, is dangerous; hatred avowed, loses the opportunity of revenge.

THE GRIEF IS SLIGHT WHICH CAN TAKE COUNSEL.
Med. 155.

Levis est dolor, qui capere consilium potest,
Et clepere sese ; magna non latitant mala.

The grief is slight which can take counsel and conceal itself; great evils cannot be hid.

FORTUNE TRAMPLES ON THE COWARD.
Med. 159.

MED. Fortuna fortes metuit, ignavos premit.
NUTR. Tunc est probanda, si locum virtus habet.
MED. Nunquam potest non esse virtuti locus.
NUTR. Spes nulla monstrat rebus adflictis viam.
MED. Qui nil potest sperare, desperet nihil.

MED. Fortune fears the valiant, but tramples on the coward. NURSE. Then valour is to be approved of, when there is room for its display. MED. There is always room for valour. NURSE. Hope points out no path in adverse circumstances. MED. He, who hopes nothing, should despair of nothing.

FORTUNE.
Med. 176.

Fortuna opes auferre, non animum, potest.

Fortune may deprive us of wealth, but not of a firm mind.

A JUDGE.
Med. 194.

Si judicas, cognosce ; si regnas, jube.

If you be a judge, investigate ; if you be a ruler, command.

HEAR THE OTHER SIDE.
Med. 199.

Qui statuit aliquid parte inaudita altera,
Æquum licet statuerit, haud æquus fuerit.

He who decides a question without hearing the other side, though he decide with justice, cannot be considered just.

This is probably the origin of the common expression :—" Audiatur et altera pars."

THE PREROGATIVE OF KINGS.

Med. 222.

Hoc reges habent
Magnificum et ingens, nulla quod rapiat dies,
Prodesse miseris, supplices fido lare
Protegere.

This noble and grand prerogative kings possess, of which they cannot be deprived, to aid the unfortunate and protect the suppliant.

THE POWERFUL NOT TO BE ATTACKED WITH SAFETY.

Med. 430.

Nemo potentes adgredi tutus potest.
None can with safety attack the powerful.

A DESPOT'S WRATH.

Med. 494.

Gravis ira regum est semper.
The wrath of kings is heavy.

THE GAINER IS THE AUTHOR OF THE ILL.

Med. 500.

Cui prodest scelus,
Is fecit.
He who profits by the villany, is the author of it.
This is the "Cui bono" of Cassius.

THE GOLDEN MEAN.

Agam. 100.

Quidquid in altum
Fortuna tulit, ruitura levat.
Modicis rebus longius ævum est.
Felix, mediæ quisquis turbæ
Sorte quietus,
Aurâ stringit littora tutâ ;
Timidusque mari credere cymbam,
Remo terras propiore legit !

The higher the pinnacle to which fortune raises man, he falls with a heavier crash. Things moderate are of longer duration. Happy the man who quietly, in the midst of the crowd, passe along the shore with a safe breeze, and, fearful to trust his bark to the sea, hugs the shore.

Modesty Never Returns.

Agam. 112.

Periêre mores, jus, decus, pietas, fides,
Et, qui redire, cum perit, nescit, pudor.

Pure morals, justice, honour, piety, and faith have disappeared, and modesty, which never returns when it has once gone.

One Crime leads to Another.

Agam. 115.

Per scelera semper sceleribus tutum est iter.

The sure way to wickedness is always through wickedness.

Time Often Heals.

Agam. 130.

Quod ratio non quit, sæpe sanavit mora.

Time often heals what reason cannot.

Extreme Remedies.

Agam. 153.

Extrema primo nemo tentavit loco.

No one has ever tried extreme remedies in the first place.

Repentance Never Too Late.

Agam. 242.

Nam sera nunquam est ad bonos mores via.
Quem pœnitet peccasse, pœne est innocens.

It is never too late to turn from the errors of our ways:
He who repents of his sins is almost innocent.

The Court.

Agam. 285.

Non intrat unquam regium limen fides.

Truth never enters within the threshold of kings.

Fidelity.

Agam. 287.

Pretio parata vincitur pretio fides.

lity, that is bought with money, may be overcome by money.

DELAY.

Agam. 426.

Omnis nimium longa properanti mora est.

Every delay, however trifling, seems too long to a man in haste.

DEATH.

Agam. 510.

In vota miseros ultimus cogit timor.

Fear of death drives the wretched to prayer.

CARES.

Agam. 665.

Magis exurunt,
Quos secretæ lacerant curæ.

Those, whom secret cares torment, suffer most.

PROSPERITY.

Agam. 934.

Poscunt fidem secunda, at adversa exigunt.

Prosperity asks for fidelity, but adversity imperatively demands it.

DEATH.

Agam. 995.

Rudis est tyrannus, morte qui pœnam exigit.
EL. Mortem aliquid ultra est?
ÆGISTH. Vita, si cupias mori.

That tyrant is foolish who inflicts death as a punishment. EL. Is there anything beyond death? ÆGISTH. Life, if you desire to die.

MISERY OF DEATH.

Her. Œt. 104.

Par ille est Superis, cui pariter dies
Et fortuna fuit ; mortis habet vices,
Lente cum trahitur vita gementibus.
Quisquis sub pedibus fata rapacia,
Et puppem posuit fluminis ultimi,
Non captiva dabit brachia vinculis,
Nec pompæ veniet nobile ferculum.

He is equal to the gods whose life and fortune close at the same moment; he feels the misery of death whose life is protracted amidst misery. Whosoever has trampled under foot Fate and the boat of Charon will not allow his arms to be bound in chains, nor to be led in triumph. That man can never be miserable who finds it easy to die.

DEATH.

Her. Œt. 122.

Felices sequeris, Mors, miseros fugis.

O Death! thou followest the happy and fliest the wretched.

Antiphanes (Fr. Com. Gr. p. 512, M.) says:—

Οὐδεὶς πώποτε,
Ὦ δέσποτ', ἀπέθαν' ἀποθανεῖν πρόθυμος ὤν,
Τοὺς γλιχομένους δὲ ζῆν κατασπᾷ τοῦ σκέλους
Ἄκοντας ὁ Χάρων ἐπὶ τὸ πορθμεῖον τ ἄγει
Σιτιζομένους καὶ πάντ' ἔχοντας ἀφθόνως.
Ὁ δὲ λιμὸς ἐστιν ἀθανασίας φάρμακον.

"No one ever, O master, being anxious to die has died, but those who are eager to live, Charon drags by the legs unwillingly to his ferry-boat, and carries them off in the full enjoyment of all the good things of life. But hunger is the means to induce a man to gain immortality."

VICISSITUDES.

Her. Œt. 228.

Felix, quisquis novit famulum
Regemque pati,
Vultusque potest variare suos!
Rapuit vires pondusque malis,
Casus animo qui tulit æquo.

Happy the man who can endure the highest and the lowest fortune. He, who has endured such vicissitudes with equanimity, has deprived misfortune of its power.

THINGS UNLAWFUL ARE PREFERRED.

Her. Œt. 357.

Illicita amantur; excidit, quidquid licet.
Fortuna amorem pejor inflammat magis.

What is unlawful is preferred; whatever one may do is little cared for. Misfortune only inflames love the more.

ANGER OF THE GODS.

Her. Œt. 441.

Cœlestis ira quos premit, miseros facit.

Those, whom the anger of Heaven attacks, it renders miserable.

The Prosperous.
Her. Œt. 713.

Semel profecto premere felices Deus
Cum cœpit, urget ; hos habent magna exitus.

When God has once begun to throw down the prosperous, He
overthrows them altogether: such is the end of the mighty.

The Guilty.
Her. Œt. 886.

Haud est nocens, quicunque non sponte est nocens.

He is not guilty, who is not guilty voluntarily.

The Shade of a Great Name.
Oct. 70.

Nunc in luctûs servata meos,
Magni resto nominis umbra.

Preserved for grief alone, I remain the shade of a great name.

Fortune.
Oct. 377.

Quid me, potens Fortuna, fallaci mihi
Blandita vultu, sorte contentum meâ
Alte extulisti, gravius ut ruerem editâ
Receptus arce, totque prospicerem metûs ?

Why, O Fortune, didst thou allure me on by thy deceitful coun-
tenance, and raise me aloft when I was satisfied with my own
humble lot ? Was it that I might fall with a heavier crash, and
be the subject of many fears ?

Father of his Country.
Oct. 444.

Servare cives major est patriœ patri.

It is higher praise for the father of his country to preserve his
fellow-citizens.

The Indolent.
Oct. 453.

Inertia est nescire, quid liceat sibi.
Id facere, laus est, quod decet ; non quod licet.

It is the act of the indolent not to know what he may lawfully
do. It is praiseworthy to do what is becoming, and not merely
what is lawful.

FAITH.

Oct. 456.

Ferrum tuetur principem. SEN. Melius fides.

The sword protects the prince. SEN. Faith better.

HIGHEST VIRTUE.

Oct. 472.

Pulchrum eminere est inter illustres viros,
Consulere patriæ, parcere afflictis, ferâ
Cæde abstinere, tempus atque iræ dare,
Orbi quietem, seculo pacem suo.
Hæc summa virtus ; petitur hâc cœlum viâ.

It is honourable to excel amongst illustrious men, to consult for the good of one's country, to spare the afflicted, to refrain from savage slaughter and anger, to give peace to the world. This is the highest virtue : by this heaven is reached.

THE NOBLE.

Oct. 575.

Majora populus semper a summo exegit.

The people always require the best example to be set by the noblest in station.

THE COUNTENANCE BETRAYS THE PASSIONS.

De Ird. i. 1.

Nec ignoro cæteros quoque affectûs vix occultari, libidinem, metumque et audaciam dare sui signa et posse prænosci. Neque enim ulla vehementior intra cogitatio est, quæ nihil moveat in vultu.

Nor am I ignorant that other affections also are scarcely concealed—that lust, fear, and boldness show themselves, and may be known beforehand. For there is no strong inward thought that does not betray itself in the countenance.

LIFE IS LIKE A SCHOOL OF GLADIATORS.

De Ird. ii. 8.

Non alia quam in ludo gladiatoria vita est, cum iisdem viventium pugnantiumque.

Life is like a school of gladiators, where men live and fight with each other.

Man subject to Diseases of the Mind as well as of the Body.

De Irâ. ii. 9.

Hâc conditione nati sumus, animalia obnoxia non pauci-oribus animi quam corporis, morbis.

We have been born under these conditions, that we should be animals liable to no fewer diseases of the mind than of the body.

Fear.

De Irâ. ii. 11.

Necesse est multos timeat, quem multi timent.

He must necessarily fear many, whom many fear.

Man not the Cause of the Revolution of Summer and Winter.

De Irâ. ii. 27.

Non enim nos causa mundo sumus, hiemem æstatemque referendi : suas ista leges habent, quibus divina exercentur.

For we are not the cause why summer and winter return in regular succession: these seasons have their own laws, and have their order arranged by heaven.

Innocence.

De Irâ. ii. 27.

Quam angusta innocentia est, ad legem bonum esse !

What a slight foundation for innocence it is, to be good only from fear of the law!

Vices of Others.

De Irâ. ii. 28.

Aliena vitia in oculis habemus ; a tergo nostra sunt.

Other men's sins are before our eyes; our own, behind our back.

See (Gr.) The Mote ; (Fr.) Wallet-bearers.

Men Angry with the Sinner, not with the Sin.

De Irâ. ii. 28.

Magna pars hominum est, quæ non peccatis irascitur sed peccantibus.

The greater part of mankind are angry with the sinner and not with the sin.

See (F- ` -'-

PUNISHMENT LOOKS TO THE FUTURE.

De Irâ. ii. 31.

Ne homini quidem nocebimus, quia peccavit, sed ne
peccet : nec unquam ad præteritum, sed ad futurum pœna
referetur : non enim irascitur sed cavet.

**We will not punish a man because he hath offended, but that
he may offend no more; nor does punishment ever look to the
past, but to the future; for it is not the result of passion, but
that the same thing may be guarded against in future.**

HATRED.

De Irâ. ii. 33.

Hoc habent pessimum animi magnâ fortunâ insolentes ;
quos læserunt et oderunt.

**Those minds, whom fortune hath made insolent, have this bad
quality, that they hate those whom they have harmed.**

IT REQUIRES TWO SIDES FOR A QUARREL.

De Irâ. ii. 34.

Cadit statim simultas, ab alterâ parte deserta : nisi pari-
ter, non pugnant.

**A quarrel is quickly settled when deserted by the one party
there is no battle unless there be two.**

INJURY.

De Irâ. iii. 5.

Aut potentior te, aut imbecillior læsit : si imbecillior,
parce illi ; si potentior, tibi.

**He who has injured thee was either stronger or weaker; if
weaker, spare him : if stronger, spare thyself.**

A MAN IS KNOWN BY HIS COMPANY.

De Irâ. iii. 8.

Sumuntur a conversantibus mores : et ut quædam in
contactos corporis vitia transiliunt, ita animus mala sua
proximis tradit.

**Manners are acquired from those with whom we live familiarly :
and as the body receives disease from contagion, so the mind is
affected by the vicious propensities of others.**

Repentance a Severe Punishment.
De Ird. iii. 26.

Maxima est factæ injuriæ pœna, fecisse : nec quisquam gravius adficitur, quam qui ad supplicium pœnitentiæ traditur.

The severest punishment a man can receive who has injured another, is to have committed the injury ; and no man is more severely punished than he who is subject to the whip of his own remorse.

"There is none Righteous, no, not One."
De Ird. iii. 26.

Omnes mali sumus. Quidquid itaque in alio reprehenditur, id unusquisque in suo sinu inveniet. Placidiores itaque invicem simus : mali inter malos vivimus. Una res nos facere potest quietos, mutuæ facilitatis conventio.

We are all wicked. Therefore whatever we blame in another, we shall find in our own bosom. Let us then be forgiving to one another, for, being of evil inclinations ourselves, we live in an evil world. One thing alone can enable us to live at peace, mutual forgiveness.

Solon (Fr. 13, Schneidewin) says :—

Οὐδὲ μάκαρς οὐδεὶς πέλεται βροτός, ἀλλὰ πονηροί
Πάντες, ὅσους θνητοὺς ἥλιος καθορᾷ.

"There is no man happy, but all are wicked, whom the sun shines upon."

We are Angry with the Gods because any one Surpasses us.
De Ird. iii. 31.

Diis irascimur, quod aliquis nos antecedat, obliti quantum hominum retro sit.

We are angry with the gods because any one is superior to us, forgetting how many are beneath us.

It is a Pleasure to have Something to Hope for.
De Irâ. iii. 31.

Inter voluptates est, superesse quod speres.

Among other pleasures it is no small one to see that there is something remaining, for which thou mayest hope.

ART.

De Brevit. Vit. 1.

Vita brevis est, longa ars.

Life is short, but art is long.

Hipparchus (Fr. Com. Gr. p. 1097, M.) says :—

Πολὺ γ' ἐστὶ πάντων κτῆμα τιμιώτατον
Ἄπασιν ἀνθρώποισιν εἰς τὸ ζῆν τέχνη.
Τὰ μὲν γὰρ ἄλλα καὶ πόλεμος καὶ μεταβολαὶ
Τύχης ἀνήλωσ', ἡ τέχνη δὲ σώζεται.

"By far the most precious possession to all men is skill in the art of living; for both war and the changes of fortune may destroy other things, but skill is preserved."

Longfellow (" A Psalm of Life ") says :—

" Art is long and Time is fleeting."

LIFE IS LONG ENOUGH.

De Brevit. Vit. 2.

Vita, si scias uti, longa est.

Life, if thou knowest how to use it, is long enough.

SHORTNESS OF LIFE.

De Brevit. Vit. 2.

Exigua pars est vitæ quam nos vivimus.

Short is that part of life which we really live.

LENGTH OF LIFE.

De Brevit. Vit. 8.

Non est itaque, quod quemquam propter canos aut rugas putes diu vixisse : non ille diu vixit, sed diu fuit.

And therefore never say that this man hath lived long, as his white head and wrinkled face show : he hath not lived long, but has only been long in existence.

Prince Metternich, in a letter to Alexander von Humboldt, (17th Sept. 1849,) congratulating him on reaching his eightieth year, says :—" Naître est peu de chose ; utiliser la vie est beaucoup. Vous comptez parmi les plus riches et vous avez fait un bien noble usage de votre fortune morale."

TIME PAST NEVER RETURNS.

De Brevit. Vit. 8.

Nemo restituet annos, nemo iterum te tibi reddet. Ibit qua cœpit ætas, nec cursum suum aut revocabit aut supprimet : nihil tumultuabitur, nihil admonebit velocitatis suæ : tacita labetur.

No one will restore the years gone past, no one will return thee to thyself. Thy days will go on as they have done hitherto, nor canst thou recall nor cause them to halt : they will move on without noise and without warning thee of their speed : they will glide on with silent step.

A Hungry People.
De Brevit. Vit. 18.

Nec rationem patitur nec æquitate mitigatur nec ulla prece flectitur populus esuriens.

A hungry people listens not to reason, nor cares for the laws of equity, nor can be bent by any prayer.

The Error of One Man Causes Another to Err.
De Vit. Beat. 1.

Quod in strage hominum magnâ evenit, quum ipse se populus premit, nemo ita cadit, ut non alium in se adtrahat ; primi exitio sequentibus sunt ; hoc in omni vitâ accidere videas licet ; nemo sibi tantummodo errat, sed alieni erroris et causa et auctor est.

As often happens in a great crowd of men, when the people press against each other, no one falls without drawing another after him, and the foremost are the cause of the ruin of those that follow : so it is in common life ; there is no man that erreth to himself, but is the cause and author of other men's error.

A Multitude.
De Vit. Beat. 2.

Non tam bene cum rebus humanis agitur, ut meliora pluribus placeant : argumentum pessimi, turba est.

Human affairs are not so happily arranged that the best things please the most men. It is the proof of a bad cause when it is applauded by the mob.

Who are the Vulgar?
De Vit. Beat. 2.

Vulgum tam chlamydatos, quam coronatos voco.

The vulgar are found in all ranks, and are not to be distinguished by the dress they wear.

Conscience.
De Vit. Beat. 20.

Nihil opinionis causâ, omnia conscientiæ faciam : populo teste fieri credam, quidquid me conscio faciam.

I will do all things, not for opinion, but for conscience' sake: I shall believe that it is done in the sight of all men, whatsoever I do with my own knowledge only.

KINDNESS TO MAN.
De Vit. Beat. 24.

Ubicumque homo est, ibi beneficio locus est.

Wherever a man is, there is an opportunity for doing a kindness.

INJURIES LEAVE A DEEPER IMPRESSION THAN KINDNESSES.
De Benef. i. 1.

Ita naturâ comparatum est, ut altius injuriæ quam merita descendant et illa cito defluant, has tenax memoria custodiat.

It has been so provided by nature that injuries make a more lasting impression than kindnesses, and while the latter quickly are forgotten, the former are retained with a most tenacious memory.

NOTHING COSTS SO MUCH AS WHAT IS BOUGHT BY PRAYERS.
De Benef. ii. 1.

Nulla res carius constat quam quæ precibus emta est.

Nothing costs so much as what is bought with prayers.

THE TIME BEFORE PUNISHMENT.
De Benef. ii. 5.

Quod antecedit tempus, maxima venturi supplicii pars est.

The time that precedes punishment, is the severest part of it.

BENEFITS.
De Benef. ii. 11.

Non est dicendum, quid tribuerimus : qui admonet, repetit. Non est instandum, non est memoria revocanda ; nisi ut aliud dando, prioris admoneas.

We ought never to disclose that which we have given : he, that upbraids a courtesy, asks it back. We must not importune ; we ought never to refresh the memory about a former kindness, except it be to second it by another.

2 K

A Benefit.
De Benef. ii. 11.

Qui dedit beneficium taceat ; narret, qui accepit.

Let him that hath done the good office conceal it ; let him that hath received it disclose it.

The Ungrateful.
De Benef. iii. 1.

Ingratus est, qui beneficium accepisse se negat, quod accepit : ingratus est, qui dissimulat : ingratus, qui non reddit : ingratissimus omnium, qui oblitus est.

He is ungrateful, who denies that he has received a kindness which has been bestowed upon him ; he is ungrateful, who conceals it ; he is ungrateful who makes no return for it ; most ungrateful of all is he who forgets it.

The Noble.
De Benef. iii. 15.

Generosi animi et magnifici est juvare, prodesse ; qui dat beneficia, Deos imitatur ; qui repetit, feneratores.

It is the property of a generous and noble mind to aid and do good to others ; he who conferreth benefits imitates the gods ; he who demands them back is like the usurers.

Virtue to be Found in all Classes.
De Benef. iii. 18.

Nulli præclusa virtus est, omnibus patet, omnes admittit, omnes invitat, ingenuos, libertinos, servos, reges, et exules : non eligit domum, nec censum ; nudo homine contenta est.

Virtue is shut out from no one ; she is open to all, accepts all, invites all, gentlemen, freedmen, slaves, kings, and exiles : she selects neither house nor fortune ; she is satisfied with a human being without adjuncts.

The Origin of All the Same.
De Benef. iii. 28.

Eadem omnibus principia eademque origo : nemo altero nobilior, nisi cui rectius ingenium et artibus bonis aptius. Qui imagines in atrio exponunt, et nomina familiæ suæ longo ordine, ac multis stemmatum illigata flexuris, in parte primâ ædium collocant : non noti magis quam nobiles

didos, sive per sordidos gradus, ad hunc prima cujusque
origo perducitur.

All men have the same beginning and the same origin : no one
is more noble than another except the man of lofty genius, with
talents fitted for the successful pursuit of the higher objects
of life. Those, who range their ancestral images in their halls, and
engrave in the entrance of their palaces the names of their illus-
trious forefathers in a long line, and their pedigree in all its rami-
fications, may be regarded as known to the world rather than
noble. The world is the parent of us all, whether we trace our
origin through a series of nobles or plebeians.

NATURE IS GOD.
De Benef. iv. 7.

Quid enim aliud est natura, quam Deus, et divina ratio,
toti mundo et partibus ejus inserta ?

What else is nature but God, and divine reason residing in the
whole world and its parts ?

FATE.
De Benef. iv. 7.

Quum Fatum nihil aliud est quam series implexa cau-
sarum, ille est prima omnium causa, ex quâ ceteræ pendent.

As Fate is an immutable ordinance, which holds all causes chained
together, God is the first cause of all, He on whom all the rest
depend.

GOD AND NATURE THE SAME.
De Benef. iv. 8.

Ergo nihil agis, ingratissime mortalium, qui te negas
Deo debere, sed naturæ : quia nec natura sine Deo est, nec
Deus sine naturâ : sed idem est utrumque nec distat officio.
Si quid a Senecâ accepisses, Annæo te diceres debere vel
Lucio ; non creditorem mutares sed nomen ; quoniam sive
prænomen ejus, sive nomen dixisses, sive cognomen, idem
tamen ille esset. Sic nunc naturam voces, fatum, fortunam ;
omnia ejusdem Dei nomina sunt, varie utentis suâ potes-
tate.

Wherefore it availeth thee nothing, thou most ungrateful of
men, to avow that thou art in no way indebted to God, but art
under obligation to nature ; for neither is nature without God nor
God without nature : both these are the same and differ in nothing.
If thou shouldst confess that thou owest to Annæus or Lucius that
which Seneca had lent thee, thou wouldst only change the name
but not the creditor. For whether thou callest him by his name

or surname, he would be the same man. Call him as thou pleasest, nature, fate, or fortune, it matters not, because they are all the names of the self-same God, who makes use of His divine providence diversely.

"God Sendeth Rain on the Just and the Unjust."
De Benef. iv. 28.

Nec poterat lex casuris imbribus dici, ne in malorum improborumque rura defluerent.

Neither was a law able to be imposed on the falling showers, that they should not water and overflow the fields of the wicked and unjust.

The Use of Adversity.
De Benef. v. 20.

Multa beneficia tristem frontem et asperam habent, quemadmodum secare et urere ut sanes et vinculis coërcere.

Many benefits have a sad and rough countenance, so as to burn and cut in order to healing.

God Never Repents.
De Benef. vi. 23.

Nec unquam primi consilii Deos pœnitet.

God never repents of what He has first resolved upon.

Truth.
De Benef. vii. 1.

Involuta veritas in alto latet.

Truth lies wrapped up and hidden in the depths.

Dr Walcott (" Birthday Ode ") says :—

" The sages say, dame Truth delights to dwell—
Strange mansion—in the bottom of a well."

What is to Make us Better lies Before us.
De Benef. vii. 1.

Quidquid nos meliores beatosque facturum est, aut in aperto aut in proximo posuit.

Whatever is to make us better and happy, God has placed either openly before us or close to us.

An Old Man.
De Tranquil. 3.

Nihil turpius est quam grandis natu senex, qui nullum

aliud habet argumentum, quo se probet diu vixisse, præter ætatem.

· There is nothing more disgraceful than that an old man should have nothing to produce as a proof that he has lived long except his years.

A Good Citizen.
De Tranquil. 3.

Nunquam inutilis est opera civis boni : auditu, enim visu, vultu, nutu, obstinatione Tacitâ, incessuque ipso prodest.

The aid of a good citizen is never without a beneficial effect ; for he assists by everything he does, by listening, by looking on, by his presence, by his nod of approbation, even by obstinate silence, and by his very gait.

To Labour Against Nature is Vain.
De Tranquil. 6.

Male enim respondent coacta ingenia : reluctante naturâ inritus labor est.

Where the mind is acting under constraint, the results are seldom good : when nature is reluctant, the labour is lost.

A Trusty Friend a Remedy for a Troubled Mind.
De Tranquil. 7.

Quantum bonum est, ubi sunt præparata pectora, in quæ tuto secretum omne descendat, quorum conscientiam minus quam tuam timeas, quorum sermo sollicitudinem leniat, sententia consilium expediat, hilaritas tristitiam dissipet, conspectus ipse delectet !

What a great blessing is a friend, with a breast so trusty that thou mayest safely bury all thy secrets in it, whose conscience thou mayest fear less than thine own, who can relieve thy cares by his conversation, thy doubts by his counsels, thy sadness by his good humour, and whose very look gives comfort to thee !

Books.
De Tranquil. 9.

Onerat discentem turba librorum, non instruit : multoque satius est paucis te auctoribus tradere quam errare per multos.

A large library is apt to distract rather than to instruct the learner ; it is much better to confine thyself to a few authors than to wander at random over many.

Milton ("Paradise Regained," iv. 819) says of books :—

> "However, many books,
> Wise men have said, are wearisome ; who reads
> Incessantly, and to his reading brings not
> A spirit and judgment equal or superior,
> (And what he brings what needs he elsewhere seek ?)
> Uncertain and unsettled still remains,
> Deep versed in books and shallow in himself."

CUSTOM.
De Tranquil. 10.

Nullo melius nomine de nobis Natura meruit, quam quod quum sciret, quibus ærumnis nasceremur, calamitatum mollimentum consuetudinem invenit, cito in familiaritatem gravissima adducens. Nemo duraret, si rerum adversarum eandem vim adsiduitas haberet, quam primus ictus. Omnes cum fortunâ copulati sumus : aliorum aurea catena est et laxa ; aliorum arta et sordida.

The greatest blessing we have received from nature is that, foreseeing to what sorrows we would be subject in this world, she found out habit as a remedy to soothe us, making thereby the greatest calamities quickly familiar and supportable. No one could endure it, if adversity continued to be as bitter as it is at its first approach. We are all chained to fortune ; some of us have a golden and loose chain, others a tight and base one.

SOME RELAXATION TO BE GIVEN TO THE MIND.
De Tranquil. 15.

Danda est remissio animis : meliores acrioresque requieti urgent. Ut fertilibus agris non est imperandum : cito enim exhauriet illos nunquam intermissa fecunditas : ita animorum impetûs adsiduus labor frangit.

Some relaxation must be given to our minds ; rest makes them better and more active. As we must not overwork our fertile fields, for in that way we shall soon exhaust them, so uninterrupted labour destroys the power of men's minds.

NO GREAT WIT WITHOUT A SPICE OF FOLLY.
De Tranquil. 15.

Nullum magnum ingenium sine mixturâ dementiæ fuit.

No great wit has ever existed without a spice of madness.

So Dryden ("Absalom and Achitophel" pt. i. l. 163) :—

> "Great wits are sure to madness near allied,
> And thin partitions do their bounds divide."

A Great Fortune is a Great Servitude.
Consolat. ad Polybium, 26.

Magna servitus est magna fortuna.

A great fortune is a great servitude.

The Paternal Affection of God.
De Provid. 1.

Inter bonos viros ac Deum amicitia est, conciliante virtute : amicitiam dico? immo etiam necessitudo et similitudo ; quoniam quidem bonus ipse tempore tantum a Deo differt, discipulus ejus, æmulatorque et vera progenies : quem parens ille magnificus, virtutum non lenis exactor sicut severi patres, durius educat.

Between good men and God there is a friendship which virtue conciliates ; a friendship, do I say? yea, a kindred and similitude ; since a good man is God's disciple and imitator and His true offspring, whom that magnificent Father, an exacter of virtue with no gentle hand, doth after the manner of severe parents educate hardly.

The Chastisement of God.
De Provid. 2.

Miraris tu si Deus ille bonorum amantissimus, qui illos quam optimos esse atque excellentissimos vult, fortunam illis cum quâ exercentur adsignat?

Are you surprised if God, who is most loving of the good, and who wishes that they should be as good and excellent as possible, gives them that kind of fortune by which they are tried?

A Man Struggling with Adversity.
De Provid. 2.

Ecce spectaculum dignum, ad quod respiciat intentus operi suo Deus : ecce par Deo dignum, vir fortis cum malâ fortunâ compositus, utique si et provocavit.

Behold a spectacle to which God may worthily turn His attention ; behold a match worthy of God, a brave man hand-in-hand with adverse fortune, at least if he has challenged the combat.

To Conquer without Danger.
De Provid. 3.

Scit eum sine gloriâ vinci, qui sine periculo vincitur.

He knows that the man is overcome ingloriously, who is overcome without danger.

Corneille (Cid, ii. 2) says:—
> "A vaincre sans péril en triomphe sans gloire."
> "We triumph without glory when we conquer without danger."

The Man Untried by Adversity.
De Provid. 3.

Nihil infelicius eo, cui nihil unquam evenit adversi, non licuit enim illi se experiri.

There is no one more unfortunate than the man who has never been unfortunate, for it has never been in his power to try himself.

A Great Mind.
De Clement. i. 5.

Magnam fortunam magnus animus decet.

A great mind becomes a great fortune.

Sin.
De Clement. i. 6.

Etiamsi quis tam bene purgavit animum, ut nihil obturbare eum amplius possit ac fallere, ad innocentiam tamen peccando pervenit.

Although a man has so well purged his mind that nothing can trouble or deceive him any more, yet he reached his present innocence through sin.

The Powerful.
De Clement. i. 8.

Ut fulmina paucorum periculo cadunt, omnium metu; sic animadversiones magnarum potestatum terrent latius, quam nocent: non sine causâ. Non enim quantum fecerit, sed quantum facturus sit, cogitatur in eo, qui omnia potest.

Even as lightning causes danger to few, but fear to all; so the punishments of mighty potentates are more full of fear than of evil, and not without reason. For in him that has power, all men considers, not what he does, but what he may do.

Severity.
De Clement. i. 22.

Severitas, quod maximum remedium habet, assiduitate amittit auctoritatem.

Severity, if it be too frequently used, loses its authority, which is its chief use.

When Economy is too Late.

Ep. 1.

Sera parsimonia in fundo est.

When we have reached the end of our property it is too late then to become economical.

Hesiodus ('Έργα, 369) says:—

δειλὴ δ' ἐνὶ πυθμένι φειδώ.

Time.

Ep. 1.

Quædam tempora eripiuntur nobis, quædam subducuntur, quædam effluunt. Turpissima tamen est jactura, quæ per negligentiam venit: et si volueris attendere, magna vitæ pars elabitur male agentibus, maxima nihil agentibus, tota aliud agentibus.

Some portion of our time is taken from us by force; another portion is stolen from us; and another slips away. But the most disgraceful loss is that which arises from our own negligence; and if thou wilt seriously observe, thou shalt perceive that a great part of life flits from those who do evil, a greater from those who do nothing, and the whole from those who do not accomplish the business which they think that they are doing.

No Satisfaction without a Companion.

Ep. 6.

Nullius boni sine sociis jucunda possessio est.

There is no satisfaction in any good without a companion.

Precepts contrasted with Example.

Ep. 6.

Longum iter est per præcepta, breve et efficax per exempla.

The road by precepts, is tedious; by example, short and efficacious.

Men Learn by Teaching Others.

Ep. 7.

Homines, dum docent, discunt.

Men, while they teach, learn.

Love.

Ep. 9.

Si vis amari, ama.

If you wish to be loved, love.

The Mind.
Ep. 9.
Omnia bona mea mecum sunt.

My all I carry with me.

How to Live.
Ep. 10.
Sic vive cum hominibus, tanquam Deus videat; sic loquere cum Deo, tanquam homines audiant.

Live with men as if God saw you; converse with God as if men heard you.

Vices not to be Removed by Wisdom.
Ep. 11.
Nullâ sapientiâ naturalia corporis aut animi vitia ponuntur: quidquid infixum et ingenitum est, lenitur arte, non vincitur.

No wisdom can remove the natural vices of the body or mind; what is infixed or inbred may be allayed by art, not subdued.

We Cannot be Deprived of Past Enjoyment.
Ep. 12.
In somnum ituri, lœti hilaresque dicamus:

Vixi! et, quem dederat cursum fortuna, peregi. Crastinum si adjecerit Deus, lœti recipiamus. Ille beatissimus est, et securus sui possessor, qui crastinum sine solicitudine expectat. Quisquis dixit "Vixi" quotidie ad lucrum surgit.

When we retire to rest, let us joyfully and contentedly say: "I have lived and finished the course which Fortune had given me." If God grant us to-morrow, let us receive it with thankfulness. Thrice happy is he, and thoroughly master of himself, who can look forward to to-morrow without anxiety. Whoever has — said, "I have lived," rises daily to the acquisition of gain.

"Sufficient to the Day is the Evil thereof."
Ep. 13.
Ne sis miser ante tempus; quum illa, quæ velut imminentia expavisti, fortasse nunquam ventura sint, certe nondum venerint. Quædam ergo nos magis torquent, quam debent; quædam ante torquent quam debent; quædam torquent, quum omnino non debeant.

Be not wretched before the time : since the things, which thou thinkest to be impending, perhaps will never happen, at all events have not yet happened. Therefore some things torment us more than they ought ; some things torment us before they ought ; some things torment us when they ought not to do it at all.

FOLLY.

Ep. 13.

Inter cætera mala hoc quoque habet stultitia, semper incipit vivere.

Among other ills, folly has this also, that it is always beginning to live.

HOW TO LIVE.

Ep. 16.

Si ad naturam vives, nunquam eris pauper ; si ad opinionem, nunquam eris dives.

If thou live according to nature, thou wilt never be poor ; if according to the opinions of the world, thou wilt never be rich.

DEBT.

Ep. 19.

Leve æs alienum debitorem facit, grave inimicum.

A slight debt makes a man a debtor, a heavy one an enemy.

MEN OF GENIUS.

Ep. 21.

Profunda supra nos altitudo temporis veniet ; pauca ingenia caput inserent, et idem quandoque silentium obitura, oblivioni resistent, ac se diu vindicabunt.

There will come after us a long course of ages ; a few men of great genius will raise their heads, and though by and by about to sink into the same silent tomb, they will resist the forgetfulness of mankind, and keep themselves a long time in reputation.

BEGINNING TO LIVE.

Ep. 23.

Molestum est, semper vitam inchoare : male vivunt, qui semper vivere incipiunt.

It is a tedious thing to be always beginning life : they live badly who always begin to live.

SELF-RESPECT.
Ep. 25.

Quum jam profeceris tantum, ut sit tibi etiam tui reverentia, licebit dimittas pœdagogum.

When thou hast profited so much that thou respectest even thyself, thou mayst let go thy tutor.

Pope ("Essay on Man," Ep. iv. l. 255) speaks thus of self-respect :—
> " One self-approving hour whole years outweighs
> Of stupid starers and of loud huzzas."

ART.
Ep. 29.

Non est ars, quæ ad effectum casu venit.

That is not art which succeeds by chance.

AN OLD MAN.
Ep. 36.

Turpis et ridicula res est elementarius senex. Juveni parandum, seni utendum est.

It is an absurd and base thing to see an old man at his A, B, C. We should lay up in our youth what we are to make use of in our old age.

MANNERS.
Ep. 36.

In mores fortuna jus non habet.

Fortune hath no power over manners.

A VICIOUS AGE.
Ep. 39.

Quæ fuerunt vitia, mores sunt.

What were vices once are now the fashion.

GOD IS IN US.
Ep. 41.

Prope est a te Deus, tecum est, intus est! ita dico, Lucili : sacer intra nos spiritus sedet, malorum bonorumque nostrorum observator et custos : hic, prout a nobis tractatus est, ita nos ipse tractat. Bonus vir sine Deo nemo est.

God is nigh to thee, He is with thee, He is in thee : I tell thee, O Lucilius, a holy spirit resideth within us, an observer a' dian of our good and our bad doings, who, as He hath been dealt with by us, so He dealeth with us ; no man is good without God.

PUNISHMENT OF WICKEDNESS.

Ep. 42.

Nec ulla major poena nequitiæ est, quam quod sibi ac suis displicet.

There is no greater punishment of wickedness than that it is dissatisfied with itself and its deeds.

GOOD CONSCIENCE.

Ep. 43.

Bona conscientia turbam advocat, mala etiam in solitudine anxia atque solicita est. Si honesta sunt, quæ facis, omnes sciant : si turpia, quid refert neminem scire, quum tu scias? O te miserum, si contemnis hunc testem.

A good conscience may have a crowd around, a bad is even in solitude anxious and care-worn. If thou dost what is honourable, all may know ; if thou actest basely, what boots it that no one knows, when thou thyself knowest. O miserable man, if thou despisest such a witness.

PEDIGREE.

Ep. 44.

Si quid est aliud in philosophiâ boni, hoc est, quod stemma non inspicit. Omnes, si ad originem primam revocentur, a Diis sunt.

If there is anything good in philosophy, it is this, that it does not regard nobility. All, if we look back to their first origin, are sprung from the gods.

THE GENTLEMAN.

Ep. 44.

Quis est generosus? ad virtutem bene a naturâ compositus. Non facit nobilem atrium plenum fumosis imaginibus. Nemo in nostram gloriam vixit : nec, quod ante nos fuit, nostrum est. Animus facit nobilem, cui ex quâcumque conditione supra fortunam licet surgere.

Who is the gentleman? He that is well prepared by nature for virtue. It does not make a nobleman to have his court full of smoky images. No man lived for our glory, neither is that, which was before us, ours. The mind makes the nobleman, which enables us to rise from the basest condition above fortune.

Spenser, in his "Faerie Queen," (vi. 3. 1,) thus speaks of the man of gentle manners :—

> " True is, that whilome that good poet said,
> The gentle mind by gentle deeds is known.
> For a man by nothing is so well bewray'd
> As by his manners."

Tennyson (" In Memoriam," cant. x.):—

> " The grand old name of gentleman
> Defamed by every charlatan,
> And soil'd with all ignoble use."

BOOKS.
Ep. 45.

Non refert quam multos libros, sed quam bonos habeas ; lectio certa prodest, varia delectat.

It is not how many books thou hast, but how good; careful reading profiteth, while that which is full of variety delighteth.

VICES UNDER THE NAME OF VIRTUES.
Ep. 45.

Vitia nobis sub virtutum nomine obrepunt.

Vices creep upon us under the name of virtues.

TO-MORROW.
Ep. 45.

Recognosce singulos, considera universos ; nullius non vita spectat in crastinum.

Examine each individual, and consider the whole world, and you will find that there is no man's life that is not aiming at to-morrow.

MANNERS.
Ep. 47.

Sibi quisque dat mores ; ministeria casus assignat.

Each giveth himself manners : chance bestoweth his office in life.

THE GOOD AND THE BAD.
Ep. 47.

Hoc habent inter cætera boni mores, placent sibi ac permanent ; levis est malitia, sæpe mutatur, non in melius, sed in aliud.

Good habits have this advantage among other things, that they give pleasure to those who possess them, and are an enduring possession ; whereas the evil-inclined are fickle, often changing, never for the better, but to something else.

SWIFTNESS OF TIME.
Ep. 49.

Infinita est velocitas temporis, quæ magis apparet respicientibus.

The swiftness of time is infinite, as is still more evident when we look back upon the past.

LANGUAGE OF TRUTH.
Ep. 49.

Veritatis simplex oratio est.

The language of truth is simple.

Æschylus (Fr.) says :—

'Απλᾶ γάρ ἐστι τῆς ἀληθείας ἔπη.

"For the words of truth are simple."

ORIGINAL SIN.
Ep. 50.

Ad neminem ante bona mens venit, quam mala.

To no man comes a good mind before an evil.

TO DO A THING WILLINGLY.
Ep. 61.

Ita dico, qui imperia libens excipit, partem acerbissimam servitutis effugit, facere quod nolit. Non, qui jussus aliquid facit, miser est : sed qui invitus facit.

I maintain that he who willingly submits to another man's command has escaped from the most cruel part of servitude,—that is to say, to do that which he is unwilling to do. The most miserable man is not he that has a command put upon him, but the man that does it against his will.

NOT LOST BUT GONE BEFORE.
Ep. 63.

Cogitemus ergo, Lucili carissime, cito nos eo perventuros, quo illum pervenisse mœremus. Et fortem (si modo sapientium vera fama est, recipitque nos locus aliquis) quem putamus perisse, præmissus est.

Let us think, therefore, dearest Lucilius, that we shall soon arrive at that place whither we grieve that he has reached. And perhaps (if only the idea of the wise is correct, and some place or other receives us) he, whom we imagine to be lost, has only gone before us.

A GREAT MAN MAY ISSUE FROM A COTTAGE.
Ep. 66.

Potest ex casâ vir magnus exire ; potest et ex deformi
humilique corpusculo formosus animus ac magnus.

A great man may spring from a cottage ; a virtuous and great
soul may be inclosed in a deformed and mean body.

WISDOM NOT TO BE ACQUIRED EASILY.
Ep. 71.

Quemadmodum lana quosdam colores semel ducit, quos-
dam nisi sæpius macerata et recocta non perbibit : sic alias
disciplinas ingenia cum accepere, protinus præstant : hæc
nisi altè descendit, et diù sedit, animum non coloravit, sed
infecit, nihil ex his quæ promiserat præstat.

As wool imbibes at once certain colours and others it does not,
unless it has been frequently soaked and doubly-dyed ; so there
are certain kinds of learning which, on being acquired, are
thoroughly mastered ; but philosophy, unless she sinks deeply into
the soul and has long dwelt there, and has not given a mere
colouring but a deep dye, performs none of the things which she
had promised.

TO LEARN.
Ep. 76.

Tamdiu discendum est, quamdiu nescias et, si proverbio
credimus, quamdiu vivas.

Thou must learn as long as thou art ignorant, and, if we give
credit to the proverb, so long as thou livest.

THE POOR MAN.
Ep. 80.

Sæpius pauper et fidelius ridet.

The poor man laughs oftener and more securely.

FEIGNED HAPPINESS.
Ep. 80.

Personata felicitas.

Happiness covered with a mask.

A GOOD MAN.
Ep. 81.

Nemo mihi videtur pluris æstimare virtutem, nemo illi

magis esse devotus, quam qui boni viri famam perdidit, ne conscientiam perderet.

No man expresses such a respect and devotion to virtue as he does, who forfeits the repute of being a good man, that he may not lose the consciousness of being such.

RETIREMENT.

Ep. 82.

Otium sine literis mors est, et hominis vivi sepultura.

Retirement without study is death and the grave of a living man.

GOD IS EVERYWHERE PRESENT.

Ep. 83.

Quid enim prodest ab homine aliquid esse secretum? nihil Deo clusum est: interest animis nostris et cogitationibus mediis intervenit. Sic intervenit, dico? tanquam discedat!

Of what consequence is it that anything should be concealed from man? nothing is hidden from God: He is present in our minds and comes into the midst of our thoughts. Comes, do I say?—as if He were ever absent!

THE WORSE TO BE GOVERNED BY THE BETTER.

Ep. 90.

Naturæ est enim, potioribus deteriora submittere.

For it is the arrangement of nature that the worse should be ruled by the better.

LIFE.

Ep. 93.

Non vixit iste, sed in vitâ moratus est; nec sero mortuus est, sed diu.

This man lived not, but merely had an abode in this life: he died not lately, but long ago.

DO AS YOU WOULD BE DONE BY.

Ep. 94.

Ab alio expectes, alteri quod feceris.

Expect from another what you do to another.

2 L

How God is to be Propitiated.
Ep. 95.

Vis Deos propitiare? bonus esto! Satis illos coluit,
quisquis imitatus est.

Dost thou wish to propitiate the gods? Be good. Whoever has
imitated them, has shown sufficient reverence.

Life is a Warfare.
Ep. 96.

Atqui vivere, militare est.

But life is a warfare.

So Æschylus (Eum. 140) says :—

'Εμοὶ δ' ὄνειδος ἐξ ὀνειράτων μολὸν,
Ἔτυψεν δίκαν διφρηλάτου·
Μεσολαβεῖ κέντρῳ
Ὑπὸ φρένας, ὑπὸ λοβὸν πάρεστι μαστίκτορος
Δαΐου, δαμίου
Βαρὺ, τὸ περίβαρυ κρύος ἔχειν.

"Reproach springing from my dreams has struck deep into my heart and
soul, like the charioteer's firmly-grasped whip; I feel horror, chill horror
creep over me from the never pitying scourge."

Voltaire (Mahomet ii. 3) says :—

"Ma vie est un combat."

Every Age will Produce a Clodius.
Ep. 97.

Omne tempus Clodios, non omne Catones feret. Ad
deteriora faciles sumus, quia nec dux potest nec comes
deesse.

We shall find Clodii in every age, seldom Catos : we are prone
to evil, because we are never without a leader or companion on
our downward way.

What is the Punishment of Transgressors.
Ep. 97.

Prima et maxima peccantium pœna est peccâsse ; Se-
cundæ vero pœnæ sunt timere semper et expavescere et
securitati diffidere et fatendum est mala facinora conscientiâ
flagellari et plurimum illic tormentorum esse, eo, quod
perpetua illam solicitudo urget ac verberat, quod sponsori-
bus securitatis suæ non potest credere.

The first and severest punishment of sinners is the feeling of
having sinned; the second is to be always afraid, to be in con-

tant dread, to have no feeling of security ; we must confess that
evil deeds are lashed by conscience, and that the greatest torture
arises on this account, because never-resting remorse oppresses
and scourges the mind, no confidence being placed in the vouchers
of its security.

PROSPERITY IS A FEEBLE REED.
Ep. 98.

Fragilibus innititur, qui adventitio lætus est.

He leans on a feeble reed, who takes pleasure on what is exter-
nal to himself.

See (Fr.) Prosperity.

A MIND ANXIOUS ABOUT THE FUTURE.
· Ep. 98.

Calamitosus est animus futuri anxius.

The mind that is anxious about future events is wretched.

THE MIND IS SUPERIOR TO EVERY KIND OF FORTUNE.
Ep. 98.

Valentior omni fortunâ animus est : in utramque par-
em ipse res suas ducit, beatæque ac miseræ vitæ sibi caussa
est.

The mind is the master over every kind of fortune : itself acts
in both ways, being the cause of its own happiness and misery.

ANTICIPATION OF EVIL.
Ep. 98.

Nil est nec miserius nec stultius quam prætimere.   Quæ
ista dementia est, malum suum antecedere ?

There is nothing so wretched or foolish as to anticipate mis-
fortunes.   What madness is it in your expecting evil before it
arrives ?

DIGNITY.
Ep. 101.

Facilius crescit dignitas quam incipit.

Dignity increases more easily than begins.

LIFE.
Ep. 101.

Quam stultum est, ætatem disponere ne crastini quidem

dominum! O quanta dementia est spes longas inchoantium!

What a foolish thing it is to promise ourselves a long life, who are not masters of even to-morrow! How mad are they who live on long hopes!

The Human Mind.
Ep. 102.

Magna et generosa res est humanus animus: nullos sibi poni, nisi communes et cum Deo terminos patitur.

The mind of man is great and noble; it allows no bounds to be put to it except what is common and with God.

Difficult Things.
Ep. 104.

Non, quia difficilia sunt, non audemus, sed, quia non audemus, difficilia sunt.

It is not, because things are difficult, that we do not dare to attempt them, but they are difficult, because we do not dare to make the attempt.

Why we Learn.
Ep. 106.

Non vitæ sed scholæ discimus.

We acquire learning not that we may improve our lives, but for the sake of learned disputation.

Fate Leads the Willing.
Ep. 107.

Ducunt volentem fata, nolentem trahunt.

Fate leads the willing and drags the unwilling.

This expression is thus paraphrased by Montaigne (Essais, b. ii. ch. 37):—

"Suyvons de par Dieu: suyvons: Il meine ceulx qui suyvent; ceulx qui ne le suyvent pas, il les entraine."

This idea of Seneca is found in a fragment of Cleanthes:—

Ἄγου δέ μ' ὦ Ζεῦ καὶ σύ γ' ἡ Πεπρωμένη,
Ὅποι ποθ' ὑμῖν εἰμὶ διατεταγμένος.
Ὡς ἕψομαι γ' ἄοκνος· ἢν δὲ μὴ θέλω
Κακὸς γενόμενος, οὐδέν ἧττον ἕψομαι.

"Lead me, O Jupiter, both thou and Fate; wheresoever I am directed by you, I shall follow without hesitation. Even if I am unwilling, being recalcitrant, nevertheless I shall be obliged to follow."

Some Passions are more easily Cut off than Regulated.

Ep. 108.

Quædam abscinduntur facilius animo quam temperantur.

Some passions cannot be regulated but must be entirely cut off.

Like Speech, Like Life.

Ep. 114.

Talis hominibus est oratio, qualis vita.

Men's conversation resembles their kind of lives.

Young Men out of a Band-box.

Ep. 115.

Nôsti complures juvenes, barbâ et comâ nitidos, de capsulâ totos : nihil ab illis speraveris forte, nihil solidum. Oratio vultus animi est.

You know some young men, with beard and hair so trimmed, as if they had stopped out of a band-box, but you could expect nothing great from such parties. The conversation is the index of the mind.

Money from any Source.

Ep. 115.

Non quare et unde ; quid habeâs tantum rogant.

They do not inquire why and whence, but only how much thou possessest.

The Being of God Proved.

Ep. 117.

Multum dare solemus præsumptioni omnium hominum et apud nos veritatis argumentum est, aliquid omnibus videri ; tanquam, Deos esse inter alia hoc colligimus, quod omnibus de Diis opinio est, nec ulla gens usquam est adeo extra leges moresque projecta ut non aliquos Deos credat.

We are wont to attribute much to what all men presume ; with us it is an argument of truth that anything seems true to all, as that there are gods, we hence collect, for that all men have engrafted in them an opinion concerning gods, neither is there any nation so void of laws or good manners that it does not believe that there are some gods.

To Strive against Nature.
Ep. 122.

Contra naturam nitentibus, non alia vita est, quam contra aquam remigantibus.

The life of those who strive against nature is no otherwise than theirs who strive against the stream.

Tale-bearers.
Ep. 123.

Pessimum genus hominum videbatur, qui verba gestarent: sunt quidam, qui vitia gestant. Horum sermo multo nocet: nam etiamsi non statim officit, semina in animo relinquit; sequiturque nos, etiam quum ab illis discessimus, resurrecturum postea malum.

Tale-bearers were reputed the worst sort of men; but some there are who spread vices. The speech of these sort of men is productive of much mischief; for although it hurts not instantly, yet it leaves some seeds in the mind, and it follows us even when we have left them, likely hereafter to enkindle in us a new evil.

Voyage to India Westward.
Nat. Quæst. Præfat. ad. i. lib.

Curiosus spectator contemnit domicilii (terræ) angustias. Quantum enim est, quod ab ultimis litoribus Hispaniæ usque ad Indos jacet? paucissimorum dierum spatium, si navem suus ventus implevit.

The inquisitive examiner who looks around him despises the narrow limits of this world in which he dwells. For how short, after all, the distance that intervenes between the remote shores of Spain and the Indies! a space passed over in a very few short days if a favourable wind fills his sails.

Proof of the Divinity of the Soul.
Nat. Quæst. Præfat. ad. i. lib.

Animus hoc habet argumentum divinitatis suæ, quod illum divina delectant.

The soul has this proof of its divine origin, that divine things delight it.

Truth and Error.
Excerpt. vol. v. p. 188, *Ed. Tauch.*

Veritati aliquid extremum est: error immensus est.

There is an end to truth; error is never-ending.

DISEASE NOT REMOVED BY THE SPLENDOUR AROUND.

Excerpt. vol. v. p. 189, *Ed. Tauch.*

Nihil refert, utrum ægrum in lecto ligneo, an in aureo colloces ; quocunque illum transtuleris, morbum suum secum transferet.

It matters not whether you place the sick man on a wooden bed or one of gold ; wherever you lay him, he carries his disease along with him.

GOD LOVETH NOT TEMPLES MADE WITH HANDS.

Fragm. vol. v. p. 204, *Ed. Tauch.*

Deum non immolationibus et sanguine multo colendum : quæ enim ex trucidatione immerentium voluptas est ? sed mente purâ, bono honestoque proposito. Non templa illi, congestis in altitudinem saxis, struenda sunt ; in suo cuique consecrandus est pectore.

God is not to be worshipped with sacrifices and blood : for what pleasure can He have in the slaughter of the innocent ? but with a pure mind, a good and honest purpose. Temples are not to be built for Him with stones piled on high : God is to be consecrated in the breast of each.

GOD.

Nat. Quæst. ii. 45.

Eundem, quem nos Jovem, sapientissimi viri intelligunt custodem rectoremque universi, animum ac spiritum, mundani hujus operis dominum et artificem, cui nomen omne convenit. Vis illum Fatum vocare ? Non errabis. Hic est, ex quo suspensa sunt omnia : ex quo sunt omnes causæ causarum. Vis illum providentiam dicere ? recte dices. Est enim, cujus consilio huic mundo providetur, ut inconfusus eat et actus suos explicet. Vis illum naturam vocare ? non peccabis. Est enim, ex quo nata sunt omnia, cujus spiritu vivimus. Vis illum vocare mundum ? non falleris. Ipse enim est, totum quod vides, totus suis partibus inditus et se sustinens vi suâ.

The same being, whom we call Jupiter, the wisest men regard as the keeper and protector of the universe, a spirit and a mind, the lord and maker of this lower world, to whom all names are suitable. Wilt thou call him Destiny ? Thou wilt not err. On him depend all things, and all the causes of causes are from him.

Wilt thou call him Providence? Thou wilt say well. For it is his wisdom that provides for this world that it be without confusion and proceed on its course without change. Wilt thou call him Nature? Thou wilt not commit a mistake. For all things have had their beginning from him, in whom we live and move and have our being. Wilt thou call him the World? Thou wilt not be deceived. For he is all that thou seest, wholly infused into its parts and sustaining himself by his own power.

The following is the *Scholium* annexed to the *Principia* of Newton, (Cambridge, 1713,) which may be considered as the germ of the celebrated argument *a priori* for the existence of God :—

"Æternus est et infinitus, omnipotens et omnisciens; id est, durat ab æterno in æternum, et adest ab infinito in infinitum. . . . Non est æternitas et infinitas, sed æternus et infinitus; non est duratio et spatium sed durat et adest. Durat semper et adest ubique, et existendo semper et ubique durationem et spatium constituit."

"God is eternal and infinite, omnipotent and omniscient; that is, he endures from everlasting to everlasting, and is present from infinity to infinity. He is not eternity nor infinity, but eternal and infinite. He is not duration or space, but he endures and is present. He endures always and is present everywhere, and by existing always and everywhere, constitutes duration and space."

SILIUS ITALICUS

BORN A.D. 25—DIED A.D. 100.

C. SILIUS ITALICUS, born about A.D. 25, became famed at an early age as a pleader at the bar. He was raised to the consulship A.D. 65, the year in which Nero perished. He passed through a prosperous life amidst very exciting scenes, and at last determined to retire from the busy world that he might enjoy the tranquillity of a literary life. He passed his time chiefly near Puteoli, at the favourite villa of Cicero, called Academia. Here he lived happily for many years, till, falling into an incurable disease, he determined to leave life, which he did by starving himself, A.D. 100. He wrote an heroic poem, in seventeen books, entitled *Punica*, which has reached us entire.

DILIGENCE IN WAR.

Pun. i. 569.

Tempore Martis
Utendum est rapto, et grassandum ad clara periclis.

In time of war we must be speedy in execution, and advance to honour through the path of danger.

SENATE OF ROME.
Pun. i. 609.

Concilium vocat augustum, castâque beatos
Paupertate Patres, ac nomina parta triumphis
Consul, et œquantem superos virtute senatum.
Facta animosa viros, et recti sacri cupido
Attollunt, hirtœque comœ, neglectaque mensa,
Dexteraque a curvis capulo non segnis aratris :
Exiguo faciles, et opum non indiga corda,
Ad parvos curru remeabant sœpe penates.

The consul summons a solemn council ; men distinguished by unstained poverty, whose names are known for triumphs in war, a senate that equals the gods in virtue. Valiant deeds and a sacred regard of right raise them aloft, unshorn hair, a simple diet, hands familiar with the crooked plough ; content with little, hearts, whom no desire of wealth torments, who often retired to their small cottage in triumphal cars.

TRUE VIRTUE.
Pun. ii. 578.

Ardua virtutem profert via : pergite primi
Nec facilem populis, nec notam invadere laudem.

True virtue advances upwards through difficulties ; go on to obtain that praise which is not easily gained by the bulk of mankind and is little known.

DEATH MUST COME IN PEACE OR WAR.
Pun. iii. 134.

Et pace et bello cunctis stat terminus œvi,
Extremumque diem primus tulit : ire per ora
Nomen in œternum paucis mens ignea donat,
Quos pater œtheriis cœlestûm destinat oris.

In peace as well as in war an end to life must at last come ; our first day gave being to our last ; a mighty spirit bestows on few a never-ending name, on those only whom the father of the gods destines for the blessed abodes above.

SLOTH.
Pun. iii. 580.

               Blandoque veneno
Desidiœ virtus paullatim evicta senescit.

Valour, when it has been gradually overpowered by the delicious poison of sloth, grows torpid.

PATIENCE.

Pun. vi. 375.

Nec tam fugisse cavendo
Adversa egregium, quam perdomuisse ferendo.

It is not so honourable to avoid misfortunes by our vigilance, as to overcome them by noble patience.

Euripides (Aiol. Fr. 20) says :—

Μοχθεῖν ἀνάγκη· τὰς δὲ δαιμόνων τύχας
'Όστις φέρει κάλλιστ', ἀνὴρ οὗτος σοφός.

"Distresses must be endured ; whoever bears with patience the inflictions of the gods, that man is wise."

MISERY REMINDS MAN OF GOD.

Pun. vii. 88.

Tanta adeo, cum res trepidæ, reverentia divûm
Nascitur : at raræ fumant felicibus aræ.

When we are in misery, then springs up a reverence of the gods: the prosperous seldom approach the sacred altar.

TO INJURE OUR COUNTRY.

Pun. vii. 554.

Accipe, et æterno fixum sub pectore serva :
Succensere nefas patriæ, nec fœdior ulla
Culpa sub extremas fertur mortalibus umbras.

Hear, and keep this fixed for ever in thy breast ; to be incensed against thy country is impious, nor is there any sin more heinous that conducts man to the grave.

THE GAULS.

Pun. viii. 16.

Quin etiam ingenio fluxi, sed prima feroces,
Vaniloquum, Celtæ, genus ac mutabile mentis,
Respectare domos : mœrebant cæde sine ullâ
(Insolitum sibi) bella geri, siccasque cruoris
Inter tela siti Mavortis hebescere dextras.

Besides, the Gauls began to look towards home, a people fierce at the first onset, but unsteady ; a race boastful in words, and of a light, inconstant mind ; they grieved to see a war carried on without slaughter, (a thing to them unknown,) and that their hands, while they stood in arms, should grow stiff and dry from blood.

Adversity Grows Greater through Fear.
Pun. x. 598.

Dura inter pavidos alitur fortuna sedendo,
Et gliscunt adversa metu.

The frowns of fortune are deepened to the timid when there is
no resistance, and adverse circumstances go on increasing by yield-
ing to fear.

Faith to be kept in Distress.
Pun. xi. 163.

Magnum, atque in magnis positum populisque virisque,
Adversam ostentare fidem.

It is noble, and regarded as the noblest, both among nations and
individuals, to keep faith in adversity.

True Kindness.
Pun. xi. 167.

Is locus officio, cum cessant prospera, cumque
Dura ad opem fortuna vocat : nam laeta fovere
Haudquaquam magni est animi decus.

Then is the time to give proof of kindly feelings, when prosperity
has fled and misfortunes call for aid ; for to show kindness to the
fortunate in no way does honour to the noble.

Peace.
Pun. xi. 595.

               Pax optima rerum,
Quas homini novisse datum est : pax una triumphis
Innumeris potior : pax, custodire salutem
Et cives aequare potens.

Peace is the best of things known to mortals ; peace brings
greater honour than innumerable triumphs ; peace that is able to
keep the common safety, and to make all citizens equal to each
other.

Be Daring in War.
Pun. xiii. 772.

          Turpis lenti sollertia Martis.
Audendo bella expedias : pigra extulit arctis
Haud unquam sese virtus. Tu magna gerendi
Praecipita tempus : mors atra impendet agenti.

Supineness in war is disgraceful. It is by daring that thou mayest bring wars to a successful result. Sloth never yet raised herself to the stars. Hasten on thy mighty deeds; black death impends over thee in the midst of thy labours.

STATIUS

BORN ABOUT A.D. 61—DIED ABOUT A.D. 96.

P. Papinius Statius was the son of P. Papinius Statius, the preceptor of Domitian, being born at Naples. Of his personal history little is known, as he is mentioned by no ancient author except Juvenal. He gained the prize three times at the Alban games, (Suet. Dom. 4.) He is said to have been stabbed with a stilus by Domitian. Several of his works are extant.

THE DEMAGOGUE.

Theb. i. 171.

Aliquis, cui mens humili læsisse veneno
Summa, nec impositos unquam cervice volenti
Ferre duces.

Then one, whose nature was to attack the noble with the poisonous slander of his tongue, and who was unwilling to submit to the leaders placed over him, rose up to speak.

A TIGER.

Theb. i. 128.

Qualis ubi audito venantum murmure tigris
Horruit in maculas, somnosque excussit inertes;
Bella cupit, laxatque genas et temperat ungues;
Mox ruit in turmas, natisque alimenta cruentis
Spirantem fert ore virum.

As the tiger, when he hears the sound of the approaching huntsmen, rustles his spotted skin, shaking off his lazy sleep; he wakes to the combat, expands his jaws and points his claws: then bounds into the midst of the bands and bears off his reeking prey, food for his bloody whelps.

The Deserving.

Theb. i. 661.

      Fors æqua merentes
Respicit.

 A just fortune awaits the deserving.

Envy.

Theb. ii. 16.

Unus ibi ante alios, cui læva voluntas
Semper, et ad superos hinc est gravis exitus, ævi
Insultare malis, rebusque ægrescere lœtis.

There is one, above all others, who always acts opposed to the
rest of the world, and therefore with difficulty reaches the gods
above, prone to insult and sickening at another's joys.

Ambition.

Theb. ii. 489.

      O cæca nocentum
Consilia! o semper timidum scelus!

O blinded counsels of the guilty! O wickedness, always full of
fearful forebodings!

Fear.

Theb. iii. 5.

      Tunc plurima versat
Pessimus in dubiis augur timor.

Then fear, the very worst prophet in misfortunes, anticipates
many evils.

To-Morrow.

Theb. iii. 562.

     Quid crastina volveret ætas,
Scire nefas homini.

It is unlawful for man to know what may be to-morrow.

Simonides of Ceos (Fr. 23, S.) says much to the same effect:—

  Ἄνθρωπος ἐὼν μή ποτε εἴπῃς ὅτι γίγνεται αὔριον,
  μηδ' ἄνδρα ἰδὼν ὄλβιον, ὅσσον χρόνον ἔσσεται·
  ὠκεῖα γὰρ οὐδὲ τανυπτερύγου μυίας
  οὕτως ἁ μετάστασις·

"Being a mortal, do not pretend to say what to-morrow will bring forth,
nor when you see a man happy, how long he will be so. For the change is
quicker than that of a long-winged fly."

BLINDNESS OF MAN.
Theb. vi. 718.

     Pro ! fors, et cæca futuri
Mens hominum.
Oh chance and the mind of man, blind to futurity !

MERCY.
Theb. vi. 816.

Pulchrum est vitam donare minori.
It is a noble act to bestow life on the vanquished.

LOVE OF LIFE.
Theb. viii. 386.

     Qui mente novissimus exit,
Lucis amor.
The love of life, the last that lingers in the human breast.

SLEEP.
Theb. x. 84.

Stat super occiduæ nebulosa cubilia noctis,
Æthiopasque alios, nulli penetrabilis astro
Lucus iners, subterque cavis grave rupibus antrum
It vacuum in montem, qua desidis atria Somni
Securumque larem segnis Natura locavit.
Limen opaca Quies, et pigra Oblivia servant,
Et nunquam vigili torpens Ignavia vultu.
Otia vestibulo, pressisque Silentia pennis
Muta sedent, abiguntque truces a culmine ventos,
Et ramos errare vetant, et murmura demunt
Altibus : non hic pelagi, licet omnia clament
Littora, non ullus cœli fragor : ipse profundis
Vallibus effugiens speluncæ proximus amnis
Saxa inter scopulosque tacet : nigrantia circa
Armenta, omne solo recubat pecus, et nova marcent
Germina, terrarumque inclinat spiritus herbas.
Mille intus simulacra dei cœlaverat ardens
Mulciber : hic hæret lateri redimita Voluptas,
Hic comes in requiem vergens Labor : est ubi Baccho,
Est ubi Martigenæ socium pulvinar Amori
Obtinet : interius tectûm in penetralibus altis
Et cum Morte jacet : nullique ea tristis imago.
Ipse autem, vacuus curis, humentia subter

Antra soporifero stipatus flore, tapetas
Incubat : exhalant vestes, et corpore pigro
Strata calent, supraque torum niger efflat anhelo
Ore vapor : manus hæc fusos a tempore lævo
Sustentat crines, hæc cornu oblita remisit.

Beside the cloudy confines of the western night and the distant Ethiopians, there is a misty grove, impenetrable to the brightest star, and under the hollow rocks an immense cave descends into the bowels of the mountain, where sluggish Nature has placed the halls of lazy sleep and the drowsy god. Motionless Rest and dark Oblivion stand on guard, and torpid Sloth with never wakeful eye. At the porch sits Ease and speechless Silence with close contracted wings, driving the murmuring winds from the roof, forbidding the foliage to rustle or the birds to twitter : here no roaring of the ocean, though all the shores resound, no crashing of the thunder ; the stream itself, gliding along the deep valleys close to the grotto, rolls silently between the rocks and cliffs ; the sable herds and flocks recline at ease on the ground ; the newly-sprung grass withers, and the vapour makes the herbage languid. Glowing Vulcan had formed a thousand statues of the god within : close by is wreathed Pleasure ; here, in attendance, is Toil inclined to rest ; here the same couch receives Love and Wine ; deep, deep within he lies with his twin-brother Death, a sad image to none. Beneath the dew-bespangled cavern the god himself, released from cares, crowned with drowsy flowers, lay on tapestry : his dress sends forth exhalations, his couch is warm with his lazy body, and above the bed a dark vapour rises from his half-shut mouth. The one hand sustains his hair hanging over his left temple, the other has dropped the horn unheeded.

The Gods are Subject to Law.

Silv. iii. 3. 53.

Habent et numina legem :
Servit et astrorum velox chorus, et vaga servit
Luna, nec injussi toties redit orbita solis.

The gods also are subject to law, the rapid choir of stars, the moon is subject, nor does the sun follow its appointed course without having been so ordained.

So Sophocles (Ajax, 669) says :—

Καὶ γὰρ τὰ δεινὰ καὶ τὰ καρτερώτατα
Τιμαῖς ὑπείκει· τοῦτο μὲν νιφοστιβεῖς
Χειμῶνες ἐκχωροῦσιν εὐκάρπῳ θέρει·
Ἐξίσταται δὲ νυκτὸς αἰανὴς κύκλος,
Τῇ λευκοπώλῳ φέγγος ἡμέρᾳ φλέγειν·
Δεινῶν τ' ἄημα πνευμάτων ἐκοίμισε
Στένοντα πόντον· ἐν δ' ὁ παγκρατὴς ὕπνος
Λύει πεδήσας, οὐδ' ἀεὶ λαβὼν ἔχει.

"For all that is dreadful and all that is mightiest gives way to law. First snow-paced winter yields to fruitful summer, and the orb of murky night gives place to the day with his white steeds to kindle his light, and the blast of the dreadful winds hath lulled the roaring main, nay, all o'erpowering sleep looses where he has bound, nor always holds us captive."

Again, Shakespeare ("Troilus and Cressida," act i. sc. 3) says :—

> "The heavens themselves, the planets, and this centre,
>   Observe degree, priority, and place,
>   Insisture, course, proportion, season, form,
> Office, and custom, in all line of order."

TACITUS

BORN ABOUT A.D. 50—DIED ABOUT A.D. 120.

P. CORNELIUS TACITUS is supposed by some to have been born at Interamna, the modern Terni, but this is doubtful. We find him advanced to office by Vespasian, and to have been a favourite of his sons Titus and Domitian. He married the daughter of C. Julius Agricola, who was consul A.D. 77. He was prætor A.D. 88, and in the reign of Nerva, A.D. 97, he was appointed consul suffectus in the place of T. Verginius Rufus, who had died in that year. He was the intimate friend of Pliny the younger, and in the collection of Pliny's letters we find eleven addressed to Tacitus. The precise time of his death is unknown, nor is it certain whether he left any family, though the emperor Tacitus claimed to be descended from the historian.

TRAITORS.

Ann. i. 58.

Proditores etiam iis, quos anteponunt, invisi sunt.

Traitors are hateful even to those who gain by their treason.

HATRED.

Ann. i. 69.

Odia in longum jaciens, quæ reconderet, auctaque promeret.

Sowing the seeds of hatred, which would lie hid for a long period, and gathering strength would spring up at some distant day.

INSTABILITY OF HUMAN AFFAIRS.
Ann. i. 72.

Cuncta mortalium incerta; quantoque plus adeptus foret, tanto se magis in lubrico dictitans.

Alleging the instability of human affairs, and the danger always increasing in proportion to the eminence which a man reaches.

DOMESTIC EXPENSES.
Ann. ii. 33.

Neque in familiâ et argento, quæque ad usum parentur, nimium aliquid aut modicum, nisi ex fortunâ possidentis. Distinctos senatus et equitum censûs, non, quia diversi naturâ, sed ut locis, ordinibus, dignationibus antistent et aliis, quæ ad requiem animi aut salubritatem corporum parentur. Nisi forte clarissimo cuique plures curas, majora pericula subeunda; delenimentis curarum et periculorum carendum esse.

In domestic expenses, such as slaves, plate, and what is necessary for life, there is nothing in itself excessive, nothing mean but what is made so by the circumstances of the parties. The only reason why the fortune of a senator should differ from the qualification of a knight is not that they are different in nature, but that they should excel each other in station, rank, and honours, and those other things which are for the recreation of the mind and the health of the body. Unless, perhaps, you are inclined to maintain that the most illustrious ought to submit to weightier anxieties and greater dangers, while they are without the means to soothe their anxieties and dangers.

FALSE COMPASSION.
Ann. ii. 38.

Languescet alioqui industria, intendetur socordia, si nullus ex se metus aut spes: et securi omnes alieni subsidia exspectabunt, sibi ignavi, nobis graves.

If we yield to false compassion, industry will go to ruin; sloth will predominate if man has nothing to hope or fear from his own exertions. All being secure of subsistence, will look to their neighbours for support, being idle in their own business and a burden to the public.

TRUTH.
Ann. ii. 39.

Veritas visu et morâ, falsa festinatione et incertis valescunt.

Truth is brought to light by time and reflection, while falsehood gathers strength from precipitation and bustle.

FALSE GRIEF.
Ann. ii. 77.

Nulli jactantius mœrent, quam qui maxime lœtantur.

None grieve with so much ostentation as those who in their hearts rejoice at the event.

DAY OF MOURNING.
Ann. iii. 4.

Dies quo reliquiæ tumulo Augusti inferebantur, modo per silentium vastus, modo ploratibus inquies.

On the day that the remains of Augustus were conveyed to the tomb, there was dreary desolation with passionate sorrow.

THE COMMONWEALTH.
Ann. iii. 6.

Principes mortales, rempublicam æternam case.

Whatever be the fate of noble families, the commonwealth is immortal.

FORTUNE TURNS EVERYTHING TO A JEST.
Ann. iii. 18.

Quanto plura recentium seu veterum revolvo, tanto magis ludibria rerum mortalium cunctis in negotiis obversantur.

When we review what has been doing in the world, is it not evident that in all transactions, whether of ancient or of modern date, some strange caprice of fortune turns all human wisdom to a jest?

LAWS IN A CORRUPT STATE.
Ann. iii. 27.

Corruptissimâ republicâ plurimæ leges.

When the state is most corrupt, the laws are most numerous.

PEACE.
Ann. iii. 44.

Miseram pacem vel bello bene mutari.

Even war is preferable to a wretched and dishonourable peace.

Saying of Tiberius.
Ann. iii. 65.

Memoriæ proditur, Tiberium, quotiens curiâ egrederetur, Græcis verbis in hunc modum eloqui solitum, "O homines ad servitutem paratos!"

We are informed by tradition that Tiberius, as often as he went from the Senate-house, used to exclaim in Greek, "Devoted men, how they rush headlong into bondage!"

Conspicuous by Absence.
Ann. iii. 76.

Eo magis præfulgebat, quod non videbatur.

He shone with the greater splendour because he was not seen.

This expression is the French "briller par son absence."

Chastity.
Ann. iv. 3.

Neque fœmina, amissâ pudicitiâ, alia abnuerit.

When a woman has lost her chastity, she will shrink from no crime.

Kindnesses.
Ann. iv. 18.

Beneficia eo usque læta sunt, dum videntur exsolvi posse : ubi multum antevenere, pro gratiâ odium redditur.

Obligations are only then acknowledged, when it seems in our power to requite them ; if they exceed our ability, gratitude gives way to hatred.

Informers.
Ann. iv. 30.

Sic delatores, genus hominum publico exitio repertum, et pœnis quidem nunquam satis coërcitum, per præmia eliciebantur.

In this way informers, a race of men the bane and scourge of society, never having been sufficiently curbed by punishment, were drawn forth by the wages of iniquity.

The British Constitution.
Ann. iv. 33.

Cunctas nationes et urbes populus aut primores aut singuli regunt : delecta ex his et consociata reipublicæ forma

laudari facilius, quam evenire, vel, si evenit, haud diuturna
esse potest.

In all nations the supreme authority is vested either in the
people, the nobles, or a single individual. A constitution com-
posed of these three simple forms may in theory be praised, but
can never exist in fact, or if it should, it will be but of short
duration.

See (Gr.) Judges, duties of; Government, best form; (Fr.) Government.

EXAMPLE.
Ann. iv. 33.

Pauci prudentiâ honesta ab deterioribus, utilia ab noxiis,
discernunt ; plures aliorum eventis docentur.

Few are able by their own reflection to draw the line between
vice and virtue, or to separate the useful from that which is the
opposite ; many learn experience by what happens to others.

THE LAST OF THE ROMANS.
Ann. iv. 34.

Cremutius Cordus postulatur, novo ac tunc primum
audito crimine, quod, editis annalibus, laudatoque M.
Bruto, C. Cassium Romanorum ultimum dixisset.

Cremutius Cordus is accused of a new and, till that time, un-
heard-of crime, that, having published a series of annals, and
eulogised M. Brutus, he had styled C. Cassius the last of the
Romans.

CALUMNY.
Ann. iv. 34.

Spreta exolescunt : si irascare, agnita videntur.

Calumny, when disregarded, is soon forgotten by the world ;
if you get in a passion, it seems to have a foundation of truth.

POSTERITY.
Ann. iv. 35.

Suum cuique decus posteritas rependit.

Posterity gives to every man his true value and proper honour.

TALENTS PROSCRIBED BY TYRANTS.
Ann. iv. 35.

Quo magis socordiam eorum inridere libet, qui præsenti
potentiâ credunt exstingui posse etiam sequentis ævi me-

PRECEDENTS.

Ann. xi. 24.

Inveterascet hoc quoque: et quod hodie exemplis tuemur, inter exempla erit.

The measure which I now defend by examples will, at a future day, become another precedent. It is now a new regulation; in time it will be history.

EMBELLISHMENT OF A STORY.

Ann. xi. 27.

Compositum miraculi causâ.

A story embellished merely to create astonishment.

POPULAR OPINION.

Ann. xiii. 19.

Nihil rerum mortalium tam instabile ac fluxum est, quam fama potentiæ, non suâ vi nixa.

In human affairs there is nothing so unstable and fluctuating as the fancied pre-ominence which depends on popular opinion, when there is no solid foundation to support it.

LOVERS' QUARRELS.

Ann. xiii. 44.

Tum, ut adsolet in amore et irâ, jurgia, preces, exprobratio, satisfactio.

Then there is the usual scene, when lovers are excited with each other, quarrels, entreaties, reproaches, and then fondling reconcilement.

DOING EVIL THAT GOOD MAY COME.

Ann. xiv. 44.

Habet aliquid ex iniquo omne magnum exemplum, quod contra singulos, utilitate publicâ rependitur.

Every striking example has some injustice mixed up with it individuals suffer, while the public derive benefit.

THE AGENTS IN EVIL ACTIONS.

Ann. xiv. 62.

Malorum facinorum ministri quasi exprobrantes aspiciuntur.

The assistants in the commission of crimes are always regarded ey were reproaching the act.

New Brooms.

Ann. xv. 21.

Initia magistratuum nostrorum meliora ferme, finis inclinat.

Magistrates discharge their duties best at the beginning, and fall off at the conclusion.

Lust of Power.

Ann. xv. 53.

Cupido dominandi cunctis affectibus flagrantior est.

The lust of power is the strongest in the human breast.

The Bold.

Ann. xv. 59.

Etiam fortes viros subitis terreri.

Even the bravest men are not proof against a surprise.

Cutting Jokes.

Ann. xv. 68.

Sæpe asperis facetiis inlusus ; quæ, ubi multum ex vero traxere, acrem sui memoriam relinquunt.

He had often made the prince the subject of his raillery ; and raillery, when seasoned with truth, never fails to leave a sting that festers in the memory.

Effect of Indolence.

Ann. xvi. 18.

Utque alios industria, ita hunc ignavia ad famam protulerat.

While other men have been advanced to eminence by industry, this man succeeded by mere sluggishness and indolence.

Arbiter of Taste.

Ann. xvi. 18.

Inter paucos familiarium Neroni adsumptus est, elegantiæ arbiter.

Being in favour at court, and cherished as the companion of Nero in his select parties, he was allowed to be the arbiter of taste and elegance.

CALUMNY.
Hist. i. 1.

Obtrectatio et livor pronis auribus accipiuntur : quippe adulationi fœdum crimen servitutis, malignitati falsa species libertatis inest.

Spleen and calumny are devoured with a greedy ear. Flattery wears a badge of servitude; while in detraction and invective there appears an unreal kind of liberty.

NO CENSORSHIP OF THE PRESS.
Hist. i. 1.

Rarâ temporum felicitate, ubi sentire, quæ velis, et, quæ sentias, dicere licet.

Through the rare felicity of the times, you are permitted to think what you please and to publish what you think.

ROMAN PEOPLE.
Hist. i. 16.

Neque enim hic, ut in ceteris gentibus, quæ regnantur, certa dominorum domus, et ceteri servi : sed imperaturus es hominibus, qui nec totam servitutem pati possunt, nec totam libertatem.

For it is not here, as in other nations subject to monarchy, that a hereditary despotism exists in a single family and slavery in all the rest ; but you are destined to bear sway over a nation who are equally incapable of entire slavery and of entire freedom.

A SUCCESSOR.
Hist. i. 21.

Suspectum semper invisumque dominantibus, qui proximus destinaretur.

The man whom the public voice has named for the succession is sure to be suspected by the reigning prince.

TO MEET DANGER WITH FORTITUDE.
Hist. i. 33.

Si cadere necesse est, occurrendum discrimini.

If a man must fall, he should manfully meet the danger.

The Coward is a Boaster after Battle.
Hist. i. 35.

Ignavissimus quisque, et, ut res docuit, in periculo non ausurus, nimii verbis, linguâ feroces.

Every coward, who showed his timidity in the hour of danger, was lavish of words and playing the braggart with his tongue after the battle.

Foreboding of a Storm.
Hist. i. 40.

Neque populi aut plebis ulla vox, sed adtoniti vultus et conversæ ad omnia aures. Non tumultus, non quies : quale magni metus et magnæ iræ silentium est.

A deep and sullen silence prevailed. The very rabble was hushed. Amazement sat on every face. Their eyes watched every motion, and their ears caught every sound. The interval was big with terror ; it was neither a tumult nor a settled calm, but rather such an awful stillness as always indicates mighty terror and mighty fury.

Not to come up to Expectations.
Hist. i. 49.

Major privato visus, dum privatus fuit, et omnium consensu capax imperii, nisi imperâsset.

While no higher than a private citizen, his merit was thought superior to his rank ; and the suffrages of mankind would have pronounced him worthy of empire, had he never made the experiment.

Dangerous Enterprises.
Hist. i. 55.

Insitâ mortalibus naturâ, propere sequi, quæ piget inchoare.

Each man, as is usual in dangerous enterprises, expecting the bold example of his comrades, ready to second the insurrection, yet not daring to begin it.

Fickleness.
Hist. i. 69.

Militis animum mitigavit, ut est mos vulgo, mutabilem subitis, et tam pronum in misericordiam, quam immodicus sævitiæ fuerat.

He had the address to soothe the minds of the soldiers, who (such is the nature of the multitude) are easily inflamed, and with a sudden transition shift to the opposite extreme.

PROSPERITY.
Hist. ii. 7.

Rebus secundis etiam egregios duces insolescere.

In the hour of prosperity even the most illustrious generals become haughty and insolent.

THE ELEVATION OF NEW MEN.
Hist. ii. 20.

Insitâ mortalibus naturâ, recentem aliorum felicitatem ægris oculis introspicere, modumque fortunæ a nullis magis exigere, quam quos in æquo videre.

Such is the nature of the human mind, disposed at all times to behold with jealousy the sudden elevation of new men, and to demand that he who has been known in an humble station, should know how to rise in the world with temper and modest dignity.

A DISSOLUTE SOLDIERY.
Hist. ii. 21.

Segnem ac desidem et circo et theatris corruptum militem.

A slothful and listless soldiery, debauched by the circus and theatres.

CONTEST FOR EMPIRE.
Hist. ii. 74.

Imperium cupientibus nihil medium inter summa et præcipitia.

When the contest is for sovereign power, there is no middle course.

POPULACE.
Hist. ii. 90.

Vulgus tamen, vacuum curis, et sine falsi verique discrimine solitas adulationes edoctum, clamore et vocibus adstrepebat : abnuentique nomen Augusti, expressere, ut adsumeret : tam frustra, quam recusaverat.

The populace, as usual, knowing neither truth nor falsehood, and indifferent about both, paid their tribute of flattery with noise and uproar. They pressed him to accept the title of Augustus ; he declined it for some time ; but the voice of the rabble prevailed. He yielded to their importunity ; but the compliance was useless, and the honour was of short duration.

POWER.

Hist. ii. 92.

Nec unquam satis fida potentia, ubi nimia est.

Power is never stable when it exceeds all bounds.

CHANGE.

Hist. ii. 95.

Magis alii homines, quam alii mores.

New men succeeded, but the measures were still the same.

QUALITIES OF A GENERAL.

Hist. iii. 20.

Ratio et consilium, propriæ ducis artes.

The proper qualities of a general are forethought and prudence.

INCONSIDERATE ACTIONS.

Hist. iii. 58.

Omnia inconsulti impetus cœpta, initiis valida, spatio languescunt.

All enterprises, which are begun inconsiderately, are violent at the beginning, but soon languish.

TUMULT.

Hist. iv. 1.

In turbas et discordias pessimo cuique plurima vis : pax et quies bonis artibus indigent.

In seasons of tumult and public distraction, the bold and desperate take the lead ; peace and good order are the work of virtue and ability.

RETALIATION.

Hist. iv. 3.

Tanto proclivius est injuriæ, quam beneficio, vicem exsolvere : quia gratia oneri, ultio in quæstu habetur.

So true it is that men are more willing to retaliate an injury than to requite an obligation ; obligation implies a debt, which is a painful sensation ; by a stroke of revenge, something is thought to be gained.

LOVE OF FAME THE LAST TO BE RESIGNED BY THE WISE.

Hist. iv. 6.

Etiam sapientibus cupido gloriæ novissima exuitur.

The love of fame is the last weakness which even the wise resign.

Thus Milton in " Lycidas " (l. 70) :—

> " Fame is the spur that the clear spirit doth raise
> (That last infirmity of noble minds)
> To scorn delights and live laborious days."

Massinger (" A Very Woman," v. 4) :—

> " Though the desire of fame be the last weakness
> Wise men put off."

Plato (Athen. xi. 507, d.) says :—

Ἔσχατον τὸν τῆς δόξης χιτῶνα ἐν τῷ θανάτῳ αὐτῷ ἀποδυόμεθα.

" The love of fame is the last vesture which we throw off at death."

LIBERTY.
Hist. iv. 17.

Libertatem naturâ etiam mutis animalibus datam.

Liberty, that best gift, dealt out by the impartial hand of Nature, even to the brute creation.

THE COWARD.
Hist. iv. 34.

Seditiosissimus quisque ignavus.

The most forward in seditious proceedings are cowards in action.

THE POOR.
Hist. iv. 38.

Vulgus, alimenta in dies mercari solitum, cui una ex republicâ annonœ cura.

The populace, who have never more than one day's provision, dreaded an approaching famine. Of all that concerns the public, the price of grain is their only care.

FAMILY UNION.
Hist. iv. 52.

Non legiones, non classes, perinde firma imperii munimenta, quam numerum liberorum. Nam amicos tempore, fortunâ, cupidinibus aliquando aut erroribus inminui, transferri, desinere : suum cuique sanguinem indiscretum, sed maxime principibus : quorum prosperis et alii fruantur, â junctissimos pertineant.

armies are not always the strongest bulwarks ; the s of the sovereign are in his own family. Friends r ; time changes the affections of men ; views of interest form new connexions ; the passions fluctuate ; desires arise that cannot be gratified ; misunderstandings follow, and friendships are transferred to others ; but the ties of blood still remain in force ; and in that bond of union consists the security of the emperor. In his prosperity numbers participate ; in the day of trouble, who, except his relations, takes a share in his misfortunes ?

Contests between Relatives.

Hist. iv. 70.

Acerrima proximorum odia,

The hatreds of relatives are most violent.

Rights of Man always a Specious Pretext for Demagogues.

Hist. iv. 73.

Cæterum libertas et speciosa nomina prætexuntur : nec quisquam alienum servitium et dominationem sibi concupivit, ut non eadem ista vocabula usurparet.

But the rights of man, and such specious language, are the pretext ; this has always been the language of those who want to usurp dominion over others.

An Armed Peace is the best Guarantee against War.

Hist. iv. 74.

Neque enim quies gentium sine armis, neque arma sine stipendiis, neque stipendia sine tributis.

For the repose of nations cannot be maintained without arms, arms without pay, nor pay without taxes.

Vices as long as there are Men.

Hist. iv. 74.

Vitia erunt, donec homines.

There will be vices as long as there are men.

The Jews.

Hist. v. 5.

Ægyptii pleraque animalia effigiesque compositas venerantur ; Judæi mente solâ unumque numen intelligunt : profanos, qui deûm imagines mortalibus materiis in hominum effingant : summum illud et æternu' mutabile neque interiturum. Igitur nulla simul· bus suis, nedum templis, sinunt.

The Egyptians worship various animals, and also ce

l representations, which are the work of men. The Jews
wledge one God only, and Him they see in the mind's eye,
Iim they adore in contemplation, condemning as impious
ors all who, with perishable materials, wrought into the
n form, attempt to give a representation of the Deity. The
of the Jews is the great governing Mind that directs and
s the whole frame of nature, eternal, infinite, and neither
le of change nor subject to decay. In consequence of this
on, no statue was to be seen in their city, much less in their
ie.

VIRTUOUS CHARACTERS.
Agric. 1.

eo virtutes iisdem temporibus optime æstimantur,
is facillime gignuntur.

is virtuous characters are most valued in those times to
they are most congenial.

ER TO DESTROY THAN REVIVE THE LOVE OF LETTERS.
Agric. 3.

turâ tamen infirmitatis humanæ tardiora sunt re-
l, quam mala; et, ut corpora lente augescunt, cito
guuntur, sic ingenia studiaque oppresseris facilius,
revocaveris. Subit quippe etiam ipsius inertiæ dul-
et invisa primo desidia postremo amatur.

from the infirmity natural to man, the remedies are slower
ration than the disease; and as the growth of bodies is slow
ogressive, their destruction rapid and instantaneous, so you
uch more easily destroy genius and the love of letters than
ill recall them into existence. For even idleness itself pos-
charms, which insensibly grow upon us: and sloth, at first
ed, is afterwards embraced with affection.

FAME.
Agric. 9.

Haud semper errat fama; aliquando et elegit.

mon fame does not always err: it sometimes even points
e man to be elected.

A HOUSEHOLD.
Agric. 19.

e suisque orsus, primum domum suam coercuit; quod
que haud minus arduum est, quam provinciam regere.

nning with himself and his friends, he first reformed his own
old—a work often attended with not less difficulty than the
istration of a province.

PLACABILITY.

Agric. 22.

Ceterum ex iracundiâ nihil supererat : secretum et silen
tium ejus non timeres. Honestius putabat offendere, quan
odisse.

His passion soon passed away and left no trace behind : yo
had no reason to fear his concealed ill-will. He thought it mor
honourable to give open offence than to indulge in secre
hatred.

DEFEAT AND SUCCESS.

Agric. 27.

Atque illi, modo cauti ac sapientes, prompti post even
tum ac magniloqui erant. Iniquissima hæc bellorum con
ditio est : prospera omnes sibi vindicant, adversa uni in
putantur.

And those who had lately prided themselves on their prudenc
and wisdom, were, after the successful result, ardent and full o
boasting. This is the unfair tax which commanders of armie
must always pay : all claim a share of success, while a bad result
is ascribed to the commander alone.

THE UNKNOWN.

Agric. 30.

Omne ignotum pro magnifico.

Everything unknown is magnified.

PEACE.

Agric. 30.

Auferre, trucidare, rapere, falsis nominibus inperium.
atque, ubi solitudinem faciunt, pacem adpellant.

To rob, to ravage, and to murder, in their imposing language.
are the arts of civil policy. When they have made the world a
solitude, they call it peace.

FEAR.

Agric. 32.

Metus et terror est, infirma vincula caritatis ; quæ ubi
removeris, qui timere desierint, odisse incipient.

Fear and awe are only weak chains to secure love ; when these
fetters are broken, the man who forgets to fear will begin to
show the effects of his hatred.

INJURIES.

Agric. 42.

Proprium humani ingenii est, odisse quem læseris.

It is the property of the human mind to hate those whom we we injured.

GLORY.

Agric. 44.

Et ipse quidem, quanquam medio in spatio integræ :atis ereptus, quantum ad gloriam, longissimum ævum regit.

And he, though carried off in the prime of life, had lived long ough for glory.

DOMITIAN.

Agric. 45.

Nero tamen subtraxit oculos, jussitque scelera, non spec-vit: præcipua sub Domitiano miseriarum pars erat, videre adspici, cum suspiria nostra subscriberentur, cum deno-ndis tot hominum palloribus sufficeret sævus ille vultus rubor, quo se contra pudorem muniebat.

Even Nero had the grace to turn away his eyes from the horrors his reign. He commanded deeds of cruelty, but never was a ectator of the scene. Under Domitian it was our wretched lot to ιhold the tyrant, and to be seen by him, while he kept a register our sighs and groans. With that fiery visage, of a dye so red ιat the blush of guilt could never colour his cheek, he marked the ιle languid countenance of the unhappy victims who shuddered ι his frown.

THE DEAD.

Agric. 46.

Si quis piorum manibus locus; si, ut sapientibus placet, on cum corpore exstinguuntur magnæ animæ: placide ιiescas, nosque, domum tuam, ab infirmo desiderio et ιuliebribus lamentis ad contemplationem virtutum tuarum ɔces, quas neque lugeri neque plangi fas est: admiratione : potius, et immortalibus laudibus, et, si natura suppe-itet, æmulatu decoremus. Is verus honos, ea conjunctis-mi cujusque pietas.

If in another world there is a pious mansion for the blessed; if, ι the wisest men have thought, the soul is not extinguished with ιe body, mayest thou enjoy a state of eternal felicity! From that ιation behold thy disconsolate family; exalt our minds from

2 N

fond regret and unavailing grief to the contemplation of thy vir-
tues. Those we must not lament; it were impiety to sully them
with a tear. To cherish their memory, to embalm them with our
praises, and if our frail condition will permit, to emulate thy
bright example, will be the truest mark of our respect, the best
tribute thy family can offer.

Young ("Night Thoughts," night ii. l. 26):—

"He mourns the dead, who lives as they desire."

THE MIND.
De Orator. c. 6.

Nam in ingenio, sicut in agro, quanquam alia diu ser-
antur atque elaborentur, gratiora tamen, quæ suâ sponte
nascuntur.

For in the mind, as in a field, though some things may be sown
and carefully brought up, yet what springs naturally, is most
pleasing.

ENVY.
De Orator. c. 18.

Vitio malignitatis humanæ vetera semper in laude, præ-
sentia in fastidio sunt.

From the maliciousness of human nature we are always praising
what has passed away, and depreciating the present.

ELOQUENCE.
De Orator. c. 36.

Magna eloquentia, sicut flamma, materiâ alitur, et moti-
bus excitatur et urendo clarescit.

It is of eloquence as of a flame; it requires matter to feed it,
motion to excite it, and it brightens as it burns.

TERENTIUS
BORN B.C. 195—DIED B.C. 159.

P. TERENTIUS AFER, born at Carthage, B.C. 195, became the slave
of P. Terentius Lucanus, a Roman senator. He gave him a good
education, and subsequently manumitted him, upon which he
assumed, according to the usual practice, his patron's name. The
success of his play "the Andria," B.C. 166, introduced him to the
most refined and intellectual circles of Rome. He is said to have

received assistance in the composition of his plays from Scipio and Lælius, who treated him more as a friend than a dependent. As he was a foreigner, and the pure idioms of the Latin language could be little known to him, it is not at all improbable that his plays should have been submitted to the revision of his friends. The calumnious attacks of his rivals are said to have driven him from Italy, when he took refuge in Greece, from which he never returned. According to one story, after embarking at Brundisium, he was never heard of more; according to others, he died in some city of the Peloponnesus. He left a daughter, but nothing is known of his family.

IGNORANCE.

And. Prol. 17.

Faciunt næ intelligendo, ut nihil intelligant.

Faith! by too much knowledge they bring it about that they know nothing.

OBSCURE DILIGENCE.

And. Prol. 20.

Quorum æmulari exoptat negligentiam
Potius, quam istorum obscuram diligentiam.

He prefers to emulate the negligence of the one, rather than the obscure diligence of the other.

KINDNESS.

And. i. 1. 16.

Sed hoc mihi molestum est : nam isthæc commemoratio,
Quasi exprobratio est immemoris benefici.

But this annoys me ; for this reminding me of your kindness is as it were a reproaching me of ingratitude.

Shakespeare ("Troilus and Cressida," act iii. sc. 3) says :—

"Time hath, my lord, a wallet at his back,
Wherein he puts alms for oblivion,
A great-sized monster of ingratitudes :
These scraps are good deeds past ; which are devour'd
As fast as they are made, forgot as soon
As done."

See (Gr.) Kindness ; (Fr.) Wallet-bearers.

EXCESS.

And. i. 1. 34.

Nam id arbitror
Adprime in vitâ esse utile, ut ne quid nimis.

For I hold this to be the golden rule of life, "Too much of any-thing is bad."

See (Gr., Fr.) Excess.

COMPLIANCE.
And. i. 1. 41.

Obsequium amicos, veritas odium parit.

Obsequiousness procures friends, plain dealing breeds hatred.

BAD HEART.
And. i. 1. 137.

Mala mens, malus animus.

From bad dispositions arise bad designs.

A SIMPLETON.
And. i. 2. 23.

Davus sum, non Œdipus.

I am a simple Davus, who can understand plain talk very well, but I have not the sagacity of an Œdipus to fathom the enigma which you propose.

DOTARDS.
And. i. 3. 13.

Inceptio est amentium, haud amantium.

This is a beginning of dotards, not of doting.

This has been shortened to "amantes, amentes," "in love, a fool." It is translated alliteratively thus in an old translation (1641):—"For they are fare as they were lunaticke and not love-sicke."

· A WISH. ·
And. ii. 1. 5.

Quoniam non potest id fieri, quod vis,
Id velis, quod possit.

Since the thing you wish cannot be had, wish for that which you can have.

THE SICK.
And. ii. 1. 9.

Facile omnes, quum valemus, recta consilia ægrotis damus.

We all, when we are well, give good advice to the sick.

Sophocles (Trachin. 731):—

Τοιαῦτα δ' ἂν λέξειεν οὐχ ὁ τοῦ κακοῦ
Κοινωνὸς, αλλ' ᾧ μηδέν ἐστ' οἴκοις βαρύ.

'Not he who shares in the grief may suggest comfort, but he to whom
re is no anxiety at home."

See (Gr., Fr.) Advice.

THANKS.

And. ii. 1. 30.

ro, Charine, neutiquam officium liberi esse hominis puto,
m is nihil promereat, postulare id gratiæ adponi sibi.

I do not by any means think it the act of an honourable man,
en he has done nothing to merit favour, to require that thanks
ould be given him.

SELF-LOVE.

And. ii. 5. 14.

Nullâne in re esse homini cuiquam fidem !
Verum illud verbum est, vulgo quod dici solet,
Omnes sibi malle melius esse, quam alteri.

s there no faith in the affairs of men ! It is an old saying, and
rue one too, " Of all mankind, each loves himself the best."
lenander says :—

Φιλεῖ ἑαυτοῦ πλείον οὐδεὶς οὐδένα.

" No one loves another better than himself."

See (Gr., Fr.) Self-love.

SAFETY.

And. iii. 1. 22.

Ego in portu navigo.

My vessel is in harbour, reckless of the troubled sea.

LOVERS.

And. iii. 3. 22.

Amantium iræ, amoris integratio est.

Quarrels of lovers but renew their love.

This idea is seized by Béranger in one of his songs :—

" Commissaire, commissaire,
Colin bat sa ménagère,
C'est un beau jour pour l'amour."

MALICE.

And. iv. 1. 1.

Hoccin' est credibile, aut memorabile,
Tanta vecordia innata cuiquam ut siet,
Ut malis gaudeant alienis, atque ex incommodis
Alterius, sua ut comparent commoda ?

Is it to be believed or told, that there is such malice in men as to rejoice in misfortunes, and from another's woes to draw delight?

Menander says :—

ταῖς ἀτυχίαις μήποτ' ἐπίχαιρε τῶν πέλας.

"Never rejoice at the misfortunes of your neighbour."

CHARITY AT HOME.

And. iv. 1. 10.

Ibi tum eorum impudentissima oratio est,
Quis tu es ? quis mihi es ? cur meam tibi ?
Heus, proximus sum egomet mihi.

Here, then, is their shameless impudence; they cry, Who, then, are you? What are you to me? Why should I give my property to you? Hark ye, I have a right to be my own best friend.

INCLINATION.

And. iv. 1. 34.

Scio : tu coactus tuâ voluntate es.

I know it; thou art constrain'd by inclination.

FROM THE HEART.

And. iv. 4. 55.

Paulum interesse censes, ex animo omnia,
Ut fert natura, facias, an de industriâ ?

Dost thou think that there is little difference whether thou dost a thing from the heart, as nature suggests, or with a purpose?

AS WE CAN.

And. iv. 5. 10.

Ut quimus, aiunt, quando ut volumus, non licet.

As we can, according to the old saying, when we cannot, as we would.

SAFETY.

And. v. 2. 4.

Omnis res est jam in vado.

All is now secure.

GRAVITY.

And. v. 2. 16.

Tristis-severitas inest in voltu, atque in verbis fides.

A grave severity is in his face.
And credit in his words.

To Hear what is Displeasing.
And. v. 4. 17.

mihi pergit, quæ volt, dicere ; ea, quæ non volt, audiet.

f he persist in saying whatever he pleases, he will hear what is
pleasing.

his seems to be a translation of a line of Alcæus (Fr. 62, S.) :—

Ἀλκ' εἴπῃς τὰ θέλεις, (ἢ κεν,) ἀκούσαις τά κεν ὁυ θέλοις.

If thou sayest what thou wishest, thou wilt hear what thou wishest not.'

r of Homer (Il. xx. 250) :—

'Οππόιόν κ' εἴπῃσθα ἔπος, τόιόν κ' ἐπακούσαις.

"Whatever words thou shalt say, the same shalt thou hear."

Ills of Life.
And. v. 6. 3.

re hominum evenit, ut quod sim nactus mali,
us rescisceres tu, quam ego illud, quod tibi evenit boni.

happens, as is usual among men, that my ills should reach
ears before thy joys reach mine.

ilton ("Samson Agonistes," l. 1538) expresses the same idea :—

"For evil news rides post, while good news bates."

Nothing New.
Eun. Prol. 41.

Nullum est jam dictum, quod non dictum sit prius.

Nothing's said now, but has been said before.

Jerome relates that his preceptor Donatus, explaining this passage,
d severely at the ancients for taking from him his best thoughts,
ng--

"Pereant, qui ante nos nostra dixerunt."

See Warton in his "Essay on Pope," in a note i. 88.

Love.
Eun. i. 1. 14.

In amore hæc omnia insunt vitia : injuriæ,
Suspiciones, inimicitiæ, induciæ,
Bellum, pax rursum.   Incerta hæc si tu postules
Ratione certa facere, nihilo plus agas,
Quam si des operam, ut cum ratione insanias.

n love there are all these ills: wrongs, suspicions, quarrels, re-
cilements, war, and peace again.   If thou wouldst try to do
igs thus uncertain by a certain method, thou wouldst act a
ely as if thou wert to run mad with reason as thy guide.

FLATTERERS.

Eun. ii. 2. 17.

Est genus hominum, qui esse primos se omnium rerum
 volunt,
Nec sunt: hos consector. Hisce ego non paro me ut
 rideant;
Sed his ultro arrideo, et eorum ingenia admiror simul.
Quidquid dicunt, laudo: id rursum si negant, laudo id
 quoque.
Negat quis? nego: ait? aio. Postremo imperavi egomet
 mihi
Omnia assentari. Is quæstus nunc est multo uberrimus.

There is a kind of men who wish to be the head of everything,
and are not: these I attend; not to make them laugh like the
buffoon, but I laugh with them, and wonder at their parts. Whatever they say, I praise: if they refuse the praise, I praise that
also. Does any deny? I too deny. Affirm? I too affirm. In a
word, I have brought myself to assent to everything. That now
is the best of all professions.

CHANGE.

Eun. ii. 2. 45.

Omnium rerum, heus, vicissitudo est.

There is, alas! a change
 In all things.

MEN OF WIT.

Eun. iii. 1. 9.

Labore alieno magnam partam gloriam
Verbis sæpe in se transmovet, qui habet salem,
Qui in te est.

They, who have the wit that is in you, often transfer to themselves the glory got by others' care and toil.

SILENCE.

Eun. iii. 2. 23.

Tacent: satis laudant.

Dumb? Praise sufficient.

This is illustrated by the sublime saying of Soanen, Bishop of Senez, when
he was proceeding to exile:—
 "La silence du peuple est la leçon des rois."

LOVE.

Eun. iv. 5. 6.

Sine cerere et libero friget Venus.

Without good eating and drinking love grows cold.

THE WAYS OF WOMEN.

Eun. iv. 7. 42.

Immo certe, novi ingenium mulierum :
Nolunt, ubi velis : ubi nolis, cupiunt ultro.

y, certainly, I know the ways of women : they won't, when
wilt, and when thou won't, they are passionately fond.
teespeare ("Hamlet," act 1. sc. 2) says :—
  " Frailty, thy name is woman ! "

NEIGHBOURHOOD.

Heaut. i. 1. 4.

Tamen vel virtus tua me, vel vicinitas,
Quod ego in propinquâ parte amicitiæ puto,
Facit, ut te audacter moneam, et familiariter :
Quod mihi videre præter ætatem tuam
Facere, et præterquam res te adhortatur tua.

either thy austere life, or else near neighbourhood, which I
ler to be the first step to friendship, causes me to warn thee
' and as a friend, that thou seemest to me to be acting in a
nsuited to thy age and otherwise than thy income requires.

HUMANITY.

Heaut. i. 1. 23.

ME. Chreme, tantumne est ab re tuâ otii tibi,·
ena ut cures ; eaque, nihil quæ ad te attinet ?
'H. Homo sum : humani nihil a me alienum puto.

Chremes, hast thou such leisure from thy own affairs that
anst lavish time on those of others, and on matters which
concern thee? CHR. I am a human being : I consider none
incidents which befall my fellow-creatures to be matters of
cern to me.

THE MIND.

Heaut. i. 2. 19.

reliqui est, quin habeat, quæ quidem in homine
icuntur bona ?
tes, patriam incolumem, amicos, genus, cognatos,
livitias ?

Atque hæc perinde sunt, ut illius animus, qui ea possidet :
Qui uti scit, ei bona : illi, qui non utitur recte, mala.

What now prevents his having every earthly blessing that man
can possess? Parents, a prosperous country, friends, high birth,
relatives, riches? Yet all these take their value from the colour
of the mind. To him who knows their proper use, they are bless-
ings : to him who misuses them, they are curses.

Spenser, in his "Faerie Queen," (vi. 9. 30,) speaks thus of the mind of
man :—

> " It is the mind that maketh good or ill,
>   That maketh wretch or happy, rich or poor :
> For some, that hath abundance at his will,
> Hath not enough, but wants in greatest store ;
> And other, that hath little, asks no more,
> But in that little is both rich and wise ;
> For wisdom is most riches : fools therefore
> They are, which do by vows devise ;
> Sith each unto himself his life may fortunise."

Experience from Others' Misfortunes.
Heaut. i. 2. 36.

Scitum est ; periculum ex aliis facere, tibi quod ex usu siet.

Remember this maxim, to draw from others' misfortunes a pro-
fitable lesson for thyself.

A Deaf Man.
Heaut. ii. 1. 10.

Astutus ! næ ille haud scit, quam mihi nunc surdo narret
    fabulam.

Cunning old gentleman ! he little knows how deaf my ears are
to the wise saws he is pouring into them.

Women take Time for Adornment.
Heaut. ii. 2. 10.

Non cogitas hinc longule esse ? et nôsti mores mulierum :
Dum moliuntur, dum comuntur, annus est.

Dost thou not know that her house is a long way off. And then
thou knowest the ways of women : while they are setting them-
selves off and tricking out their persons, it is an age.

Simplicity in Dress.
Heaut. ii. 3. 47.

Sine auro, tum ornatam, ita uti quæ ornantur sibi :
Nullâ malâ re esse expolitam muliebri.

nd her dressed without gold or trinkets, as ladies who
d only for themselves, set off with no female paints and

No Famous Deed without Danger.
Heaut. ii. 3. 73.

fit sine periclo facinus magnum et memorabile.

at and famous deed is accomplished without danger.

A Lover.
Heaut. ii. 3. 130.

o te autem novi, quam esse soleas impotens :
versa verba, eversas cervices tuas,
mitus, screatus, tussis, risus, abstine.

thee, how little command thou hast over thyself ; no
sanings, turning thy neck round to leer, sighs, hems,
tittering.

License.
Heaut. iii. 1. 72.

ntam fenestram ad nequitiam patefeceris !
autem porro ut non sit suave vivere.
a deteriores omnes sumus licentiâ.
dcunque inciderit in mentem, volet : neque id
abit, pravum an rectum siet, quod petet.

at an opening for profligacy thou wilt make ! so that in
time life itself will be a burden.   For we all become
n too much liberty.   Whatever comes into his head, he
nor will he consider whether it be right or wrong.

Nature of Mankind.
Heaut. iii. 1. 96.

Dî vostram fidem !
nparatam esse hominum naturam omnium,
ut melius videant, et dijudicent,
sua ! an eo fit, quia in re nostrâ, aut gaudio
præpediti nimio, aut ægritudine ?
ihi quanto nunc plus sapit, quam egomet mihi !

that the nature of mankind should be such that they
wisdom, and determine better, in the affairs of others
heir own !   Does this superior wisdom arise because,
r own interest is concerned, we are prevented from
roperly either by excessive joy or grief ?   How much
ly does my neighbour here think for me than I do for

TRIFLES.

Heaut. iv. 1. 8.

Magno jam conatu magnas nugas. - --
> She 'll take mighty pains
> To be deliver'd of some mighty trifle.

INDUSTRY.

Heaut. iv. 2. 8.

Nihil tam difficile est, quin quærendo investigari possiet.
> Nothing so difficult but may be won by industry.

Antiphanes (Fr. Com. Gr. p. 500, M.) says :—
> Τῆς ἐπιμελίας δοῦλα πάντα γίνεται.
> "Everything yields to industry."

AN IF.

Heaut. iv. 3. 41.

Quid si redeo ad illos, qui aiunt: quid si nunc coelum ruat?
> Suppose, as some folk say, the sky should fall!

STRICT LAW.

Heaut. iv. 5. 48.

Dicunt, jus summum sæpe summa est malitia.
> For 'tis a common saying and a true,
> That strictest law is oft the highest wrong.

AGAINST THE GRAIN.

Heaut. iv. 6. 1.

Nulla est tam facilis res, quin difficilis siet,
Quum invitus facias.
> There is nothing so easy in itself but grows difficult when it is
> performed against one's will.

HABIT.

Heaut. iv. 7. 11.

Quam multa injusta ac prava fiunt moribus!
> How many unjust and wicked things are done from mere habit!

HOPE.

Heaut. v. 2. 28.

Modo liceat vivere; est spes.
> So we do but live,
> There 's hope.

A Father's Fears.

Adelph. i. 1. 10.

Ego, quia non redit filius, quæ cogito !
Et quibus nunc sollicitor rebus ! ne aut ille alserit,
Aut uspiam ceciderit, aut perfregerit
Aliquid, vah : quemquamne hominem in animum insti-
 tuere, aut
Parare, quod sit carius, quam ipse est sibi ?

What a world of fears now possess me, because my son has not returned! And with what apprehensions am I even now distracted! lest he should have taken cold, or had a fall or broken a limb! That any human being should entertain in his mind, or by his acts provide a thing, which should be dearer than he is to himself.

Children.

Adelph. i. 1. 30.

Nam qui mentiri, aut fallere insuêrit patrem, aut
Audebit : tanto magis audebit cœteros.
Pudore et liberalitate liberos
Retinere satius esse credo, quam metu.

For he, who has acquired the habit of lying or deceiving his father, will do the same with less remorse to others. I believe that it is better to bind your children to you by a feeling of respect and by gentleness than by fear.

Kindness.

Adelph. i. 1. 40.

Et errat longe, meâ quidem sententiâ,
Qui imperium credat gravius esse, aut stabilius,
Vi quod fit, quam illud, quod amicitiâ adjungitur.
Mea sic est ratio, et sic animum induco meum :
Malo coactus qui suum officium facit,
Dum id rescitum iri credit, tantisper cavet :
Si sperat fore clam, rursus ad ingenium redit.
Ille, quem beneficio adjungas, ex animo facit :
Studet par referre : præsens, absensque idem erit.
Hoc patrium est, potius consuefacere filium,
Suâ sponte recte facere, quam alieno metu.

The man is very much mistaken, in my opinion at least, who fancies that authority is more firm and stable that is founded on force than what is built on friendship. This is my way, this is my idea ; he who does his duty, driven to it by severity, while he thinks his actions are observed, so long only is he on his guard ;

if he hopes for secrecy, he goes back to his own ways again. He, whom you have made your own by kindness, does it of good will, is anxious to make a due return, acting present or absent evermore the same. This, then, is the duty of a father, to make a son embrace a life of virtue rather from choice than from terror or constraint.

Ben Jonson ("Every Man in his Humour," act i.) thus expresses the idea:—

> "There is a way of winning more by love,
> And urging of the modesty than fear.
> Force works on servile natures, not the free.
> He that's compell'd to goodness may be good;
> But 'tis but for that fit; where others, drawn
> By softness and example, get a habit."

To Despise Money is Gain.

Adelph. ii. 2. 8.

Pecuniam in loco negligere, maximum interdum est lucrum.

> To seem upon occasion to slight money,
> Proves, in the end, sometimes the greatest gain.

Hope.

Adelph. ii. 2. 11.

San. Ego spem pretio non emo.
Syrus. Nunquam rem facies! abi, nescis inescare homines, Sannio.
San. Credo istuc melius esse : verum ego nunquam adeo astutus fui,
Quin, quidquid possem, mallem auferre potius in præsentiâ.

San. I never purchase hope with ready money. Syr. Thou 'lt never make a fortune: away with thee, thou dost not know how to ensnare men, Sannio. San. Well, perhaps, thy way is best; yet I was never so cunning, but I had rather, when it was in my power, receive prompt payment.

True Wisdom.

Adelph. iii. 3. 32.

Istuc est sapere, non quod ante pedes modo est
Videre, sed etiam illa, quæ futura sunt,
Prospicere.

That is to be wise to see not merely that which lies before your feet, but to foresee even those things which are in the womb of futurity.

WISDOM.

Adelph. iii. 3. 40.

Tu, quantus quantus, nihil nisi sapientia es :
Ille, somnium. Sineres vero tu illum tuum
Facere hœc ? DEM. Sincerem illum ! an non sex totis men-
    sibus ·
Prius olfecissem, quam ille quidquam cœperit ?

Thou, from head to foot, art nought but wisdom's self : he a
more dotard. Wouldst thou ever permit thy boy to do such
things? DEM. Permit him? I? Or should I not much rather
smell him out six months before he did but dream of it?

CHILDREN.

Adelph. iii. 3. 46.

Ut quisque suum volt esse, ita est.

As fathers form their children, so they prove.

Euripides (Fr. Antiop. 17) says :—

Πᾶσι δ' ἀγγέλλω βροτοῖς,
'Εσθλῶν ἀπ' ἀνδρῶν εὐγενῆ σπείρειν τέκνα.

" I announce to all men, that noble children are sprung from noble sires.'

HOME EDUCATION.

Adelph. iii. 3. 59.

Domi habuit unde disceret.

He need not go from home for good instruction.

EDUCATION.

Adelph. iii. 3. 60.

Nihil prætermitto : consuefacio : denique
Inspicere, tanquam in speculum, in vitas omnium
Jubeo, atque ex aliis sumere exemplum sibi.
Hoc facito. SYR. Recte sane. DEM. Hoc fugito. SYR. Cal-
    lide.
DEM. Hoc laudi est. SYR. Istœc res est. DEM. Hoc vitio
    datur.
SYR. Probissime.

I spare no pains, neglect no means ; in a word, I bid him look
into the lives of all, as into a mirror, and thence draw from others
an example for himself. "Do this." SYR. Good. DEM. "Fly
that." SYR. Very good. DEM. "This deed is highly commend-
able." SYR. That's the thing. DEM. "That's reprehensible."
SYR. Most excellent.

EDUCATION.

Adelph. iii. 3. 76.

Inepta hæc esse, nos quæ facimus, sentio :
Verum quid facias ? ut homo est, ita morem geras.

I perceive that the things which we do are silly : but what
can one do? According to men's habits and dispositions, so one
must yield to them.

LAW.

Adelph. iii. 4. 44.

Quod vos jus cogit, id voluntate impetret.

Grant her, then, freely, what law else will claim.

RESULT OF INDULGENCE.

Adelph. iii. 4. 64.

Nimia illæc licentia
Profecto evadet in aliquod magnum malum.

But this immoderate indulgence must assuredly produce some
terrible misfortune in the end.

SPEAK OF THE DEVIL.

Adelph. iv. 1. 21.

Lupus in Fabulâ.

The wolf i' th' fable.

I AM A FRAIL MAN.

Adelph. iv. 2. 40.

Cense'n hominem me esse ? erravi.

Do you not remember that I am a frail human being ? and there-
fore I have erred.

This is probably the origin of the phrase "errare humanum est," which
first appears in the "Antilucretius sive de deo et naturâ," a didactic poem
of the Cardinal de Polignac, (Paris, 1747.) It is found in b. v. 1. 59.

THE POOR ARE SUSPICIOUS OF NEGLECT.

Adelph. iv. 3. 14.

Omnes, quibus res sunt minus secundæ, magis sunt, nescio
quomodo,
Suspiciosi : ad contumeliam omnia accipiunt magis :
Propter suam impotentiam se semper credunt negligi.

All, whose fortunes are less prosperous, are, I know not how,
the more suspicious ; they take everything as if insult were in-

tended: on account of their peculiar state of indigence, they always think themselves to be slighted.

A BLUSH.

Adelph. iv. 5. 9.

Erubuit : salva res est.

He blushes. All 's safe, I find.

Diphilus (Fr. Com. Gr. p. 1091, M.) says :—

'Ὃς δ' οὔτ' ἐρυθριᾶν οἶδεν οὔτε δεδιέναι,
Τὰ πρῶτα πάσης τῆς ἀναιδείας ἔχει.

" The man that neither blushes nor fears, has the initiative to every kind of shamelessness."

Young, " Night Thoughts," (night vii. 496) :—

" The man that blushes is not quite a brute."

LIFE OF MAN LIKE A GAME AT DICE.

Adelph. iv. 7. 21.

Ita vita est hominum, quasi, quum ludas tesseris :
Si illud, quod maxime opus est jactu, non cadit ;
Illud, quod cecidit forte, id arte ut corrigas.

The life of man is like a game at dice : if the favourable throw be not cast, that which chance sends, you must strive to amend by skill.

Alexis (Fr. Com. Gr. p. 607, M.) says :—

Τοιοῦτο τὸ ζῆν ἐστιν ὥσπερ οἱ κύβοι·
Οὐ ταὔτ' ἀεὶ πίπτουσιν, οὐδὲ τῷ βίῳ
Ταὐτὸν διαμένει σχῆμα, μεταβολὰς δ' ἔχει.

" Such a life is like dice : the same throws do not always turn up, nor does the same form remain to life, but it has changes."

PROVIDENCE UNABLE TO SAVE SOME MEN.

Adelph. iv. 7. 43.

Ipsa, si cupiat, Salus,
Servare prorsus non potest hanc familiam.

'Tis not in the power
Of Providence herself, howe'er desirous,
To save from ruin such a family.

TWO DOING THE SAME THING.

Adelph. v. 3. 37.

Duo quum idem faciunt, sæpe ut possis dicere,
Hoc licet impune facere huic, illi non licet :
Non quod dissimilis res sit, sed quod is sit.

2 o

When two persons do the self-same thing, it oftentimes falls out, that in the one it is criminal, in the other it is not so,—not that the thing itself is different, but he who does it.

This is evidently the origin of the common expression :—

"Duo quum faciunt idem, non est idem."

RULE OF LIFE CHANGED BY EXPERIENCE.

Adelph. v. 4. 1.

Nunquam ita quisquam bene subductâ ratione ad vitam
  fuit,
Quin res, ætas, usus, semper aliquid adportet novi,
Aliquid moneat, ut illa, quæ te scire credas, nescias :
Et quæ tibi putâris prima, in experiundo repudies.

Never did man lay down so wise a rule of life, but fortune, age, experience made some change in it, and taught you that those things which you thought you knew, you did not know; and the things which you deemed your chief perfections, from experience you threw by.

GENTLENESS.

Adelph. v. 4. 7.

                    Re ipsâ reperi,
Facilitate nihil esse homini melius neque clementiâ.

I have found by dear experience that there is nothing so advantageous for man as mildness and a forgiving disposition.

OLD MEN.

Adelph. v. 8. 31.

Vitium commune omnium est,
  Quod nimium ad rem in senectâ attenti sumus.

It is the common failing of old men
To be too much intent on worldly matters.

TO FOIL A MAN AT HIS OWN WEAPONS.

Adelph. v. 8. 35.

Suo sibi hunc gladio jugulo.

I foil him at his own weapons.

MISFORTUNE.

Hecyr. iii. 1. 6.

Nam nos omnes, quibus est alicunde aliquis objectus labos,
Omne quod est interea tempus, prius quam id rescitum est,
  lucro est.

For when mischance befalls us, all the interval between its happening, and our knowledge of it, may be esteemed clear gain.

WOMEN ARE WEAK OF SOUL.
Hecyr. iii. 1. 28.

Nam sæpe est, quibus in rebus alius ne iratus quidem est ;
Quum de eâdem causâ est iracundus factus inimicissimus,
Pueri inter sese quam pro levibus noxiis iras gerunt !
Quapropter ? quia enim, qui eos gubernat animus, infirmum
    gerunt.
Itidem illæ mulieres sunt ferme, ut pueri, levi sententiâ ;
Fortasse unum aliquod verbum inter eas iram hanc con-
    civerit.

For often a trifling cause, which would not move another's spleen, makes the choleric man your most bitter enemy. For how slight causes children squabble ! Why ? Because they are governed by a feeble mind. Women, like children, are impotent and weak of soul. A single word, perhaps, has kindled all this enmity between them.

WE RISE OR FALL ACCORDING TO OUR FORTUNE.
Hecyr. iii. 3. 20.

Omnibus nobis ut res dant sese, ita magni atque humiles
    sumus.

All of us, according as our affairs prosper, are elated or cast down.

MEN OF PLEASURE.
Hecyr. iii. 5. 9.

              Homo voluptati obsequens
Fuit, dum vixit : et qui sic sunt haud multum heredem
    juvant.
Sibi vero hanc laudem relinquunt : vixit, dum vixit, bene.

He was, his whole life-time, a man of pleasure : and those, who are so, do not much enrich their heir ; yet they leave this praise behind them : " While he lived, he lived well."

PAYMENT OF DEBTS.
Phorm. i. 2. 6.

Præsertim ut nunc sunt mores : adeo res redit :
Si quis reddit, magna habenda est gratia.

As times go now, things are come to such a pass that if a man pays you what he owes, you are much beholden to him.

MOUNTAINS OF GOLD.

Phorm. i. 2. 18.

Montes auri pollicens.

Promising mountains of gold.

This proverbial expression is found in Sallust, (Cat. 22,) being derived from the Persians boasting of mountains of gold, as that metal abounded with them.

See Persius (Sat. iii. 65.)

TO KICK AGAINST THE PRICKS.

Phorm. i. 2. 27.

Nam quæ inscitia est,
Advorsum stimulum calces?

For what a foolish task
To kick against the pricks!

See (Gr.) To kick; Acts ix. 5.

PATIENCE.

Phorm. i. 2. 88.

Quod fors feret, feremus æquo animo.

Whate'er chance brings, I will patiently endure.

Alexis (Fr. Com. Gr. p. 752, M.) says:—

Σοφοῦ γὰρ ἀνδρὸς τὰς τύχας ὀρθῶς φέρειν.

"For it is the part of a wise man to bear the buffets of fortune with patience."

And Hurdis says:—

"The noblest fortitude, is still to bear
Accumulated ills and never faint."

DISCONTENT.

Phorm. i. 3. 20.

Ita plerique ingenio sumus omnes, nostri nosmet pœnitet.

We are almost all of this disposition, that we are never satisfied with our own.

FORTUNE FAVOURS THE BRAVE.

Phorm. i. 4. 26.

Fortes fortuna adjuvat.

Fortune favours the brave.

ALL ALIKE.

Phorm. ii. 1. 34.

DE. Ecce autem similia omnia : omnes congruunt :
Unum cognôris, omnes nôris.
PH. Haud ita est.
DE. Hic in noxâ est : illa ad defendendam causam adest :
Quum ille est, hic prœsto est : tradunt operas mutuas.

DE. See all alike! the whole gang hangs together: know one,
and you know all. PH. Nay, it is not so. DE. One is in fault,
the other is at hand to bear him out : when the other slips, he is
ready ; each in their turn.

BORROWING EASILY SAID.

Phorm. ii. 1. 70.

GE. Non ratio, verum argentum deerat.
DE. Sumeret alicunde.
GE. Alicunde ! nihil est dictu facilius.

GE. It was not the reckoning, but money that was wanting.
DE. He might have borrowed. GE. Have borrowed it! easily
said.

FLEECE THE SIMPLE.

Phorm. ii. 2. 16.

Quia non rete accipitri tenditur, neque miluo,
Qui male faciunt nobis : illis, qui nihil faciunt, tenditur.
Quia enim in illis fructus est : in illis opera luditur.

Because the net is not stretched to catch the hawk or kite,
who do us wrong : it is laid for those who do us none at all. In
them there is something to be got, in these it is mere labour lost.

FIRST ATTACK.

Phorm. ii. 2. 32.

Prima coitio est acerrima.
The first attack's the fiercest.

PEDIGREE.

Phorm. ii. 3. 46.

Si talentûm rem reliquisset decem.
DE. Dî tibi male faciant !
PH. Primus esses, memoriter
Progeniem vostram usque ab avo atque atavo proferens.

If he had left behind him a property of some ten talents. DE.
Out upon you. PH. Then you would have been the first to trace
your descent from grandsire and great-grandsire.

A MATTER SETTLED.

Phorm. ii. 3. 72.

Actum, aiunt, ne agas.

Oh! that matter is all settled:
Think on 't no more.

MANY MEN, MANY MINDS.

Phorm. ii. 4. 14.

Quot homines, tot sententiæ : suus cuique mos.

Many men, many minds.

Euripides (Fr. Rhadam. 1) says :—

Ἔρωτες ἡμῖν εἰσι παντοῖοι βίου.
Ὁ μὲν γὰρ εὐγένειαν ἱμείρει λαβεῖν
Τῷ δ' οὐχὶ τούτου φροντίς, ἀλλὰ χρημάτων
Πολλῶν κεκλῆσθαι βούλεται πατὴρ δόμοις·
Ἄλλῳ δ' ἀρέσκει μηδὲν ὑγιὲς ἐκ φρενῶν
Λέγοντι πείθειν τοὺς πέλας τόλμῃ κακῇ·
Οἱ δ' αἰσχρὰ κέρδη πρόσθε τοῦ καλοῦ βροτῶν
Ζητοῦσιν, οὕτω βίοτος ἀνθρώπων πλάνη.
Ἐγὼ δὲ τούτων οὐδενὸς χρῄζω τυχεῖν,
Δόξαν δὲ βουλοίμην ἂν εὐκλείας ἔχειν.

" Various are the inclinations of man: this one longs for high descent:
to this other there is no such thought, but he wishes to be called the master
of much wealth in his house: this other, who can speak nothing sensible,
tries to persuade his neighbours with sheer shamelessness : some men seek
base gain before what is honourable, in such various ways do men stray.
I, however, wish none of these, but would desire to have the glory of high
fame."

TO HARP ON THE SAME STRING.

Phorm. iii. 2. 10.

Cantilenam eandem canis.

You are harping on the same string.

GIVE PLACE TO YOUR BETTERS.

Phorm. iii. 2. 37.

Reperi qui det, neque lacrumet : da locum melioribus.

I have found a ready paymaster, no sniveller: give place then to
your betters!

WORD TO THE WISE.

Phorm. iii. 3. 8.

Ah ! dictum sapienti sat est.

A word to the wise.

TWO STRINGS TO MY BOW.

Phorm. iv. 2. 13.

Commodius esse opinor duplici spe utier.

I think it better to have two strings to my bow.

A HANGING MATTER.

Phorm. iv. 4. 5.

Ad restim mihi quidem res rediit planissime.

Nothing indeed remains for me but that I should hang myself.

A TALE.

Phorm. iv. 4. 15.

          Nihil est, Antipho,
Quin male narrando possit depravarier.

Many a tale is spoilt in telling, Antipho.

FORTUNE.

Phorm. v. 1. 30.

      Quam sæpe forte temere
Eveniunt, quæ non audeas optare !

How often Fortune blindly brings about
More than we dare to hope for !

KNAVERY.

Phorm. v. 2. 6.

His nunc præmium est qui recta prava faciunt.

Knavery's now its own reward.

TIBULLUS

BORN ABOUT B.C. 59—DIED ABOUT B.C. 18.

ALBIUS TIBULLUS was born about B.C. 59, of equestrian rank, but of his youth and education we know nothing. His property was situated at Pedum, between Tibur and Præneste, and, like many others, in consequence of the civil wars, he was deprived of a large portion of it. He accompanied his patron, Messala, when he was despatched by Augustus to suppress a formidable insurrection which had broken out in Aquitania, a province of Gaul, and subsequently proceeded with Messala on his way to the East, whither he was sent to reorganise that part of the empire. Being taken ill, he was obliged to remain at Corcyra, (Corfu,) whence he returned to Rome, and thus ended the active life of Tibullus. He spent the remainder of his short life in composing those poetical effusions which have come down to us.

LOVE.
i. 2. 15.

Tu quoque ne timide custodes, Delia, falle :
Audendum est : fortes adjuvat ipsa Venus.

Delia, be not afraid to elude thy guards : thou must be courageous : Venus herself aids the adventurous maiden.

PERJURIES OF LOVERS.
i. 4. 20.

Nec jurare time ; Veneris perjuria venti
　　Irrita per terras et freta summa ferunt,
Gratia magna Jovi ; vetuit pater ipse valere,
　　Jurâsset cupide quicquid ineptus amor.

Fear not to swear ; the winds carry the perjuries of lovers without effect over land and sea, thanks to Jupiter ; the father of the gods himself has denied effect to what foolish lovers in their eagerness have sworn.

PASSAGE OF TIME.
i. 4. 27.

At si tardus eris, errabis : transiit ætas
　　Quam cito ! non segnis stat remeatve dies.

Quam cito purpureos deperdit terra colores!
  Quam cito formosas populus alba comas!
Quam jacet, infirmæ venere ubi fata senectæ,
  Qui prior Eleo est carcere missus equus!
Vidi ego jam juvenem, premeret cum serior ætas,
  Mœrentem stultos præteriisse dies.
Crudeles divi! serpens novus exuit annos;
  Formæ non ullam fata dedere moram.
Solis æterna est Phœbo Bacchoque juventas;
  Nam decet intonsus crinis utrumque deum.

But, if thou delayest, thou wilt be wrong: how swiftly time
passes! the day moves not sluggishly nor goes back. How quickly
the earth loses its gay colours! how quickly the white poplar
its leafy honours! How slothfully lies the horse, which flew when
young in the Olympic course, when it is unnerved by age! I have
seen the youth, when age has come upon him, bewail the days he
has passed in folly. Ye cruel gods! the serpent strips off his
years and renews his youth: fate allows no delay to beauty.
Apollo and Bacchus are the only gods that know no change: their
looks are ever unfading.

WINE.

i. 7. 39.

Bacchus et agricolæ magno confecta labore
  Pectora lætitiâ dissoluenda dedit:
Bacchus et afflictis requiem mortalibus affert,
  Crura licet durâ compede pulsa sonent.

Bacchus causes country swains oppressed with cares to forget
themselves in joys: Bacchus gives respite to the wretch's pains,
though his legs be galled with rattling chains.

Pindar (Fr. Incert. 61) says something to the same effect:—

> Ἀλικ᾽ ἀνθρώπων καματώδεες
> Οἴχονται μέριμναι στηθέων ἔξωθεν,
> Πελάγει δ᾽ ἐν πολυχρύσῳ πλοῦτον
> Πάντες ἴσα νέομεν ψευδῆ πρὸς ἀκτάν.
> Ὃς μὲν ἀχρήμων, ἀφνειὸς τότε,
> Τοὶ δ᾽ αὖ πλουτέοντες, ἀέξονται,
> Φρένας ἀμπελίνοις τόξοις δαμέντες.

"When the wearying cares of men fly from their breasts, and we all alike
sail in a sea of gold-abounding plenty to a false shore: the poor become
rich, the rich abound still more, with their minds under the influence of
wine."

See (Gr.) Wine.

DECEIT.

i. 9. 3.

Ah miser ! et si quis primo perjuria celat,
  Sera tamen tacitis Poena venit pedibus.

Ah wretch! even though one may be able at first to conceal his perjuries, yet punishment creeps on though late with noiseless step.

DECEIT.

i. 9. 23.

Nec tibi celandi spes sit peccare paranti ;
  Est deus, occultos qui vetat esse dolos.

When thou art preparing to commit a sin, think not that thou wilt conceal it ; there is a God that forbids crimes to be hidden.

See (Gr.) Crime.

EARLY AGES.

i. 10. 7.

Divitis hoc vitium est auri : nec bella fuerunt,
  Faginus adstabat cum scyphus ante dapes ;
Non arces, non vallus erat ; somnumque petebat
  Securus varias dux gregis inter oves.

This vice proceeds from greedy thirst of gold : there were no wars when draughts were quaffed from beechen cups ; then there were no towers, no ramparts ; the shepherd slept secure amidst his numerous flocks.

PLEASURES OF COUNTRY LIFE.

i. 10. 39.

Quam potius laudandus hic est, quem prole paratâ
  Occupat in parvâ pigra senecta casâ !
Ipse suas sectatur oves, at filius agnos ;
  Et calidam fesso comparat uxor aquam.
Sic ego sim ; liceatque caput candescere canis,
  Temporis et prisci facta referre senem.

How much more wise the man who, surrounded by his children, spends his old age in some small cottage ! He tends the sheep, his son the lambs ; while his wife prepares warm water for his weary feet. Such may I be, and may I with hoary locks relate in my old age the deeds of earlier times.

See (Gr.) Country Life.

DEATH.

i. 10. 33.

Quis furor est atram bellis arcessere mortem?
Imminet, et tacito clam venit illa pede.
Non seges est infra, non vinea culta ; sed audax
Cerberus, et Stygiæ navita turpis aquæ.

What madness is it to summon gloomy death by wars? It is always impending and advancing secretly with noiseless step. In the regions below there are no corn fields, no clustering vines, but fierce Cerberus and the filthy ferryman of the Stygian waters.

PEACE.

i. 10. 45.

Interea Pax arva colat.   Pax candida primum
Duxit araturos sub juga curva boves.
Pax aluit vites, et succos condidit uvæ,
Funderet ut nato testa paterna merum.
Pace bidens vomerque vigent : at tristia duri
Militis in tenebris occupat arma situs.

Meanwhile may Peace cultivate the fields.   It was auspicious Peace that first instructed the oxen to draw the crooked plough. It was Peace that planted the vines and gave juice to the grapes, that the paternal jar may furnish wine to cheer the son.   In piping times of Peace the rake and the plough ply with diligence, while rust eats into the gloomy arms of the fierce soldiers in darkness.

Aristophanes (Fr. Com. Gr. I. p. 284, M.) says :—

A. Τοῖς πᾶσιν ἀνθρώποισιν Εἰρήνης φίλης
    Πιστὴ τροφός, ταμία, συνεργός, ἐπίτροπος,
    Θυγάτηρ, ἀδελφή, πάντα ταῦτ' ἐχρῆτό μοι.
B. Σοὶ δ' ὄνομα δὴ τί ἐστιν; A. Ὅ, τι; Γεωργία.

"A. The faithful nurse, housekeeper, co-operator, guardian, daughter, sister of Peace, the friend of all men, all these names are used by me. B. What is your name? A. What? Agriculture."

AN EPITAPH.

ii. 4. 49.

Et, "Bene," discedens dicet, "placideque quiescas ;
· Terraque securæ sit super ossa levis !"

And at departure he will say, "Mayest thou rest soundly and quietly, and may the light turf lie easy on thy bones."

HAPPY FAMILY.

ii. 5. 89.

Ille levis stipulæ sollennes potus acervos .
    Accendet, flammas transilietque sacras ;
Et fetus matrona dabit, natusque parenti
    Oscula comprensis auribus eripiet.
Nec tædebit avum parvo advigilare nepoti,
    Balbaque cum puero dicere verba senem.

Warmed by wine, he will kindle heaps of light straw and leap across the sacred flames ; the mother will bring forward her children, and the child, seizing his father by the ears, will snatch kisses. And the grandsire will delight to watch his little grandchild, and in his old age will lisp words to the boy.

HOPE.

ii. 6. 19.

Jam mala finissem leto ; sed credula vitam
    Spes fovet, et fore cras semper ait melius.
Spes alit agricolas ; spes sulcis credit aratis
    Semina, quæ magno fœnore reddat ager.
Hæc laqueo volucres, hæc captat arundine pisces,
    Cum tenues hamos abdidit ante cibus.
Spes etiam validâ solatur compede vinctum :
    Crura sonant ferro ; sed canit inter opus.

I would long ere this have quenched my sorrows in death, had not flattering hope cherished life, and always whispered that to-morrow would be happier than to-day. It is hope that cheers the peasant, hope that intrusts the seed to the furrows to be returned with abundant interest. It is hope that catches birds with gins, fishes with the rod, when the bait has concealed the slender hook. Hope also comforts the prisoner bound in chains ; his legs rattle with the fetters, but he sings in the midst of his work.

Shakespeare (" Richard III.," act v. sc. 2) :—

    " True hope is swift, and flies with swallows' wings,
      Kings it makes gods, and meaner creatures kings."

WINE.

iii. 6. 13.

Ille facit dites animos deus ; ille ferocem
    Contudit, et dominæ misit in arbitrium.
Armenias tigres et fulvas ille leænas
    Vicit, et indomitis mollia corda dedit.

The joyous god enlarges the soul : he subdued the stubborn hero, (Hercules,) and made him subservient to his mistress. He overcame Armenian tigresses and tawny lionesses, giving a soft heart to the ungovernable.

Forced Laughter.

iii. 6. 33.

Hei mihi ! difficile est imitari gaudia falsa ;
Difficile est tristi fingere mente jocum :
Nec bene mendaci risus componitur ore ;
Nec bene sollicitis ebria verba sonant.

Ah, me ! how difficult it is to imitate false mirth ; how difficult to mimic cheerfulness with a sad heart : a smile suits not well a countenance that belies it ; nor do drunken words sound well from an anxious mind.

Woes of Another.

iii. 6. 43.

Felix, quicunque dolore
Alterius disces posse carere tuo.

Happy thou who canst learn to guard against thy own ills by observing those of another.

Perjuries of Lovers.

iii. 6. 47.

Etsi perque suos audax jurabit ocellos,
Junonemque suam, perque suam Venerem ;
Nulla fides inerit : perjuria ridet amantûm
Jupiter, et ventos irrita ferre jubet.

Though she shall boldly swear by her eyes, by Juno and her Venus, there is nothing in it : Jupiter laughs at the perjuries of lovers, and throws them idly to the winds.

A Lover's Prayer.

iii. 6. 53.

Quam vellem longas tecum requiescere noctes,
Et tecum longos pervigilare dies !

How could I, blest with thee, long nights employ !
And how with thee the longest day enjoy !

The Will for the Deed.

iv. 1. 7.

Est nobis voluisse satis.   Nec munera parva
Respueris.

Let the will be taken for the deed, nor refuse the gift of my humble muse.

VARRO

BORN B.C. 116—DIED B.C. 28.

M. TERENTIUS VARRO, the most learned of the Romans, was born B.C. 116, being ten years younger than Cicero. He received his early education from L. Ælius Stilo Præconinus, who was fond of antiquarian pursuits, and from him no doubt he imbibed his literary tastes, which makes St Augustine remark, "That he had read so much that it is astonishing he should have found time to write anything, and he wrote so much that it is difficult to believe that any one could find time to read all that he had written." In what way he rose in the service of the state has not been handed down to us, but he was employed in the wars against the pirates and Mithridates. He was attached to the party of the senate, and shared its fortunes at the battle of Pharsalia, B.C. 48. He submitted to the clemency of the conqueror, and was received into favour by Cæsar, though not before Antony had plundered and destroyed his villa, with all his books, at Casinum, which Cicero bitterly laments. He was proscribed in the second triumvirate, though he was more lucky than Cicero, as he contrived to conceal himself till he had secured the favour of Augustus. From this time he devoted himself to the seclusion of literary life, and employed himself in composing works, which amounted at last to four hundred and ninety books. They are nearly all lost.

To Pack up our Baggage at End of Life.
De Re Rust. i. 1.

Annus enim octogesimus admonet me, ut sarcinas colligam, antequam proficiscar e vitâ.

For my eightieth year warns me to pack up my baggage before I leave life.

God made the Country, Man the Town.
De Re Rust. iii. 1.

Nec mirum quod divina natura dedit agros, ars humana ædificavit urbes.

Nor is it surprising because it is Providence that has given us the country and the art of man that has built the cities.

Cowper ("The Task," l. 745) has appropriated this idea :—
  "God made the country, and man made the town."

"HE WHO RUNS MAY READ."

De Ling. Lat. v.

Legisti currens, ludens.

Thou hast read what I have written, I may say, running and playing.

Habakkuk (ii. 2.) says:—"Write the vision, and make it plain upon tables, that he may run that readeth it."

THE CHILD.

Fragm. ex Nonio.

Educit enim obstetrix, educat nutrix, instituit pœdagogus, docet magister.

For the midwife delivers the child, the nurse brings it up, the attendant slave forms its manners, and the master teaches it.

VIRGILIUS

BORN B.C. 70—DIED B.C. 19.

P. VIRGILIUS MARO was born on the 18th October B.C. 70, at Andes, a small village near Mantua in Cisalpine Gaul. His father had a small estate which he cultivated; his mother's name was Maia. Virgil was educated at Cremona and Mediolanum, (Milan,) and is said to have studied subsequently at Naples under Parthenius, a native of Bithynia. It is evident from his writings that he had received a learned education, but his health was feeble, and he did not attempt to rise to eminence by any of those means by which a Roman earned distinction. After the defeat of Brutus and Cassius, B.C. 42, the inhabitants of the north of Italy were deprived of their property that the victorious soldiery might be provided with land, and among others Virgil suffered. Through the intervention, however, of his friends at Rome, his property was restored, and the first eclogue is supposed to have been written to commemorate his gratitude to Augustus. When Augustus was returning from Samos, where he had spent the winter of B.C. 20, he met Virgil at Athens. It is said that the poet had intended to make a tour of Greece, but he accompanied the emperor to Megara and thence to Italy. His health, which had been long declining, was now completely broken down, and he died soon after his arrival at Brundisium on the 22d September

B.C. 19. His remains were transferred to Naples, which had been his favourite residence, and placed on the road from Naples to Puteoli, where his tomb is still shown.

EXILE.

E. i. 3.

Nos patriæ fines et dulcia linquimus arva.

We are leaving our country and its sweet fields.

Euripides (Fr. Aiol. 23) says :—

> Ἀλλ' ὅμως
> Οἰκτρὸς τις αἰὼν πατρίδος ἐκλιπεῖν ὅρους.

"But yet it is a sad life to leave the fields of our native country."

So Shakespeare (" Richard II.," act i. sc. 3) says :—

> "Then England's ground, farewell; sweet soil, adieu;
> My mother, and my nurse, that bears me yet!
> Where'er I wander, boast of this I can,
> Though banish'd, yet a true-born Englishman."

See (Gr.) Exile.

ENVY.

E. i. 11.

Non equidem invideo ; miror magis.

For my part I have no feeling of envy at your fortune; I rather am surprised at your luck.

COMPARISONS.

E. i. 23.

Sic canibus catulos similes, sic matribus hædos
Nôram ; sic parvis componere magna solebam.

Thus I knew that whelps were like to their sires, kids to their mothers ; so I used to compare great things with small.

BRITAIN.

E. i. 67.

Et penitus toto divisos orbe Britannos.

And Britons wholly separated from the rest of the world.

CIVIL DISCORD.

E. i. 72.

Barbarus has segetes ? en quo discordia cives
Produxit miseros !

Shall some barbarian plant and sow these fields? See to what a state civil discord has brought wretched citizens !

See (Gr., Fr.) Discord.

COUNTRY LIFE.
E. i. 80.

Hic tamen hanc mecum poteras requiescere noctem
Fronde super viridi ; sunt nobis mitia poma,
Castaneæ molles, et pressi copia lactis :
Et jam summa procul villarum culmina fumant,
Majoresque cadunt altis de montibus umbræ.

This night, at least, you might remain with me on the green
leaves ; we have plenty of excellent apples, soft chestnuts, with
curds and cream ; see, too, the curling smoke is rising from the
cottages, and the lofty mountains are throwing out their lengthen-
ing shadows.

TRUST NOT TO BEAUTY.
E. ii. 16.

Quamvis ille niger, quamvis tu candidus esses.
O formose puer, nimium ne crede colori.

Though he was black and thou art heavenly fair, O fair boy,
trust not too much to thy beauty.

EACH FOLLOWS HIS OWN PLEASURE.
E. ii. 65.

Te Corydon, o Alexi : trahit sua quemque voluptas.

Alexis, thou art chased by Corydon ; every one pursues his own
pleasure.

EVENING.
E. ii. 66.

Adspice, aratra jugo referunt suspensa juvenci,
Et sol crescentes decedens duplicat umbras :
Me tamen urit amor ; quis enim modus adsit amori ?

See, the steers are bringing back the ploughs suspended from
the yoke ; and the setting sun is doubling the lengthening sha-
dows ; yet still I am burned by love ; what bounds can be set to
love ?

SERVANTS.
E. iii. 16.

Quid domini faciant, audent quum talia fures !

What would their masters do, when their knavish servants
prate at such a rate !

SPRING.
E. iii. 56.

Et nunc omnis ager, nunc omnis parturit arbos,
Nunc frondent sylvæ, nunc formosissimus annus.

And now every field is clothed with grass, every tree with leaves;
now the woods put forth their blossoms; now the year assumes its
gayest attire.

So Shakespeare ("Winter's Tale," act iv. sc. 3) says:—

> "O Proserpina
> For the flowers now, that, frighted, thou let'st fall
> From Dis's waggon! daffodils
> That come before the swallow dares, and take
> The winds of March with beauty; violets, dim,
> But sweeter than the lids of Juno's eyes
> Or Cytherea's breath; pale primroses,
> That die unmarried, ere they can behold
> Bright Phœbus in his strength, a malady
> Most incident to maids; bold oxlips, and
> The crown imperial; lilies of all kinds,
> The flower-de-luce being one."

Spenser ("Faerie Queen," vi.):—

> "So forth issued the seasons of the year:
> First lusty spring all dight in leaves of flowers,
> That freshly budded and new blooms did bear,
> In which a thousand birds had built their bowers,
> That sweetly sung to call forth paramours."

BAD TASTE.
E. iii. 90.

Qui Bavium non odit, amet tua carmina, Mævi:
Atque idem jungat vulpes, et mulgeat hircos.

Let him who does not hate Bavius, love thy verses, Mævius;
and let him join foxes in the yoke and milk he-goats.

THE SECRET SNAKE.
E. iii. 92.

Qui legitis flores et humi nascentia fraga,
Frigidus, o pueri, fugite hinc, latet anguis in herbâ.

Ye boys, who are gathering flowers, and low-growing flowers,
fly hence, a cold snake is lurking among the grass.

DECISION DIFFICULT.
E. iii. 108.

Non nostrum inter vos tantas componere lites.

It does not belong to us to settle such a mighty dispute.

Poet.
E. v. 45.

Tale tuum carmen nobis, divine poeta,
Quale sopor fessis in gramine, quale per æstum
Dulcis aquæ saliente sitim restinguere rivo.

O divine poet, thy poetry is as charming to our ear as sleep to the weary swain, as to the feverish traveller the crystal stream with which he quenches his thirst.

Poets' Fame.
E. v. 76.

Dum juga montis aper, fluvios dum piscis amabit,
Dumque thymo pascentur apes, dum rore cicadæ;
Semper honos nomenque tuum laudesque manebunt.

While the boar delights in the mountain-tops, the fish in the rivers, while the bees feed on thyme, so long will the glory of thy name and thy praise remain.

To Seem is Enough.
E. vi. 24.

Solvite me, pueri; satis est potuisse videri.

Loose me, boys; it is enough that you have seemed able to overpower me.

Arcadians.
E. vii. 4.

Ambo florentes ætatibus, Arcades ambo,
Et cantare pares, et respondere parati.

Both in the flower of their age, both Arcadian swains, able to sing and to answer in alternate verses.

Byron ("Don Juan," cant. iv. st. 93) thus uses the expression:—

"Arcades ambo, id est."
"Blackguards both."

Beauties of Country.
E. vii. 65.

Fraxinus in sylvis pulcherrima, pinus in hortis,
Populus in fluviis, abies in montibus altis:
Sæpius at si me, Lycida formose, revisas,
Fraxinus in sylvis cedat tibi, pinus in hortis.

The ash is the fairest tree in the woods, the pine in the gardens, the poplar by the brooks, the fir on the high mountains; but, O fair Lycidas, if thou wilt oft visit me, the ash in the woods shall yield to thee and the pine in the gardens.

DIFFERENCE OF POWERS.
E. viii. 63.

Non omnia possumus omnes.

We are not all able to accomplish the same things.

MANTUA.
E. ix. 28.

Mantua væ miseræ nimium vicina Cremonæ !

Ah, Mantua, too near to the wretched Cremona !

A GOOSE.
E. ix. 36.

Argutos inter strepit anser olores.

The goose gabbles midst the melodious swans.

TIME.
E. ix. 51.

Omnia fert ætas, animum quoque.

Time destroys all things, even the powers of the mind.

LOVE IS NEVER SATISFIED.
E. x. 29.

Nec lacrymis crudelis Amor, nec gramina rivis,
Nec cytiso saturantur apes, nec fronde capellæ.

Love is never satisfied with tears, sooner are the meadows with the waters of the rivulets, the bees with the cytisus and the goats with leaves.

LOVE CONQUERS ALL THINGS.
E. x. 69.

Omnia vincit Amor ; et nos cedamus Amori.

Love conquers all ; and we must yield to Love.

MAN.
G. i. 63.

Unde homines nati, durum genus.

Whence men, a hard, laborious kind were born.

INDUSTRY.

G. i. 121.

Pater ipse colendi
Haud facilem esse viam voluit ; primusque per artem
Movit agros, curis acuens mortalia corda ;
Nec torpere gravi passus sua regna veterno.

The father of the gods himself did not desire that the art of cultivating the ground should be easily acquired ; he was the first to turn up the soil by skill, whetting human industry by care, nor did he allow his reign to grow torpid by sluggishness.

NECESSITY MOTHER OF INVENTION.

G. i. 129.

Ille malum virus serpentibus addidit atris,
Prædarique lupos jussit, pontumque moveri :
Mellaque decussit foliis, ignemque removit,
Et passim rivis currentia vina repressit :
Ut varias usus meditando extunderet artes
Paullatim, et sulcis frumenti quæreret herbam ;
Ut silicis venis abstrusum excuderet ignem.

Jove added venom to the black vipers, commissioned wolves to gather their prey, and the sea to be lashed by the raging storms : honey he shook from the leaves, removing from human reach the cheerful fire, and stopping the wine that ran in rivulets, that man might gradually through experience explore useful arts, raising corn from the furrows, and forcing the hidden fire from the clashing flints.

INDUSTRY.

G. i. 145.

Tum variæ venere artes : labor omnia vincit
Improbus, et duris urguens in rebus egestas.

Then various arts succeeded each other ; persevering labour overcomes everything and pressing want in the midst of hard penury.

Franklin says :—" Sloth makes all things difficult, but Industry all easy ; and he that riseth late must trot all day, and shall scarce overtake his business at night ; while Laziness travels so slowly that Poverty soon overtakes him."

DEGENERACY OF MANKIND.

G. i. 200.

Sic omnia fatis
In pejus ruere, ac retro sublapsa referri.
Non aliter, quam qui adverso vix flumine lembum

Remigiis subigit, si brachia forte remisit,
Atque illum in præceps prono rapit alveus amni.

Thus all things by the decree of Fate are turned to worse and carried back, just as the rower, who stems the current, if he but slack his arm, is borne down the channel with headlong haste.

THUNDER-STORM.
G. i. 328.

Ipse Pater, mediâ nimborum in nocte, corusca
Fulmina molitur dextrâ ; quo maxima motu
Terra tremit ; fugere feræ ; et mortalia corda
Per gentes humilis stravit pavor : ille flagranti
Aut Atho, aut Rhodopen, aut alta Cerunia telo
Dejicit ; ingeminant Austri, et densissimus imber ;
Nunc nemora ingenti vento, nunc littora plangunt.

The father of the gods himself, shrouded in dark storms, darts his fiery bolts with flashing right hand, making the mighty earth to tremble ; the wild beasts fly ; dark horror seizes every human breast ; Athos, Rhodope, and lofty Ceraunus topple down from their old foundations ; the winds redouble their fury ; woods and shores roar, lashed by the furious winds.

CUSTOM.
G. ii. 272.

Adeo in teneris consuescere multum est.
So much power has custom over tender minds.

COMPETENCY.
G. ii. 412.

Laudato ingentia rura,
Exiguum colito.
Praise spacious vineyards, but be content to cultivate those of less extent.

COUNTRY LIFE.
G. ii. 458.

O fortunatos nimium, sua si bona nôrint,
Agricolas ; quibus ipsa, procul discordibus armis,
Fundit humo facilem victum justissima tellus.
Si non ingentem foribus domus alta superbis
Mane salutantûm totis vomit ædibus undam ;
Nec varios inhiant pulchrâ testudine postes,

Illusasque auro vestes, Ephyreïaque æra ;
Alba nec Assyrio fucatur lana veneno ;
Nec casiâ liquidi corrumpitur usus olivi ;
At secura quies, et nescia fallere vita,
Dives opum variarum ; at latis otia fundis,
Speluncæ, vivique lacus ; at frigida Tempe,
Mugitusque boum, mollesque sub arbore somni
Non absunt ; illic saltus ac lustra ferarum ;
Et patiens operum, exiguoque assueta juventus ;
Sacra deum, sanctique patres ; extrema per illos
Justitia excedens terris vestigia fecit.

O too happy swains, if they only knew their happy state, who, far removed from civil broils, enjoy the fruits poured forth by Nature's bounty. Though no lofty palace with spacious gates sends forth crowds of early visitants from every entrance, with eager eyes devouring variegated posts of beautiful tortoise-shell, gold-embroidered dresses, figures of Corinthian brass, arras purple-dyed, and the smell of costly perfumes, yet he enjoys easy quiet, a harmless life that knows not to deceive, rich in home-bred plenty, the joys of a wide-extending country, grots, and crystal lakes, cool groves, the lowing of cattle, and sweet repose at night ; woods abounding in untamed beasts ; there we find youth inured to labour and accustomed to homely fare, sacred shrines and sires of venerable age : here Astræa, as she left the earth, showed the last traces of her departing steps.

THE HAPPY MAN.

G. ii. 490.

Felix, qui potuit rerum cognoscere causas,
Atque metus omnes et inexorabile fatum
Subjecit pedibus, strepitumque Acherontis avari !

Happy the man who has been able to dive into Nature's laws and has trampled under foot fears and unyielding Fate, laughing at the approach of all-subduing death.

THE VARIOUS LIVES OF MAN.

G. ii. 503.

Sollicitant alii remis freta cæca ; ruuntque
In ferrum ; penetrant aulas et limina regum ;
Hic petit excidiis Urbem miserosque Penates,
Ut gemmâ bibat, et Sarrano indormiat ostro ;
Condit opes alius, defossoque incubat auro ;
Hic stupet attonitus rostris : hunc plausus hiantem

Per cuneos (geminatur enim) plebisque patrumque
Corripuit; gaudent perfusi sanguine fratrum,
Exilioque domos et dulcia limina mutant,
Atque alio patriam quærunt sub sole jacentem.

Some pass their lives at sea, some in the camp, others freque
the palace and courts of kings; another aims at the destruction
the city and its gods, that he may get riches to enable him
drink from bowls enchased with gems, and stretch his limbs
Tyrian purple; another hides his wealth, brooding over h
buried store; this man is fond of popular praise, the applause
lords and commoners delighting his ear from both benches. Son
take pleasure in the slaughter of their brethren, exchanging the
sweet homes for exile and seeking lands that lie beneath anoth
sun.

FAME.
G. iii. 8.

Tentanda via est, qua me quoque possim
Tollere humo, victorque virûm volitare per ora.

I must attempt new ways, by which I may raise myself fro
the ground and wing my flight to fame.

Theognis has the same idea (l. 237):—

ττέρ' ἔδωκα . . . πολλῶν κείμενος ἐν στόμασιν.

"I have given myself wings . . . re-echoed from the mouths of many."

LIFE OF MAN.
G. iii. 66.

Optima quæque dies miseris mortalibus ævi
Prima fugit; subeunt morbi, tristisque senectus,
Et labor, et duræ rapit inclementia mortis.

Youth, the best part of life, flies quickly from miserable mo
tals; diseases succeed, sad old age, anxious labour, and death
inexorable doom hurry them off.

Diphilus (Fr. Com. Gr. p. 1078, M.) says:—

Ἀπροσδόκητον οὐδὲν ἀνθρώποις πάθος·
Ἐφημέρους γὰρ τὰς τύχας κεκτήμεθα.

"Man may look for trouble, for we fall in with woes day after day."

NO REST.
G. iii. 110.

Nec mora, nec requies.
No stop, no stay.

EDUCATION.

G. iii. 164.

Viamque insiste domandi,
Dum faciles animi juvenum, dum mobilis ætas.

Begin early the course of education, while the mind is pliant
and age is flexible.

See (Gr.) Education.

LOVE.

G. iii. 242.

Omne adeo genus in terris hominumque ferarumque,
Et genus æquoreum, pecudes, pictæque volucres,
In furias ignemque ruunt : amor omnibus idem.

Thus every creature on earth, man and beast, fish, cattle, and
birds with variegated plumage, rush into the fire of love ; Love
is the lord of all.

Sir W. Scott ("The Lay of the Last Minstrel," cant. iii. st. 1) thus para-
phrases the idea :—

    "In peace Love tunes the shepherd's reed ;
    In war, he mounts the warrior's steed ;
    In halls, in gay attire is seen ;
    In hamlets, dances on the green.
    Love rules the court, the camp, the grove,
    And men below, and saints above ;
    For love is heaven, and heaven is love."

LOVE EXEMPLIFIED BY LEANDER.

G. iii. 258.

Quid juvenis, magnum cui versat in ossibus ignem
Durus amor ? nempe abruptis turbata procellis
Nocte natat cœcâ serus freta ; quem super ingens
Porta tonat cœli, et scopulis illisa reclamant
Æquora ; nec miseri possunt revocare parentes,
Nec moritura super crudeli funere virgo.

What did the youth Leander, whom love's unerring dart trans-
fixed ; alone, by night amidst the tempest's roar, he swims across
the strait ; over him the rolling thunder rattles, and around him
the billows dashed against the rocks roar ; neither can his miser-
able parents call him back nor the virgin (Hero) doomed to die on
his sad pile.

TIME.

G. iii. 284.

Fugit irreparabile tempus.

Time flies not to be recalled.

Vice.

G. iii. 454.

Alitur vitium, vivitque tegendo.

The vice is fed and gathers strength by its very concealment.

Pleasures of Country Life.

G. iii. 525.

Quid labor, aut benefacta juvant? quid vomere terras
Invertisse graves? atqui non Massica Bacchi
Munera, non illis epulæ nocuere repostæ :
Frondibus et victu pascuntur simplicis herbæ ;
Pocula sunt fontes liquidi, atque exercita cursu
Flumina ; nec somnos abrumpit cura salubres.

What avails their well-deserving toil ? to turn up the sluggish
soil ; but no draughts of Massic wine nor undigested feasts injur
their stomachs; they live on salad and simple food ; their drink
is the crystal springs and the running stream ; no care deprive
them of healthful sleep.

Labour.

G. iv. 6.

In tenui labor ; at tenuis non gloria.

Slight is the subject, but the praise not small.

Mighty Souls.

G. iv. 83.

Ingentes animos angusto in pectore versant.

They have mighty souls in tiny bodies.

The Grave.

G. iv. 87.

Hi motus animorum atque hæc certamina tanta
Pulveris exigui jactu compressa quiescent.

All this commotion of spirit and this deadly fray will soon rest
under a few handfuls of dust, scattered over their bodies.

The Studies of Inglorious Ease.

G. iv. 564.

Studiis florentem ignobilis oti.

Indulging in the pursuits of inglorious ease.

Resentment in Heavenly Minds.

Æn. i. 11.

Tantæne animis cœlestibus iræ?

Is there so great wrath to be found in the breasts of the heavenly gods?

We find this expression in Boileau (Lutrin i. 12) under the ironical form :—
"Tant de fiel entre-t-il dans l'âme des dévots?"

And Milton ("Paradise Lost," book vi.) says :—
"In heavenly spirits could such perverseness dwell?"

Secret Resentment Cherished.

Æn. i. 26.

Manet altâ mente repostum
Judicium Paridis spretæque injuria formæ.

The decision of Paris, and the affront offered to her slighted beauty, remain deeply treasured up in her mind.

Here and There.

Æn. i. 118.

Apparent rari nantes in gurgite vasto ;
Arma virûm, tabulæque, et Troïa gaza per undas.

A few appear swimming here and there amid the vast and roaring abyss, arms of men, pictures and Trojan treasure are seen scattered over the waves.

A Tumult.

Æn. i. 148.

Ac veluti magno in populo quum sæpe coorta est
Seditio, sævitque animis ignobile vulgus ;
Jamque faces et saxa volant ; furor arma ministrat :
Tum pietate gravem ac meritis si forte virum quem
Conspexere, silent, arrectisque auribus adstant ;
Iste regit dictis animos, et pectora mulcet.

And as in a mighty crowd, when a tumult has arisen and the shouting varletry rage, firebrands and stones fly, their fury supplies them with arms ; then, if it chances that they see some man of great influence by his piety and merits, they are silent and stand with listening ears ; he directs them by his words, and soothes their angry mood.

Scenery.

Æn. i. 159.

Est in secessu longo locus : insula portum
Efficit objectu laterum, quibus omnis ab alto

Frangitur inque sinus scindit sese unda reductos.
Hinc atque hinc vastæ rupes geminique minantur
In cœlum scopuli, quorum sub vertice late
Æquora tuta silent ; tum sylvis scena coruscis
Desuper, horrentique atrum nemus imminet umbrâ.
Fronte sub adversâ scopulis pendentibus antrum ;
Intus aquæ dulces, vivoque sedilia saxo,
Nympharum domus.

There is a place at the bottom of a deep recess; an island forms a secure harbour by the jutting out of its sides, against which every wave from the deep is broken, and divides itself into receding curves. On this side and on that are vast rocks, and twin-like cliffs raise their threatening heads towards the sky, at the base of which the waters far and wide lie unruffled and calm ; then again, crowning the high grounds, is a wall of foliage, formed of waving trees, while a grove, dark with gloomy shade, hangs threatening over. Beneath the brow, as it fronts the view, there is a cave amid hanging cliffs ; within sweet water and seats in the natural rock, the dwelling of the Nymphs.

THE LONGEST DAY COMES TO AN END.

Æn. i. 198.

O socii, neque enim ignari sumus ante malorum ;
O passi graviora, dabit deus his quoque finem.

O my companions, O ye, who have endured greater hardships, (for we are not unacquainted with previous ills,) God will put an end to these too.

PAST MISFORTUNES REMEMBERED WITH PLEASURE.

Æn. i. 201.

Vos et Cyclopia saxa
Experti. Revocate animos, mœstumque timorem
Mittite. Forsan et hæc olim meminisse juvabit.

You, too, know the rocky shore, where dwell the Cyclops. Resume your courage and away with gloomy fear. Perhaps it will delight us hereafter to recal to mind even the present dangers.
See (Gr.) Past labours.

PERSEVERANCE.

Æn. i. 207.

Durate, et vosmet rebus servate secundis.

Be of stout heart, and preserve yourselves for better times.

DISSIMULATION.
Æn. i. 209.

> Curisque ingentibus æger,
> Spem vultu simulat, premit altum corde dolorem.

And sick at heart with mighty cares, he assumes an appearance of hope in his look, keeping deep sorrow down in his breast.

Shakespeare ("Macbeth," act i. sc. 5) says:—

> "To beguile the time,
> Look like the time; bear welcome in your eye,
> Your hand, your tongue: look like the innocent flower,
> But be the serpent under it."

ROMANS.
Æn. i. 279.

> Quin aspera Juno,
> Quæ mare nunc terrasque metu cœlumque fatigat,
> Consilia in melius referet, mecumque fovebit
> Romanos rerum dominos, gentemque togatam.

Nay, the harsh-spirited Juno herself, who now wearies out, by the fears she excites, the sea, the earth, and the heaven, shall change her counsels for the better, and shall cherish with me the Romans, the lords of the world and the gowned nation.

THE GOLDEN AGE SHALL RETURN.
Æn. i. 292.

> Cana Fides, et Vesta, Remo cum fratre Quirinus,
> Jura dabunt; diræ ferro et compagibus arctis
> Claudentur belli portæ: Furor impius intus,
> Sæva sedens super arma, et centum vinctus aënis
> Post tergum nodis, fremet horridus ore cruento.

The Faith of the good old times, Vesta, Romulus, with his brother Remus, shall administer justice: the cruel gates of War shall be closed with bolts and iron bars: impious Fury within, seated on savage arms and bound with a hundred brazen chains, shall roar horribly with blood-stained mouth.

VENUS.
Æn. i. 402.

> Dixit, et avertens roseâ cervice refulsit,
> Ambrosiæque comæ divinum vertice odorem
> Spiravere; pedes vestis defluxit ad imos;
> Et vera incessu patuit dea.

She said, and, turning away, flashed on the view with her rosy neck, and from her head the ambrosial locks breathed a heavenly odour : her robes descended to the ground in a sweep, and in her gait the true goddess was displayed to view.

BEES.

Æn. i. 430.

Qualis apes æstate novâ per florea rura
Exercet sub sole labor ; quum gentis adultos
Educunt fetus, aut quum liquentia mella
Stipant, et dulci distendunt nectare cellas ;
Aut onera accipiunt venientum, aut agmine facto
Ignavum fucos pecus a præsepibus arcent :
Fervet opus, redolentque thymo fragrantia mella.

Such toil is theirs, as that of bees, beneath the rays of the sun, throughout the flowery fields, in the beginning of summer, when they lead forth their grown-up offspring, or when they stow away the liquid honey and fill the cells with sweet nectar ; or receive the loads of the bees coming in, or, forming a band, drive from the hives the lazy drones : the work goes busily forward, and the fragrant honey is redolent of thyme.

Shakespeare ("Henry V.," act i. sc. 2) says :—

> "So work the honey bees ;
> Creatures, that by a rule in nature teach
> The art of order to a peopled kingdom.
> They have a king, and officers of sorts ;
> Where some, like magistrates, correct at home ;
> Others, like merchants, venture trade abroad ;
> Others, like soldiers, armed in their stings,
> Make boot upon the summer's velvet buds ;
> Which pillage they with merry march bring home
> To the tent-royal of their emperor ;
> Who, busied in his majesty, surveys
> The singing masons building roofs of gold ;
> The civil citizens kneading up the honey ;
> The poor mechanic porters crowding in
> Their heavy burdens at his narrow gate ;
> The sad-eyed justice, with his surly hum,
> Delivering o'er to executors pale
> The lazy yawning drone."

So Homer (Il. ii. 87) says :—

> ἠΰτε ἔθνεα εἶσι μελισσάων ἀδινάων,
> πέτρης ἐκ γλαφυρῆς αἰεὶ νέον ἐρχομενάων·
> βοτρυδὸν δὲ πέτονται ἐπ' ἄνθεσιν εἰαρινοῖσιν·
> αἱ μέν τ' ἔνθα ἅλις πεποτήαται, αἱ δέ τε ἔνθα·

"As the swarms of thick-flying bees, issuing ever fresh from a hollow rock, fly in clusters on the vernal flowers : in crowds here and in crowds there."

Milton, too, ("Paradise Lost," i. 742,) says :—

> "As bees
> In spring-time, when the sun with Taurus rides,

Pour forth their populous youth about the hive
In clusters ; they among fresh dews and flowers,
Fly to and fro, or on the smoothed plank,
The suburb of their straw-built citadel,
Now rubb'd with balm, expatiate and confer
Their state affairs."

TEARS.

Æn. i. 461.

En Priamus. Sunt hic etiam sua præmia laudi ;
Sunt lacrymæ rerum ; et mentem mortalia tangunt.
Solve metus ; feret hæc aliquam tibi fama salutem.
Sic ait, atque animum pictura pascit inani.

See, here is our Priam. Even here has praiseworthy conduct
its reward ; even here are tears for misfortunes, and human affairs
exert a touching influence on the heart. Away with fear; this
fame of our deeds of glory will bring safety. Thus he speaks and
dotes on the unreal picture.

THE GODS ARE JUST.

Æn. i. 542.

Si genus humanum et mortalia temnitis arma :
At sperate deos memores fandi atque nefandi.

If you pay no attention to the opinion which men will have of
such conduct, and despise the vengeance which they may seek to
inflict, at least recollect that the gods are mindful of right and
wrong.

TROJAN AND TYRIAN.

Æn. i. 574.

Tros Tyriusque mihi nullo discrimine agetur.

Trojan and Tyrian shall be treated by me without distinction.

ÆNEAS.

Æn. i. 588.

Restitit Æneas, claráque in luce refulsit,
Os humerosque deo similis : namique ipsa decoram
Cæsariem nato genetrix, lumenque juventæ
Purpureum, et lætos oculis afflárat honores :
Quale manus addunt ebori decus, aut ubi flavo
Argentum, Pariusve lapis, circumdatur auro.

There stood Æneas, and shone forth in full effulgence, in visage
and in shoulders like a god : for his mother herself had breathed
upon her son beautiful locks and the bright light of youth, kind-
ling up sparkling graces in his eyes ; such beauty as the hand of
the artist imparts to ivory or silver or Parian marble, when the
skill of the artist has been expended upon them.

ETERNAL FAME.
Æn. i. 603.

Di tibi, si qua pios respectant numina, si quid
Usquam justitia est et mens sibi conscia recti,
Præmia digna ferant.   Quæ te tam læta tulerunt
Sæcula ? qui tanti talem genuere parentes ?
In freta dum fluvii current, dum montibus umbræ
Lustrabunt convexa, polus dum sidera pascet :
Semper honos, nomenque tuum, laudesque manebunt,
Quæ me cunque vocant terræ.

May the gods give thee a just reward, if there be any gods that
have a regard to the pious, if justice and a mind conscious to itself
of rectitude be anywhere aught save an empty name.   What time
so fortunate have produced thee? what so illustrious parents have
brought thee forth?   As long as the rivers shall flow into the sea,
as long as the shadows of the mountains shall traverse their pro-
jecting sides, as long as heaven shall feed the stars, thy honour,
thy name, and praises shall ever survive, in whatever land I may
be fated to live.

TO PITY OTHERS' WOES FROM HAVING FELT THEM.
Æn. i. 630.

Non ignara mali miseris succurrere disco.

Not ignorant of misfortune, I learn from my own woes to suc-
cour the wretched.

Delille translates it very expressively :—
> " Malheureux j'appris à plaindre le malheur."

Gray (" Hymn to Adversity ") :—
> " What sorrow was, thou bad'st her know,
> And from her own, she learn'd to melt at others' woe."

Campbell (" Gertrude of Wyoming," part i. v. 23) :—
> " He scorn'd his own, who felt another's woe."

Rousseau (Emile liv. iv.) says of this maxim :—
> " Rien de si beau, de si profond, de si touchant, de si vrai."

See (Gr., Fr.) Woes, to melt at others'.

DESTRUCTION OF TROY.
Æn. ii. 3.

Infandum, regina, jubes renovare dolorem :
Trojanas ut opes et lamentabile regnum
Eruerint Danai ; quæque ipse miserrima vidi,
Et quorum pars magna fui.   Quis talia fando
Myrmidonum, Dolopumve, aut duri miles Ulixi

Temperet a lacrymis !   Et jam nox humida cœlo
Præcipitat, suadentque cadentia sidera somnos.
Sed, si tantus amor casus cognoscere nostros,
Et breviter Trojæ supremum audire laborem ;
Quanquam animus meminisse horret, luctuque refugit ;
Incipiam.

O Queen, thou orderest me to renew unutterable woe ; to tell
how the Greeks overthrew the Trojan power and kingdom, as well
as those sad scenes which I myself beheld, and in which I per-
sonally took a conspicuous share. Who of the Myrmidons or Dolo-
pians, or what soldier of the cruel Ulysses could refrain from tears
as he relates such things? And now dewy night rushes downward,
and the sinking stars invite to repose. But if thou art really
anxious to become acquainted with our misfortunes, and to hear
briefly the last sad fate of Troy, though my mind shudders at the
remembrance, and shrinks back through grief, I nevertheless will
begin.

The Vulgar.

Æn. ii. 39.

Scinditur incertum studia in contraria vulgus.

The wavering populace are divided into conflicting opinions.

The Greeks.

Æn. ii. 49.

Timeo Danaos et dona ferentes.

I dread the Greeks even when bringing gifts.

Sophocles (Ajax, 665) says to the same effect :—

Εχθρῶν ἄδωρα δῶρα κ' οὐκ ὀνήσιμα.

"The gifts of enemies are no gifts, and pernicious."

And Milton ("Paradise Regained," book ii. l. 391) expresses the same
dea :—

"Thy pompous delicacies I contemn,
And count thy specious gifts no gifts, but guiles."

Infatuation of Man.

Æn. ii. 54.

Si mens non læva fuisset.

If our own minds had not been infatuated.

A Sample.

Æn. ii. 65.

Accipe nunc Danaûm insidias, et crimine ab uno
Disce omnes.

Listen now to the treachery of the Greeks, and from one instan of their wicked conduct learn the character of the whole nation

INSINUATIONS.

Æn. ii. 99.

>   Hinc spargere voces
> In vulgum ambiguas.

From this time they begin to spread ambiguously-word rumours among the crowd.

ALL PLEASED THAT THE THREATENED DANGER SHOULI FALL ON ANOTHER.

Æn. ii. 131.

>   Quæ sibi quisque timebat,
> Unius in miseri exitium conversa tulere.

Those very things, which each feared would happen to himse he endured with patience, when he saw that they were to eff the ruin of another.

HECTOR.

Æn. ii. 274.

> Hei mihi, qualis erat ! quantum mutatus ab illo
> Hectore, qui redit exuvias indutus Achilli.

Ah me, how he looked ! how changed from that Hector w returned from the battle-field arrayed in the spoils of Achilles.

Wordsworth ("Poems of the Imagination," xxix.) adopts this idea :—
"Like—but oh ! how different."

DESCRIPTION OF FIRE AND TORRENTS.

Æn. ii. 304.

> In segetem veluti cum flamma furentibus austris
> Incidit, aut rapidus montano flumine torrens
> Sternit agros, sternit sata læta boumque labores,
> Præcipitesque trahit silvas ; stupet inscius alto
> Accipiens sonitum saxi de vertice pastor.

As when fire has seized on a field of standing corn, while t wind rages, or a rapid mountain torrent lays waste the fields, t joyous crops, and the labours of the oxen, carrying down with the woods, the astonished shepherd listens to the loud upre from the top of some rock.

A Neighbour's House on Fire.
Æn. ii. 312.

Proximus ardet Ucalegon.

The house of Ucalegon that is next, catches fire.

Patriotism.
Æn. ii. 314.

Arma amens capio : nec sat rationis in armis :
Sed glomerare manum bello, et concurrere in arcem
Cum sociis ardent animi. Furor iraque mentem
Praecipitant ; pulchrumque mori succurrit in armis.

I madly seize my arms ; and yet there was little sense in doing
so : I burn, however, to gather a band for the conflict, and to dash
with my associates into the citadel. Fury and passion urge me
forward, and I feel that it is honourable to die in arms.

See (Gr.) Country, to die for.

Destruction of Troy.
Æn. ii. 324.

Venit summa dies et ineluctabile tempus
Dardaniæ. Fuimus Troes ; fuit Ilium, et ingens
Gloria Teucrorum.

The last day and doom of Troy has come. We were once
Trojans ; Troy once stood, and the mighty glory of the Trojans.

Despair of Life.
Æn. ii. 354.

Una salus victis, nullam sperare salutem.

The only safety that remains for the vanquished is to expect no
safety.

Corneille says :—

"Le courage est souvent un effet de la peur."

Description of Battle.
Æn. ii. 367.

Quondam etiam victis redit in praecordia virtus ;.
Victoresque cadunt Danai : crudelis ubique
Luctus, ubique pavor, et plurima mortis imago.

At times courage returns even to the breasts of the vanquished ;
and the victorious Greeks bite the ground : everywhere you see
sad lamentation, everywhere consternation and many a form of
death.

FORTUNE SMILES.

Æn. ii. 385.

Adspirat primo Fortuna labori.

Thus fortune on our first endeavour smiled.

AN ENEMY.

Æn. ii. 390.

Dolus, an virtus, quis in hoste requirat?

Whether it be deceit or bravery, who inquires in the case of
enemy?

THE GODS UNWILLING.

Æn. ii. 402.

Heu, nihil invitis fas quenquam fidere Divis!

Alas! no one need feel confidence when the gods are opposed

THE GODS.

Æn. ii. 428.

Dis aliter visum.

Heaven thought not so.

THESE TIMES WANT OTHER AIDS.

Æn. ii. 519.

Quæ mens tam dira, miserrime conjux,
Impulit his cingi telis? aut quo rûis? inquit.
Non tali auxilio, nec defensoribus istis
Tempus eget.

O most wretched husband, why has so fearful a resolut
urged thee to array thyself in these arms? or whither rush
thou? she says. The crisis requires not such aid nor such
fenders as thou art.

A FEEBLE WEAPON.

Æn. ii. 544.

Telumque imbelle sine ictu.

A feeble weapon inflicting no wound.

DEATH OF PRIAM.

Æn. ii. 554.

Hæc finis Priami fatorum : hic exitus illum
Sorte tulit, Trojam incensam et prolapsa videntem

Pergama ; tot quondam populis terrisque superbum
Regnatorem Asiæ.   Jacet ingens littore truncus,
Avulsumque humeris caput, et sine nomine corpus.

Such was the close of Priam's life : this was his doom to see
Troy in flames and her houses in ruins, the proud queen of Asia
over so many nations and lands.   He lies on the shore a huge
trunk, his head torn from his shoulders and a nameless body.

PUNISHMENT OF A WOMAN.
Æn. ii. 583.

Namque etsi nullum memorabile nomen
Fœmineâ in pœnâ est, nec habet victoria laudem ;
Extinxisse nefas tamen, et sumsisse merentis
Laudabor pœnas ; animumque explêsse juvabit
Ultricis flammæ, et cineres satiâsse meorum.

For though there be no glory in the punishment of a woman,
nor is there in such a victory any cause for joy, yet I shall be
lauded for having got rid of an abandoned wretch, and exacted
from her well-merited punishment; and I shall be delighted to
have sated my burning desire of vengeance, and rendered full
atonement to the ashes of my countrymen.

THE WANT OF A GRAVE.
Æn. ii. 646.

Facilis jactura sepulchri est.

To be without a grave matters little.

DANGER.
Æn. ii. 709.

Quo res cunque cadent, unum et commune periclum.

Whatever may be our lot, there is one common danger.

PACES UNEQUAL.
Æn. ii. 724.

Non passibus æquis.

And with unequal paces tript along.

A SPECTRE.
Æn. ii. 771.

Quærenti, et tectis urbis sine fine furenti,
Infelix simulacrum, atque ipsius umbra Creüsæ
Visa mihi ante oculos, et notâ major imago.
Obstupui, steteruntque comæ et vox faucibus hæsit.

While I was searching and rushing unceasingly through the houses of the city, the unhappy spectre and shade of Creusa herself rose before my eyes and her image larger than life. I was astonished, my hair stood on end, and my tongue clung to the roof of my mouth.

GOLD.

Æn. iii. 57.

Quid non mortalia pectora cogis,
Auri sacra fames !

Cursed craving for gold, what dost thou not force mortals to perpetrate.

Anget, in his " Pistolles, ou l'injure du siècle," one of his satires, says :—
" Si le diable étoit or, il deviendroit monnoie."

ADMONITIONS.

Æn. iii. 188.

Moniti meliora sequamur.

Admonished, let us follow better counsels.

THE SIBYL.

Æn. iii. 443.

Insanam vatem adspicies, quæ rupe sub imâ
Fata canit, foliisque notas et nomina mandat.
Quæcumque in foliis descripsit carmina virgo,
Digerit in numerum, atque antro seclusa relinquit.
Illa manent immota locis, neque ab ordine cedunt.
Verum eadem, verso tenuis cum cardine ventus
Impulit, et teneras turbavit janua frondes,
Nunquam deinde cavo volitantia prendere saxo,
Nec revocare situs, aut jungere carmina curat.
Inconsulti abeunt, sedemque odere Sibyllæ.

Thou shalt behold a wild, raving prophetess, who, in a deep cavern, reveals the decrees of fate and commits her oracles to leaves. Whatever oracular responses she has placed on leaves, she arranges in order, and leaves them shut up in her cave. They remain immovable, nor issue from the order in which they have been placed. And yet these same, when, on the hinge being turned, a slight current of air has set them in motion, and the opening door hath disturbed the tender leaves, she never afterwards cares to arrest, as they flutter through the hollow cave, or to restore their former positions, nor connect once more her predictions. They, who apply, depart in this way without a response, and hate the habitation of the Sibyl.

FORTUNE.

Æn. iii. 493.

Vivite felices, quibus est fortuna peracta
Jam sua : nos alia ex aliis in fata vocamur.

Live happy ye, the course of whose fortune is now completely
run ; we are summoned from one fate to another.

ÆTNA.

Æn. iii. 571.

Sed horrificis juxta tonat Ætna ruinis,
Interdumque atram prorumpit ad œthera nubem,
Turbine fumantem piceo et candente favillâ ;
Attollitque globos flammarum, et sidera lambit :
Interdum scopulos avulsaque viscera montis
Erigit eructans, liquefactaque saxa sub auras
Cum gemitu glomerat, fundoque exæstuat imo.

But Ætna thunders close by with frightful crashings, and some-
times bursting, it sends forth a black cloud to the air, smoking
with pitchy whirlwind and glowing ember ; and raises fire-balls,
licking the stars ; sometimes with loud explosions it casts up
rocks and the torn bowels of the mountain ; and with a deep
internal roar, it heaps up melted stones high in air, and boils
violently from its lowest bottom.

A MONSTER.

Æn. iii. 657.

Monstrum horrendum, informe, ingens, cui lumen adem-
tum.
Trunca manum pinus regit, et vestigia firmat.
Lanigeræ comitantur oves : ea sola voluptas,
Solamenque mali.

A horrid monster, misshapen, huge, from whom sight had been
taken away. A pine-tree in his hand, lopped of its branches,
guides and steadies his steps. Woolly sheep accompany him ;
that is the only pleasure and solace for his misfortune.

TRACES OF ANCIENT FLAME.

Æn. iv. 23.

Agnosco veteris vestigia flammæ.
I again feel the flame of love, as I formerly felt it.

The Manes.
Æn. iv. 34.

Id cinerem aut Manes credis curare sepultos ?

Do you think that the ashes of the dead, or the manes laid at
rest in the tomb, care for that ?

Love.
Æn. iv. 67.

Tacitum vivit sub pectore vulnus.

The hidden wound keeps rankling in the breast.

Love.
Æn. iv. 73.

Hæret lateri lethalis arundo.

The fatal dart sticks in her side.

Ascanius.
Æn. iv. 156.

At puer Ascanius mediis in vallibus acri
Gaudet equo ; jamque hos cursu, jam præterit illos :
Spumantemque dari pecora inter inertia votis
Optat aprum, aut fulvum descendere monte leonem.

But the boy Ascanius, in the midst of the valley, delights in
his spirited steed ; and passes now these, now those in the course,
and wishes a foaming boar to be given to his prayers amid the un-
warlike herds, or that a tawny lion should descend from the
mountain.

Beautiful Description of Fame.
Æn. iv. 173.

Extemplo Libyæ magnas it Fama per urbes :
Fama malum, quo non aliud velocius ullum ;
Mobilitate viget, viresque acquirit eundo :
Parva metu primo ; mox sese attollit in auras,
Ingrediturque solo, et caput inter nubila condit.
Illam Terra parens, irâ irritata deorum,
Extremam, ut perhibent, Cœo Enceladoque sororem
Progenuit, pedibus celerem et pernicibus alis.
Monstrum horrendum, ingens ; cui, quot sunt corpore
    plumæ,
Tot vigiles oculi subter, mirabile dictu,

Tot linguæ, totidem ora sonant, tot subrigit aures.
Nocte volat cœli medio terræque, per umbram
Stridens, nec dulci declinat lumina somno.
Luce sedet custos aut summi culmine tecti,
Turribus aut altis, et magnas territat urbes ;
Tam ficti praviquc tenax, quam nuntia veri.

Forthwith a Rumour passes through the mighty cities of Libya :
rumour, an evil, than which there is no greater ; she flourishes
by her very activity, and gains strength as she moves along ;
small at first through fear ; by and by she raises herself into the
air, stalking upon the ground, and at the same time hiding her
head among the clouds. Parent Earth, incensed at the anger of
the gods, brought her forth the youngest sister, as they say, to
Cœus and Enceladus, quick in feet and wings. A monster, hor-
rible and huge, to whom, as many feathers as there are upon her
body, so many sleepless eyes are there beneath, wonderful to be
said, so many tongues, so many mouths babble forth, so many
ears she pricks up. By night she flies midway between heaven
and earth through the gloom, with a rushing sound of her pinions,
nor does she close her eyes in sweet sleep. By day, she sits as a
spy, either on the top of some lofty house or some high tower,
terrifying mighty cities : as tenacious of what is false and wicked
as an announcer of what is true.

To Choose the Softest Hours.
Æn. iv. 291.

Sese interea, quando optima Dido
Nesciat, et tantos rumpi non speret amores,
Tentaturum aditus, et quæ mollissima fandi
Tempora, quis rebus dexter modus.

That he meanwhile, since the generous Dido is ignorant of what
is passing, and does not imagine that such love can be broken,
will try gentle avenues of approach to her feelings, and what may
be the most fitting moments for addressing her ; what mode of
proceeding may be most favourable.

Jealousy.
Æn. iv. 296.

At regina dolos (quis fallere possit amantem ?)
Præsensit, motusque excepit prima futuros ;
Omnia tuta timens.

But the queen had a presentiment of their hidden projects, (for
who can deceive a lover ?) and was the first to discover their in-
tended movements, fearing all things, though they seemed to be

A Hardened Wretch.
Æn. iv. 365.

Nec tibi diva parens, generis nec Dardanus auctor,
Perfide ; sed duris genuit te cautibus horrens
Caucasus, Hyrcanæque admôrunt ubera tigres.

No goddess was thy mother nor Dardanus thy forefather, thou
traitor; but Caucasus, in horror drest with its flinty rocks, gave
thee being, and the Hyrcanian tigress gave thee suck.

Faithlessness.
Æn. iv. 373.

Nusquam tuta fides.
Nowhere is there faith on earth.

Ants.
Æn. iv. 402.

Ac veluti ingentem formicæ farris acervum
Cum populant, hiemis memores, tectoque reponunt ;
It nigrum campis agmen, prædamque per herbas
Convectant calle angusto ; pars grandia trudunt
Obnixæ frumenta humeris ; pars agmina cogunt,
Castigantque moras : opere omnis semita fervet.

As when ants plunder a large heap of grain, mindful of winter,
and lay it up in their nests; the black column issues into the fields,
carrying their booty through the grass in a narrow track ; some,
struggling, push forward with their shoulders large piles of corn ;
others keep together the column of march and chastise the dila-
tory : the whole path glows with industrious labour.

Love.
Æn. iv. 412.

Improbe amor, quid non mortalia pectora cogis.
All-powerful Love, to what dost thou not force mortals?

Description of Night.
Æn. iv. 522.

Nox erat, et placidum carpebant fessa soporem
Corpora per terras, sylvæque et sæva quiêrant
Æquora : cum medio volvuntur sidera lapsu,
Cum tacet omnis ager, pecudes, pictæque volucres,

Quæque lacus late liquidos, quæque aspera dumis
Rura tenent, somno positæ sub nocte silenti
Lenibant curas, et corda oblita laborum.

It was night, and weary mortals were enjoying quiet rest on
earth, the woods and murmuring seas were still; it was when the
stars were rolling in mid-course, when the whole country was
silent, cattle and parti-coloured birds, both those which occupy
the liquid lakes, and those which haunt the fields rough with
bushes; buried in sleep during the silent night, they were lulling
to rest their cares, and their hearts were now forgetful of toils.

This is in imitation of Apollonius Rhodius (Argon. iv. 1058) :—

Στρευγομένοις δ᾽ ἀν᾽ ὅμιλον ἐπήλυθεν εὐήτειρα
Νὺξ ἔργων ἀνδρεσσι, κατευκήλησε δὲ πᾶσιν
Γᾶιαν ὅμως·

"Sleep-bringing night had spread itself over the crowds of weary men,
and had given rest to the whole earth."

Milton ("Paradise Regained," i., at the end) :—

"Now began
Night with her sullen wings to double-shade
The desert; fowls in their clay nests were couch'd,
And now wild beasts came forth, the woods to roam."

WOMAN.
Æn. iv. 569.

Eia age, rumpe moras. Varium et mutabile semper
Fœmina.

Come, away! break through all delays; woman is a fickle and
changeful thing.

END OF LIFE.
Æn. iv. 653.

Vixi et, quem dederat cursum fortuna, peregi;
Et nunc magna mei sub terras ibit imago.

I have lived and finished the course which fortune had given
me; now a mighty fame of me shall spread through the earth.

AN ANNIVERSARY OF A FATHER'S DEATH.
Æn. v. 49.

Adest, quem semper acerbum,
Semper honoratum, (sic dî voluistis,) habebo.

The day is at hand, which I shall reckon for ever sad, for ever
dear, so it has willed the gods.

RAINBOW.

Æn. v. 88.

Ceu nubibus arcus
Mille jacit varios adverso sole colores.

As the bow in the clouds sends forth a thousand varied colours from the reflection of the sun's rays.

FLY DANGER.

Æn. v. 163.

Littus ama, altum alii teneant.

Keep close to the shore; let others launch into the main.

THE DOVE.

Æn. v. 213.

Qualis speluncâ subito commota columba,
Cui domus et dulces latebroso in pumice nidi,
Fertur in arva volans, plausumque exterrita pennis
Dat tecto ingentem : mox aëre lapsa quieto
Radit iter liquidum, celeres neque commovet alas.

As the dove, suddenly roused from her covert, whose home and beloved nest are in some rock full of hiding-places, rushes flying into the fields, and scared from her abode, gives forth a loud flapping with her wings; by and by, gliding through the still air, she skims along her liquid way nor moves her swift wings.

A CONQUEROR.

Æn. v. 229.

Hi proprium decus, et partum indignantur honorem,
Ni teneant ; vitamque volunt pro laude pacisci.
Hos successus alit : possunt, quia posse videntur.

These are indignant should they not retain their own glory and the honours already in their grasp, willing to barter life for fame. Those success feeds with fresh hopes ; they are able to conquer, because they seem to be able.

NEXT, BUT AT A LONG INTERVAL.

Æn. v. 320.

Longo sed proximus intervallo.

Next, but at a long interval.

BEAUTY.
Æn. v. 344.

Gratior et pulchro veniens in corpore virtus.

And merit appearing more beautiful in a beauteous form.

A BOXER.
Æn. v. 479.

Durosque reductâ

Libravit dextrâ media inter cornua cæstus
Arduus, effractoque illisit in ossa cerebro.
Sternitur, exanimisque tremens procumbit humi bos.

Having drawn back his right hand, he levelled from on high his hard gauntlet between the horns, and drove it into the bones, dashing the brains out; the ox, quivering, falls lifeless.

TO RETIRE FROM ACTIVE LIFE.
Æn. v. 484.

Hic victor cæstus artemque repono.

From this time I lay aside my gauntlets and renounce my profession.

PATIENCE.
Æn. v. 709.

Quo fata trahunt retrahuntque, sequamur.
Quicquid erit, superanda omnis fortuna ferendo est.

Let us follow whithersoever the Fates lead us. Whatever shall befall us, every kind of fortune is to be surmounted by patiently enduring it.

COWARDS.
Æn. v. 750.

Transscribunt urbi matres, populumque volentem
Deponunt, animos nil magnæ laudis egentes.

They enrol mothers for the city, and set apart the people that wished it, souls that dare not hazard life for future fame.

Euripides (Fr. Archel. 9) says :—

Ἐμὲ δ᾽ ἄρ᾽ οὐ

Μοχθεῖν δίκαιον ; τίς δ᾽ ἄμοχθος εὐκλεής ;
Τίς τῶν μεγίστων δειλὸς ὢν ὠρέξατο.

"Is it not right for me to endure toils? Without toils, what man has become glorious? Who, that is a craven, has reached the highest fame?"

VALOUR.
Æn. v. 754.

Exigui numero, sed bello vivida virtus.

Few in number, but ardent for war.

SEA TREACHEROUS.
Æn. v. 848.

Mene salis placidi vultum fluctusque quietos
Ignorare jubes ? mene huic confidere monstro ?

**Dost thou bid me be ignorant of the aspect of the calm sea and
of its quiet waters ? Shall I trust this treacherous appearance ?**

A PLAYTHING TO THE WINDS.
Æn. vi. 75.

Ludibria ventis.

To become the plaything of the winds.

FROWNS OF FORTUNE.
Æn. vi. 95.

Tu ne cede malis ; sed contra audentior ito,
Quâ tua te fortuna sinet.

**Do not yield to misfortunes, but advance against them with a
bolder front, in whatever way fortune shall permit thee.**

TRUTH CONCEALED.
Æn. vi. 100.

Obscuris vera involvens.

Some truths reveal'd, in terms involv'd the rest.

PLUTO'S PORTALS ALWAYS OPEN.
Æn. vi. 124.

Talibus orabat dictis, arasque tenebat ;
Cum sic orsa loqui vates : Sate sanguine divûm,
Tros Anchisiada, facilis descensus Averno ;
Noctes atque dies patet atri janua Ditis :
Sed revocare gradum, superasque evadere ad auras,
Hoc opus, hic labor est. Pauci, quos æquus amavit
Jupiter, aut ardens evexit ad æthera virtus,
Dîs geniti, potuere.

**He was entreating thus and kept clinging to the horns of the
altar, when the prophetess thus began to speak : O thou that art**

sprung from the blood of the gods, Trojan son of Anchises, the descent to the world below is easy, the gate of gloomy Pluto lies open night and day, but to retrace one's steps and reach again the upper air, this is the real labour, this the true difficulty. A few, whom the favour of heaven or brilliant merit hath exalted to the skies, sons of the gods, have been able to effect it.

THE BRANCH OF GOLD.
Æn. vi. 142.

Hoc sibi pulchra suum ferri Proserpina munus
Instituit. Primo avulso, non deficit alter
Aureus ; et simili frondescit virga metallo.

The fair Proserpine has ordained that this gift be brought as one peculiarly dear. One branch being plucked, another golden one occupies its place, and a twig of similar metal puts forth leaves.

THE PROFANE.
Æn. vi. 258.

Procul o, procul este profani.

Far hence be souls profane!

NOW THERE IS NEED OF FIRMNESS.
Æn. vi. 261.

Nunc animis opus, Ænea, nunc pectore firmo.

Now there is need of courage, Æneas, now of a firm purpose.

SHADES BELOW.
Æn. vi. 263.

Di quibus imperium est animarum, umbræque silentes,
Et Chaos, et Phlegethon, loca nocte tacentia late,
Sit mihi fas audita loqui : sit, numine vestro,
Pandere res altâ terrâ et caligine mersas.
Ibant obscuri solâ sub nocte per umbram,
Perque domos Ditis vacuas, et inania regna :
Quale per incertam lunam sub luce malignâ
Est iter in sylvis, ubi cœlum condidit umbrâ
Jupiter, et rebus nox abstulit atra colorem.

Ye gods, who preside over the souls of the dead, and silent shades, Chaos and Phlegethon, places wrapped in silent night, let me be allowed to tell what I have heard ; may it be allowed me, by your divine permission, to disclose things hidden in the depth of the earth and in darkness. They moved along, amidst the gloom of night's dark pall, through the empty halls of Pluto and solitary kingdom ; as men journey in woods by the unsteady rays of the moon, beneath the faint and glimmering light when Jupiter obscures the heaven in clouds, and gloomy night has robbed surrounding objects of their hue.

THE VESTIBULE OF PLUTO'S REALMS.
Æn. vi. 273.

Vestibulum ante ipsum primisque in faucibus Orci
Luctus et ultrices posuere cubilia Curæ ;
Pallentesque habitant Morbi, tristisque Senectus,
Et Metus, et malesuada Fames, ac turpis Egestas,
Terribiles visu formæ ; Letumque, Laboæque ;
Tum consanguineus Leti Sopor ; et mala mentis
Gaudia ; mortiferumque adverso in limine Bellum ;
Ferreique Eumenidum thalami, et Discordia demens,
Vipereum crinem vittis inexa cruentis.

Before the porch itself, within the jaws of Hell, Grief and avenging Cares have placed their couches; there dwell pale Diseases, sorrowing Age, Despondency, and ill-prompting Hunger, and loathsome Want, shapes terrible to see : Death, and Labour, and Sleep, twin-born with Death, and the criminal Lusts of the heart, and death-bringing War near the opening door ; and the iron bed-chambers of the Furies and maddening Discord, her viper's tresses bound up with bloody fillets.

OLD AGE.
Æn. vi. 304.

Jam senior, sed cruda deo viridisque senectus.

Though advanced in years, the god has a fresh and green old age.

LEAVES IN AUTUMN.
Æn. vi. 309.

Quam multa in sylvis autumni frigore primo
Lapsa cadunt folia ; aut ad terram gurgite ab alto
Quam multæ glomerantur aves, ubi frigidus annus
Trans pontum fugat, et terris immittit apricis.

Thick as leaves that fall in the woods on the first cold of autumn, or dense as birds that flock to the land from the troubled deep, when frigid winter sends them across the sea to sunny climes.

See (Fr.) Leaves.

SHADES BELOW.
Æn. vi. 322.

Anchisâ generate, deûm certissima proles,
Cocyti stagna vides, Stygiamque paludem,

Dî cujus jurare timent, et fallere numen.
Hæc omnis, quam cernis, inops inhumataque turba est:
Portitor ille, Charon : hi, quos vehit unda, sepulti.
Nec ripas datur horrendas, nec rauca fluenta
Transportare prius, quam sedibus ossa quiêrunt.
Centum errant annos, volitantque hæc litora circum :
Tum demum admissi stagna exoptata revisunt.

Son of Anchises, undoubted offspring of the gods, thou seest the streams of Cocytus and Stygian marsh, whose divinity the gods fear to swear by, and fail in their oath. All that thou seest, is a wretched unburied crowd : yon ferryman, is Charon ; those, who are being ferried across, have obtained the rites of burial : for it is not allowed to carry them across those fearful banks or hoarse-sounding waters before their bones have rested in the grave ; they wander about for one hundred years and hover about these shores : then at length being admitted into the boat, they behold the much-wished-for waters.

FATES INEXORABLE.
Æn. vi. 376.

Desine fata deûm flecti sperare precando.

Cease to think that the fixed decrees of heaven can be changed by prayers.

RETRIBUTIVE JUSTICE.
Æn. vi. 620.

" Discite justitiam moniti, et non temnere divos."
Vendidit hic auro patriam.

Warned by my fate, learn to observe justice and not to despise the gods. This man sold his country for gold.

ELYSIUM.
Æn. vi. 638.

Devenere locos lætos, et amœna vireta
Fortunatorum nemorum, sedesque beatas.
Largior hic campos æther et lumine vestit
Purpureo ; solemque suum, sua sidera nôrunt.
Pars in gramineis exercent membra palæstris ;
Contendunt ludo, et fulvâ luctantur arenâ :
Pars pedibus plaudunt choreas, et carmina dicunt.

They reached pleasant spots, the delightful verdure of the Fortunate groves, and abodes of the happy. A freer and purer sky here clothes the fields with resplendent light ; they enjoy their own sun, their own stars. Some are exercising their limbs in grassy plains, are contending in play and struggling on the yellow sand: some are striking the ground with their feet in the loud resounding dance, and singing songs.

Milton at the end of "Comus" thus beautifully expresses the idea :—

> " To the ocean now I fly,
> And these happy climes; that lie
> Where day never shuts his eye."

See (Gr., Fr.) Elysium.

ABODES OF THE BLESSED.

Æn. vi. 656.

Conspicit ecce alios dextrâ lævâque per herbam
Vescentes, lætumque choro pæana canentes,
Inter odoratum lauri nemus ; unde superne
Plurimus Eridani per sylvam volvitur amnis.
Hic manus, ob patriam pugnando vulnera passi,
Quique sacerdotes casti, dum vita manebat,
Quique pii vates, et Phœbo digna locuti.

Behold he sees some right and left feasting on the grass, and singing joyfully in chorus, beneath a sweet-smelling laurel grove ; where mighty Po rolls through a wood from the world above. Here are found bands of those who have suffered wounds fighting for their country, and who were priests of unblemished life while they lived, and who were holy bards delivering songs worthy of Apollo.

INVENTORS.

Æn. vi. 663.

Inventas aut qui vitam excoluere per artes,
Quique sui memores alios fecere merendo.

Or those who have improved life by their inventions, and those who, by deserving well, have handed their names down to posterity.

BEES.

Æn. vi. 707.

Ac veluti in pratis, ubi apes æstate serenâ
Floribus incidunt variis, et candida circum
Lilia funduntur ; strepit omnis murmure campus.

As in meadows, where bees, on a calm summer's day, light on various flowers and flutter round white lilies; the whole field resounds with their busy hum.

MIND.

Æn. vi. 727.

Mens agitat molem, et magno se corpore miscet.

The thinking principle moves the whole mass and mingles itself
with the great body.

OUR OWN BURDEN MUST BE BORNE.
Æn. vi. 743.

Quisque suos patimur Manes.

We endure each the burden of punishment imposed upon our
Manes in the world below.

Apolloderus (Fr. Com. Gr. p. 1112, M.) says :—

Χαλεπὸν τύχη 'στὶ πρᾶγμα, χαλεπόν· ἀλλὰ δεῖ
Αὐτὴν φέρειν κατὰ τρόπον ὥσπερ φορτίον.

" Fortune is a sad, sad thing ; but we must bear her as we best may as a
burden."

Galatians (vi. 5) :— ·

" For every man shall bear his own burden."

MIGHTY EMPIRE.
Æn. vi. 794.

Super et Garamantas et Indos
Proferet imperium.

He shall extend his sway over the Garamantes and Indians.

NUMA.
Æn. vi. 812.

Curibus parvis et paupere terrâ
Missus in imperium magnum.

Sent from humble cares and a poor estate to a great empire.

FABIUS.
Æn. vi. 844.

Quo fessum rapitis, Fabii ? tu Maximus ille es,
Unus qui nobis cunctando restituis rem.

Whither, ye Fabii, do you hurry me, exhausted? Thou art
that Maximus, greatest of the name, who alone by delays re-
storest our empire.

DESCRIPTION OF ROMANS.
Æn. vi. 847.

Excudent alii spirantia mollius æra,
Credo equidem, vivos ducent de marmore vultus ;
Orabunt causas melius, coelique meatus
Describent radio, et surgentia sidera dicent :

Tu regere imperio populos, Romane, memento ;
Hæ tibi erunt artes ; pacisque imponere morem,
Parcere subjectis, et debellare superbos.

Others, I do not doubt, will mould the breathing brass more like to nature, draw features more instinct with life from marble, plead causes with more eloquence, describe better with the rod the movements in the heavens, and explain more clearly the rising of the stars, do thou, Roman, rule nations with firmness : such be thy distinctive character, and to impose terms of peace, to spare the vanquished, and trample on the proud.

MARCELLUS.

Æn. vi. 678.

Heu pietas, heu prisca fides, invictaque bello
Dextera ! non illi quisquam se impune tulisset
Obvius armato, seu cum pedes iret in hostem,
Seu spumantis equi foderet calcaribus armos.
Heu miscrande puer ! si quâ Fata aspera rumpas,
Tu Marcellus eris.   Manibus date lilia plenis :
Purpureos spargam flores, animamque nepotis
His saltem accumulem donis, et fungar inani
Munere.

What piety shall be his ! what integrity like that of the good old times and unyielding bravery ! No antagonist could have met him in arms with impunity, whether advancing on foot or on horseback. Alas, boy to be pitied, if in any way thou canst break through the rigid decrees of fate, thou shalt be Marcellus. Scatter lilies in handfuls ; let me scatter the dark-hued flowers on his tomb, heap up these gifts at least to the shade of my descendant and discharge an unavailing duty.

SLEEP.

Æn. vi. 893.

Sunt geminæ somni portæ : quarum altera fertur
Cornea, quâ veris facilis datur exitus umbris :
Altera candenti perfecta nitens elephanto ;
Sed falsa ad cœlum mittunt insomnia Manes.

There are two gates to the palace of sleep : the one said to be formed of horn, gives an easy exit to true visions : the other, brightly shining, is skilfully wrought with white ivory, but through this the Manes send false dreams to the world above.

So Homer (Odyss. xix. 560) :—

ξεῖν', ἦτοι μὲν ὄνειροι ἀμήχανοι ἀκριτόμυθοι
γίγνοντ', οὐδέ τι πάντα τελείεται ἀνθρώποισιν.

δοιαὶ γάρ τε πύλαι ἀμενηνῶν εἰσὶν ὀνείρων·
αἱ μὲν γὰρ κερδεσσι τετεύχαται, αἱ δ᾽ ἐλέφαντι·
τῶν οἱ μέν κ᾽ ἔλθωσι διὰ πριστοῦ ἐλέφαντος,
οἱ ῥ᾽ ἐλεφαίρονται, ἔπε᾽ ἀκράαντα φέροντες·
οἱ δὲ διὰ ξεστῶν κεράων ἔλθωσι θύραζε,
οἱ ῥ᾽ ἔτυμα κραίνουσι, βροτῶν ὅτε κέν τις ἴδηται.

"Stranger, dreams are certainly of difficult and uncertain interpretation, nor do men find them always accomplished. For there are two gates, through which issue dreams of doubtful import. The one is formed of horn, and the other of ivory; those of them that come through smooth ivory deceive with empty hopes, bearing promises never to be accomplished; others again that issue out from polished horn, predict what is true, whenever any mortal shall see them."

Shakespeare ("Romeo and Juliet," act i. sc. 4) says :—

"I talk of dreams ;
Which are the children of an idle brain,
Begot of nothing but vain fantasy ;
Which is as thin of substance as the air ;
And more inconstant than the wind, which woos
Even now the frozen bosom of the north,
And, being anger'd, puffs away from thence,
Turns his face to the dew-dropping south."

DETERMINATION.
Æn. vii. 312.

Flectere si nequeo superos, Acheronta movebo.

If I am unable to bend the gods above, I shall try to move the gods below.

CAMILLA.
Æn. vii. 803.

Hos super advenit Volscâ de gente Camilla,
Agmen agens equitum, et florentes ære catervas,
Bellatrix : non illa colo calathisve Minervæ
Fœmineas assueta manus ; sed prœlia virgo
Dura pati, cursuque pedum prævertere ventos.

With those comes Camilla of the Volscian nation, leading a squadron of cavalry and bands armed in resplendent brass, a heroine ; with hands unused to the spindle and housewife's basket, but, though a virgin, inured to the hardships of war and to outstrip the wind in speed.

REFLECTIONS OF THE SUN'S RAYS.
Æn. viii. 22.

Sicut aquæ tremulum labris ubi lumen aënis
Sole repercussum, aut radiantis imagine lunæ,
Omnia pervolitat late loca, jamque sub auras
Erigitur, summique ferit laquearia tecti.

As when the trembling light of the water in brasen cauldrons, reflected by the sun's rays or by the bright moon, penetrates all the space around, is raised aloft and strikes the fretted ceilings of the lofty palace.

This seems to be an imitation of Apollonius Rhodius (iii. 755) :—

Ἠελίου ὡς τίς τε δόμοις ἐνιπάλλεται αἴγλη
Ὕδατος ἐξανιοῦσα, τὸ δὴ νέον ἠὲ λέβητι,
Ἠέ που ἐν γαυλῷ κέχυται· ἡ δ' ἔνθα καὶ ἔνθα
Ὠκείῃ στροφάλιγγι τινάσσεται αἰσσουσα.

" As the ray of the sun is reflected in some palace, issuing from water freshly poured from a cauldron or else some milk-pail—darting; here and there it is moved rapidly with swift whirling."

LIGHTNING.
Æn. viii. 426.

His informatum manibus jam parte politâ
Fulmen erat ; toto genitor quæ plurima cœlo
Dejicit in terras ; pars imperfecta manebat.
Tres imbris torti radios, tres nubis aquosæ
Addiderant, rutuli tres ignis, et alitis austri.
Fulgores nunc horrificos, sonitumque, metumque
Miscebant operi, flammisque sequacibus iras.

These had in hand an unfinished thunderbolt, part being already polished off, of the kind which father Jupiter hurls in numbers on the earth from every region of the sky ; part remained unfinished. They had just added three shafts of hail, three of the rain-cloud, three of gleaming fire, and three of the storm-winged southern blast. They were now intermingling with the work terror-inspiring gleamings and uproar and fear, and the wrath of heaven with its vengeful flames.

Shakespeare (" King Lear," act iv. sc. 7) says :—

" To stand against the deep dread-bolted thunder,
In the most terrible and nimble stroke
Of quick, cross lightnings."

A FATHER'S PRAYER FOR HIS SON.
Æn. viii. 572.

At vos, o superi, et divum tu maxime rector
Jupiter, Arcadii, quæso, miserescite regis,
Et patrias audite preces : Si numina vestra
Incolumem Pallanta mihi, si fata reservant,
Si visurus eum vivo, et venturus in unum :
Vitam oro ; patiar quemvis durare laborem.
Sin aliquem infandum casum, Fortuna, minaris :

Nunc, o, nunc liceat crudelem abrumpere vitam,
Dum curæ ambiguæ, dum spes incerta futuri.
Dum te, care puer, mea sera et sola voluptas,
Complexu teneo ; gravior ne nuntius aures
Vulneret.

Ye gods, and thou Jupiter, mightiest of the gods, I pray thee,
have pity on the Arcadian king, and listen to a father's prayers;
if your divine pleasure, if the fates reserve my Pallas for me, if I
am again to behold and meet him, I beg for life, let me sustain
the worst of pain. But if thou, O Fortune, threatenest some sad
bereavement, now, oh now, let me break off the tie that binds me
to an unhappy existence, while my cares still hang in suspense,
while the hope of the future is uncertain, while I strain thee to
my bosom, my dear boy, the only solace of my declining years,
lest too painful news should wound my ears.

A Horse Galloping.

Æn. viii. 595.

It clamor, et agmine facto
Quadrupedante putrem sonitu quatit ungula campum.

A shout arises, and in united band the hoof shakes the dusty
plain with the sound of the courser's tramp.

This line is supposed to imitate the sound of cavalry in quick motion.

Time.

Æn. ix. 6.

Quod optanti divûm promittere nemo
Auderet, volvenda dies en attulit ultro.

What none of the gods dared to promise to thy prayers, lo, time,
as it rolls on, has bestowed of its own accord.

Pindar (Fr. Incert. 50) says :—

Ἄνακτα τῶν πάντων ὑπερβάλλοντα χρόνον μακάρων.

"Time that rules all, superior even to the gods."

Man makes a God of his Desire.

Æn. ix. 184.

Nisus ait : Dîne hunc ardorem mentibus addunt,
Euryale ? an sua cuique deus fit dira cupido.

Nisus says: Euryalus, do the gods inspire thee with this
warmth ? Or is that, which one earnestly desires, to be regarded
as a divine inspiration ?

Filial Piety.

Æn. ix. 280.

Contra quem talia fatur
Euryalus : Me nulla dies tam fortibus ausis
Dissimilem arguerit ; tantum : fortuna, secunda
Aut adversa, cadat. Sed te super omnia dona
Unum oro : genitrix Priami de gente vetustâ
Est mihi, quam miseram tenuit non Ilia tellus
Mecum excedentem, non mœnia regis Acestæ.
Hanc ego nunc, ignaram hujus quodcunque pericli est,
Inque salutatam linquo : nox et tua testis
Dextera, quod nequeam lacrymas perferre parentis.
At tu, oro, solare inopem, et succurre relictæ.
Hanc sine me spem ferre tui : audentior ibo
In casus omnes. Percussâ mente dederunt
Dardanidæ lacrymas ; ante omnes pulcher Iulus,
Atque animum patriæ strinxit pietatis imago.

To him Euryalus replied : No day of my life shall, I trust, prove me unworthy of an attempt so bold as this ; this I am able to promise, let fortune fall out favourable or unfavourable. But above all I entreat this of thee : Of Priam's royal race my mother came, whom, when I departed, neither Troy nor the walls of king Acestes could detain. Her, now ignorant of this danger, whatever it is, and without taking farewell, I leave. Let the darkness of the night and thy right hand be witness that I am unable to endure the tears of my mother. But I entreat thee, comfort her in want and assist her, whom I leave behind me. Allow me to entertain this hope of thee ; I shall go with more confidence to meet every danger. The Trojans, deeply affected, wept, above all the fair Iulus, and this image of affection for his mother moved his bosom powerfully.

Friendship.

Æn. ix. 427.

Me, me, (adsum, qui feci,) in me convertite ferrum.

Me, me, (here am I, who did it,) turn your weapons against me.

Death of a Young Man.

Æn. ix. 435.

Purpureus veluti cum flos, succisus aratro,
Languescit moriens ; lassove papavera collo
Demisere caput, pluviâ cum forte gravantur.

As some bright flower, cut over by the plough, langu...

ı death, or poppies hang their heads with wearied neck when
ısy are overcharged with rain.

(See Fr.) Young man, death of.

POWER OF POETRY.
Æn. ix. 446.

Fortunati ambo, si quid mea carmina possunt,
Nulla dies unquam memori vos eximet ævo ;
Dum domus Æneæ Capitoli immobile saxum
Accolet, imperiumque pater Romanus habebit.

Happy both, if my poetry can avail anything, no time, however
ng, shall ever blot you out of remembrance, as long as the line
Æneas shall dwell beside the Capitol, and Augustus, the father
his people, shall hold the reins of empire.

COWARDS.
Æn. ix. 617.

O vere Phrygiæ, neque enim Phryges.

O Phrygian women truly, for ye are not Phrygian men.

BY VIRTUE WE GO TO HEAVEN.
Æn. ix. 641.

Macte novâ virtute, puer ; sic itur ad astra.

Go on and grow in valour, O boy! this is the path to im-
ortality.

FORTUNE.
Æn. x. 42.

Speravimus ista,
Dum fortuna fuit.

Such hopes I had indeed, while Heaven was kind.

THE ALL-SUBDUING POWER OF GOD.
Æn. x. 100.

Eo dicente, deûm domus alta silescit,
Et tremefacta solo tellus ; silet arduus æther ;
Tum Zephyri posuere ; premit placida æquora pontus.

As Jupiter spoke, the lofty palace of the gods was hushed in
ence, and the earth trembled to its foundations ; the high
aven gives forth no sound ; the Zephyrs are lulled ; the sea
oves not.

So Homer (Il. i. 528) :—

> Ἦ καὶ κυανέῃσιν ἐπ' ὀφρύσι νεῦσε Κρονίων
> ἀμβρόσιαι δ' ἄρα χαῖται ἐπερρώσαντο ἄνακτος
> κρατὸς ἀπ' ἀθανάτοιο· μέγαν δ' ἐλέλιξεν Ὄλυμπον.

"The son of Saturn spoke and nodded with his dark eyebrows. Then the ambrosial hair streamed down from the head of the immortal king : and he shook the mighty Olympus."

And Milton ("Paradise Lost," iii.) says :—

> "Thus while God spake, ambrosial fragrance fill'd
> All heaven, and in the blessed spirits elect
> Sense of new joy ineffable diffused."

See Catullus (Carm. 64, l. 206.)

THE FATES WILL FIND THEIR WAY.
Æn. x. 111.

Sua cuique exorsa laborem
Fortunamque ferent. Rex Jupiter omnibus idem.
Fata viam invenient.

The deeds of each will bring suffering or success. Jupiter looks with the same eye on all. The fates will find their way.

A GEM.
Æn. x. 134.

Qualis gemma micat, fulvum quæ dividit aurum
Aut collo decus, aut capiti ; vel quale per artem
Inclusum buxo, aut Oricia terebintho
Lucet ebur ; fusos cervix cui lactea crines
Accipit, et molli subnectens circulus auro.

As a gem sparkles, enchased in gold, the ornament of neck or head ; or like ivory inclosed with artistic skill in box-wood or the turpentine wood of Oricus ; his flowing locks hang down upon his ivory neck, while around his brow he wears a band of thin, ductile gold.

FORTUNE FAVOURS THE BOLD.
Æn. x. 284.

Audentes Fortuna juvat.
Fortune befriends the bold.

SHORTNESS OF LIFE LENGTHENED BY VIRTUE.
Æn. x. 467.

Stat sua cuique dies ; breve et irreparabile tempus
Omnibus est vitæ : sed famam extendere factis,
Hoc virtutis opus.

Every one has his allotted time upon earth; a brief and irretrievable space is given to all, but it is virtue's work alone to stretch the narrow space by noble deeds.

Bailey ("Festus") :—

> " We live in deeds, not years ; in thoughts, not breaths ;
> In feelings, not in figures on a dial.
> We should count time by heart-throbs. He most lives
> Who thinks most, feels the noblest, acts the best."

Man Ignorant of Futurity.

Æn. x. 501.

Nescia mens hominum fati sortisque futuræ,
Et servare modum, rebus sublata secundia.

The mind of men is ignorant of fate and future lot, and how to practise moderation, elated by prosperity.

He Dies and Thinks of his Country.

Æn. x. 781.

Sternitur infelix alieno vulnere, cœlumque
Adspicit, et dulces moriens reminiscitur Argos.

Unhappy he falls by a wound intended for another, looking up to heaven, and dying, thinks of his native Argos.

Shortness of Life.

Æn. x. 861.

Rhœbe, diu (res si quâ diu mortalibus ulla est)
Viximus.

O Rhœbus, we have lived too long, if there be anything long with mortals.

A Flower Plucked.

Æn. xi. 68.

Qualem virgineo demessum pollice florem,
Seu mollis violæ, seu languentis hyacinthi ;
Cui neque fulgor adhuc, necdum sua forma recessit ;
Non jam mater alit tellus, viresque ministrat.

Like the flower of a soft violet or languishing hyacinth, plucked by virgin hands, that has not yet lost its brilliant hue nor beauty, nor does its parent earth any longer afford it nurture and give it strength.

Experience.

Æn. xi. 283.

Experto credite, quantus
In clypeum assurgat, quo turbine torqueat hastam.

Believe me, who know by experience, with what might he rise
to his shield, and with what force he hurls his spear.

A DEMAGOGUE.

Æn. xi. 338.

Largus opum, et linguâ melior, sed frigida bello
Dextera, consiliis habitus non futilis auctor,
Seditione potens.

Rich, bold in language, but with a right hand slow in battle
in counsels deemed no trivial adviser, powerful in faction.

FORTUNE SHIFTS THE SCENE.

Æn. xi. 424.

Cur ante tubam tremor occupat artus ?
Multa dies variique labor mutabilis ævi
Rettulit in melius, multos alterna revisens
Lusit, et in solido rursus Fortuna locavit.

Why does fear seize us before the trumpet sounds? Time, and
the changes naturally connected with it, have changed many
things for the better: fortune, from time to time visiting many
has at one moment mocked them, and again placed them on a
firm basis.

MEDICINE PROVOKED THE PAIN.

Æn. xii. 46.

Ægrescitque medendo.

And grows more distempered by the very attempt that is made
to heal.

A VIRGIN.

Æn. xii. 67.

Indum sanguineo veluti violaverit ostro
Si quis ebur ; vel mixta rubent ubi lilia multâ
Alba rosâ : tales virgo dabat ore colores.

As when one has stained the Indian ivory with the blood-red
purple ; or when the white lilies look red, mingled with many
rose : such was the colour which the virgin's face exhibited.

CHANGE OF FORTUNE.

Æn. xii. 153.

Forsan miseros meliora sequentur.

Perhaps a better fate will attend the wretched.

A Royal Sceptre.
Æn. xii. 206.

Ut sceptrum hoc (dextra sceptrum nam forte gerebat)
Nunquam fronde levi fundet virgulta neque umbras,
Cum semel in sylvis, imo de stirpe recisum,
Matre caret, posuitque comas et brachia ferro ;
Olim arbos ; nunc artificis manus ære decoro
Inclusit, patribusque dedit gestare Latinis.

As this sceptre (for his right hand happened to bear a sceptre)
will never henceforth give forth shady branches with rustling
leaves, since the time, when cut down in the forest by its lowest
root, it was separated from the mother-tree, and stripped of its
foliage and twigs by the axe ; once a tree, now the skill of the
artificer has surrounded it with ornamental brass and given it to
be borne by the Latin fathers.

See Hom. Il. i. 234.

Education.
Æn. xii. 435.

Disce, puer, virtutem ex me, verumque laborem ;
Fortunam ex aliis.

Boy, learn from me the lesson of duty and patience under
afflictions, the pursuit of fortune from others.

Whirlwind.
Æn. xii. 451.

Qualis ubi ad terras abrupto sidere nimbus
It mare per medium : miseris, heu, præscia longe
Horrescunt corda agricolis ; dabit ille ruinas
Arboribus, stragemque satis ; ruet omnia late ;
Ante volant, sonitumque ferunt ad littora venti.

As when a storm bursting forth rushes over the sea to land,
the wretched husbandman, alas ! prescient of danger from afar,
shudders : it will uproot the trees and lay low the corn, destroying
all things far and wide : the winds fly before, carrying the sound
to the shores.

Swallows.
Æn. xii. 473.

Nigra velut magnas domini cum divitis ædes
Pervolat, et pennis alta atria lustrat hirundo,
Pabula parva legens, nidisque loquacibus escas ;
Et nunc porticibus vacuis, nunc humida circum
Stagna sonat.

As when the black swallow flies through the great courts
rich lord, traversing the lofty halls, gathering scanty food
nutriment for its chirping young, and now it twitters thr
the empty porticoes, now around the marshy pools.

A HERO.

Æn. xii. 644.

Turnum fugientem hæc terra videbit ?
Usque adeone mori miserum est ? vos o mihi Manes
Este boni : quoniam superis aversa voluntas.
Sancta ad vos anima, atque istius inscia culpæ
Descendam, magnorum haud unquam indignus avor

Shall this land see Turnus flying from his foe ? Is it su
wretched thing to die ? Ye gods of the lower world be propiti
since the gods above are unwilling to save me, I shall go dov
you, a pure spirit, and unsullied with the shame of flight, n
unworthy of my mighty sires.

A BULL FIGHT.

Æn. xii. 715.

Ac velut ingenti Silâ, summove Taburno,
Cum duo conversis inimica in prœlia tauri
Frontibus incurrunt, pavidi cessere magistri ;
Stat pecus omne metu mutum, mussuntque juvencœ.
Quis nemori imperitet, quem tota armenta sequantu
Illi inter sese multâ vi vulnera miscent,
Cornuaque obnixi infigunt, et sanguine largo
Colla armosque lavant ; gemitu nemus omne remugi

As in the lofty mountains of Sila or Taburnus, when two l
rush with hostile fronts to battle, the frightened herdsmen fly
whole herd stand mute with fear, the cows faintly low, doub
who shall command the pasture-ground, which of them the h
shall follow ; they inflict wounds on each other with great f
and struggling, fix their horns in each other, bathing their n
and shoulders in streams of blood ; the whole forest re-ec
with their bellowing.

SUPPLEMENT.

'HE following passages are of a later date; but, as they
ave become "household words," they deserve to be con-
ected with the "Beautiful Thoughts" of classic authors.
have given their origin so far as they have as yet been
ble to be traced; others I have added without being able
› fix the source from which they are derived. I have
› express my obligations to correspondents in that valu-
ble publication, *Notes and Queries*, for tracing the origin
f many of them.

TIMES ARE CHANGED.

Omnia mutantur, nos et mutamur in illis;
Illa vices quasdam res habet, illa suas.

All things are changed, we too are changed with them; the one
us certain changes, the other has its own.

In the "Deliciæ Poetarum Germanorum," i. 685, we have the poems of
atthias Borbonius, and there we find the words in the mouth of Lotharius
who flourished about A.D. 830.

In Pope ("Moral Essays," ep. i. l. 172) we have the same idea:—

"Manners with fortunes, humours turn with climes,
Tenets with books, and principles with times."

TRUTH.

Magna est veritas et prævalebit.
Truth is great and will prevail.

This is found in the Apocrypha (1 Esdras iv. 41):—

'Et desiit loquendo: et omnes populi clamaverunt et dixerunt: 'Magna
v eritas et prævalebit.'"

The Man of one Book.

Homo unius libri.

This expression is said to belong originally to St Thomas Aquir

See Bishop Taylor's "Life of Christ," part ii. s. xii. 1

To do a Deed by the Hand of Another.

Qui facit per alium est perinde ac si faciat per seipsum

He who does a deed by the hand of another is the same as if did it himself.

This is one of the maxims of Boniface VIII., (Sexti Decret. lib. v. tit. de Reg. Jur. c. 72,) derived according to the glossary from the maxim Paulus, (Digest. lib. i. tit. 17 de Div. Reg. Jur. i. 180.) Quod jussu alter solvitur, pro eo est quasi ipsi solutum est.

Love of Truth.

Amicus Plato, amicus Socrates, sed magis amica verita

Plato is my friend, Socrates is my friend, but truth is a frie that I value above both.

The origin of this saying is found in Aristotle Eth. Nicom. c. iv., wh he is disputing against Plato :—

Ἀμφοῖν φίλοιν ὄντοιν, ὅσιον προτιμᾶν τὴν ἀλήθειαν.

See Plato (de Repub. x. c. i. p. 595 B.

A Third Generation.

De male quæsitis gaudet non tertius hæres.

A third heir seldom enjoys property dishonestly got.

These words are found, with a slight variation, in Bellochii Praxis Mor. Theologiæ, de casibus reservatis, &c. Venetiis, 1627, 4to. :—

"Divino judicio permittitur ut tales surreptores rerum sacrarum diu i rebus furtivis non lætentur, sed imo ab aliis nequioribus furibus præi res illis abripiantur, ut de se ipso fassus est ille qui in suis ædibus distichon inscripsit, ut refert.".

So Bonif. lib. de furt. contrectatio, num. 134 in fin. :—

"Congeries lapidum variis constructa rapinia,
Aut uret, aut ruet, aut raptor alter habebit."

Et juxta illud :—

"De rebus male acquisitis, non gaudebit tertius hæres."

And an earlier citation occurs in Walsingham's Hist. Angl. :—

"Quia de male quæsitis vix gaudet tertius hæres
Nec habet eventus sordida præda bonos."

P. 280, ed. Franof. 100:

A Wise Question.

Dimidium scientiæ, prudens quæstio.

A wise questioning is the half-way towards knowledge.

This is found in Bacon, "De Augmentis Scientiarum," lib. v. cap. 116:—

"Prudens interrogatio quasi dimidium scientiæ."

Pleasing Recollection.

Heu ! quanto minus est cum reliquis versari quam tui meminisse.

Alas ! how much less delightful it is to live with those that survive, than it is to cherish a recollection of you.

This is Shenstone's epitaph on Miss Dolmen at the Leasowes.

Moore ("I Saw Thy Form") imitates this idea:—

"To live with them is far less sweet
Than to remember thee."

Unity, Liberty, Charity.

In necessariis unitas, in dubiis libertas, in omnibus caritas.

Unity in things necessary, liberty in what is doubtful, charity in all things.

This is a quotation from Melanchthon, and is found sculptured in stone over a doorway leading into the garden, formerly the residence of Archdeacon Coxe, in the Close at Salisbury.

Thus Passes away the Glory of this World.

Sancte Pater, sic transit gloria mundi.

O Holy Father, thus passes away the glory of the world.

The master of the ceremonies at the Pope's inauguration bears two dried reeds, whereof the one hath on the top a candle to kindle the other, crying aloud unto the Pope.

See Paradinus, Symbola Heroica O. P. et Gabrielis Symeonis de Gallicâ Linguâ in Latinum conversâ. Antv. 1583.

The Scotch.

Præfervidum ingenium Scotorum.

The fiery genius of the Scotch.

This occurs in the Jesuita Vapulans of Andreas Rivetus, a Calvinistic minister and professor of theology at Leyden in the middle of the seventeenth century. The phrase is found in the following passage :—"These books I will in some things no otherwise commend than Andreas Rivetus, professor of Leyden, did the doctrine of Buchanan and Knox : whose rashness he ascribed præfervido Scotorum ingenio et ad audendum prompto." Sir T. Urquhart's Tracts. Edin. 1774, p. 134.

2 s

OUR PREDECESSORS IN LEARNING.

Pereant qui ante nos nostra dixerunt.

May those perish who have anticipated us in our knowledge.

This phrase was used by Ælius Donatus, the commentator on Terence and Virgil, as is stated in the following extract from Jerome's Exposition of Ecclesiastes, i. 9 :—

"Quid est quod fuit? ipsum quod erit. . . . Huic quid simile sententiæ et Comicus ait: Nihil est dictum quod non dictum sit prius (Ter. Eun. Prolog. 41.) Unde præceptor meus Donatus cum ipsum versiculum exponeret ‘ Pereant, inquit, qui ante nos nostra dixerunt.’"

A LITTLE KNOWLEDGE.

Breves haustus in philosophiâ ad Atheismum ducunt, largiores autem reducunt ad Deum.

Small draughts of knowledge lead to Atheism, but larger bring man back to God.

This is a saying of Bacon.

THE DEAD.

De mortuis nil nisi bonum.

Of the dead nothing should be said except what is good.

This is a saying of Solon in Plutarch.

THE VOICE OF THE PEOPLE.

Vox populi, vox Dei.

The voice of the people is the voice of God.

This is No. 97 among the Aphorismi Politici ex Ph. Cominæo per Lambertum Danæum collecti, Lugd. Bat. 1609.

A THIRD SOMETHING.

Tertium quid.

"A third something" produced by the union or collision of two opposite forces.

This saying appears to have originated with the Pythagoreans, who said :—

"Ἄνθρωπος δίπους ἐστί, καὶ ὄρνις καὶ τρίτον ἄλλο.

" Sunt bipes homo et avis et tertium quid."

THE PEOPLE.

Populus vult decipi, decipiatur.

The people wish to be deceived, let it be deceived.

It was Paul IV.'s legate, Cardinal Carafa, that spoke thus of the devout Parisians :—

"Quandoquidem populus decipi vult, decipiatur."

See Matthias Prideaux's " Easy and Compendious Introduction for Reading all Texts of Histories," 6th ed, Oxford, 1682.

SCYLLA AND CHARYBDIS.

Incidis in Scyllam, cupiens vitare Charybdim.

You fall into Scylla, desiring to avoid Charybdis.

This line is from the "Alexandreis" of Philippe Gaultier. The following are the lines :—

> " Nactus equum Darius, rorantia cæde suorum
> Retrogrado fugit arva gradu. Quo tendis inertem,
> Rex periture, fugam? nescis, heu perdite, nescis
> Quem fugias, hostes incurris dum fugis hostem :
> Incidis in Scyllam, cupiens vitare Charybdim."

" Darius, having found a horse, flies away from the fields bedewed with the blood of his men. Whither, O king doomed to die, dost thou fly in so cowardly a way ? Alas ! lost man, thou knowest not whom thou fliest ; thou runnest into the midst of enemies, whilst thou fliest the enemy : thou fallest into Scylla, while thou avoidest Charybdis."

RIDICULE.

Castigat ridendo mores.

He chastises manners by ridicule.

This was improvised by Santeuil for the Harlequin Dominique.

CERTAINTY.

Certum quia impossibile.

It is certain because it is impossible.

This is from the fifth chapter of Tertullian, De carne Christi.

MAN.

Deus aut bestia.

Man is a god or a brute.

This is from Aristotle, Polit. lib. L c. 2.

A HARBOUR OF SAFETY.

Inveni portum ; spes et fortuna valete :
Sat me lusistis, ludite nunc alios.

I have found a harbour ; hope and fortune, farewell ; you have made sufficient sport of me, sport with others now.

This is a version of a Greek epigram in the Anthologia :—

Εἰς τύχην.

Ἐλπὶς καὶ σὺ τύχη μέγα χαίρετε· τὸν λιμέν' εὗρον·
Οὐδὲν ἐμοὶ χ' ὑμῖν· παίζετε τοὺς μετ' ἐμέ·

To Fortune.

" Hope and fortune, a long farewell : I have found a harbour : you and I have no farther dealings : make sport of those with me."

DECEIT.

Nulli fraus tuta latebris. -

Deceit is safe to no one in any lurking place.

This is found in Camerarius, Emblem. cent. ii. 40.

THE UNLEARNED AND LEARNED.

Indocti discant et ament meminisse periti.

The unlearned may here learn, and the learned may reflect on what they knew before.

This is a hexameter verse of Henault, made by him for the motto of his " Abrégé Chronologique de l'Histoire de France."

It is a translation of two lines of Pope (l. 740, 741) " Essay on Criticism:"—

" Content, if hence the unlearn'd their wants may view,
The learn'd reflect on what before they knew."

BOOKS HAVE THEIR FATE.

Terentianus Maurus, Carmen Heroicum, v. 288.

Pro captu lectoris habent sua fata libelli.

Little books have their fates according to the taste of the reader.

This line is found in the didactic poem of Terentianus Maurus :—

" De literis, syllabis, pedibus et metris."

A WICKED ACT.

Permissum fit vile nefas.

A thing forbidden becomes little thought of, when it is allowed.

This is found in the elegies (iii. v. 77) of C. Cornelius Gallus.

TO REJOICE IN CRIME.

O miseri, quorum gaudia crimen habent.

Wretched are those who take pleasure in their crimes.

This is found in Pseudo-Gallus (l. 180) in the collection of six elegies published under the name of C. Cornelius Gallus, by Pomponius Gauricus. (Venice, 1501, 4to.)

DIFFERENT THINGS DELIGHT DIFFERENT PEOPLE.

Diversos diversa juvant, non omnibus annis
Omnia conveniunt.

Different things are required to give pleasure to different tastes ; all things do not suit all ages.

This passage also is found in Pseudo-Gallus (l. 104.)

TO BE IN THE UTMOST MISERY.

Qui jacet in terrâ non habet unde cadat.

He who lies on the ground cannot fall.

This phrase is found in the Liber parabolarum (Opera Moralia, 1654, p. 424) of Alanus de Insulis.

The Abbé de Longuerue gives the following anecdote, in which the expression is used by Charles I. :—

"Un François m'a dit qu'etant à Londres, il avoit un commerce avec la femme d'un des principaux ennemies du roy Charles Ier, qui étoit alors arrêté, mais gardé fort negligemment : ayant appris de cette femme que le dessein étoit arrêté de faire périr le roy sur un échafaud, il en avertit M. de Bellièvre, qui alla sur-le-champ en donner avis à ce prince. On fit attendre longtemps Bellièvre ; enfin le roy vint, et lui dit : 'J'étois à la représentation d'une comédie qui est la plus plaisante chose du monde.' 'Sire,' repondit Bellièvre, 'c'est d'une tragédie qu'il est question.' Et lui ayant vendu compte de tout ce qu'il savoit, le roy répliqua froidement à la proposition de se sauver par un bateau que l'on feroit trouver au-dessous de sa maison :

"Qui jacet in terrà non habet unde cadat.
'Sire,' dit Bellièvre, 'on peut lui faire tomber la tête.' "

Butler ("Hudibras," pt. I. cant. iii. l. 877) has adopted this idea :—

"I am not now in fortune's power :
He that is down can fall no lower."

THE CONCLUSIVE ARGUMENT OF KINGS.
Ultima ratio regum.

The conclusive argument of kings.

Louis XIV. caused these words to be inscribed on his cannon.

JUPITER.
Quem Jupiter vult perdere, prius dementat.

Whom God wishes to destroy, he first deprives of his senses.

In a note on a fragment of Euripides there is the following Greek proverb :—

Ὅταν δὲ Δαίμων ἀνδρὶ πορσύνῃ κακά,
Τὸν νοῦν ἔβλαψε πρῶτον.

"When God is contriving misfortunes for man, He first deprives him of his reason."

See Duport's "Gnomologia Homerica," p. 282. Cantab. 1660. Athenagoras quotes Greek lines, and renders them in Latin, (p. 121.) Oxon. 1682 :—

"At dæmon, homini quum struit aliquid malum,
Pervertit illi primitus mentem suam."

WORDS.
Vox et præterea nihil.

Words and nothing more.

This saying is found in Plutarch's Laconic Apothegms, ("Plutarchi Opera Moralia," ed. Dan. Wyttenbach, vol. i. p. 649.) Philemon Holland has turned it into English thus :—

"Another Laconian having plucked all the feathers off from a nightingale, and seeing what a little body it had, 'Surely,' quoth he, 'thou art all voice, and nothing else.' "

To Stand on the Old Ways.

Stare super antiquas vias.

To stand on the old ways.

This is a sentence of Jeremiah, (vi. 16,) which is often quoted by Lord Bacon in his "Essay on Innovations." It is found in the Vulgate, and is thus rendered in our English version :—"Ask for the old paths, where is the good way and walk therein."

Question Solved.

Solvitur ambulando.

The question is solved by walking.

This is Aldrich's first answer to the ancient sophism of Achilles and the tortoise.

PASSAGES FROM UNKNOWN AUTHORS.

Leisure.

Otium cum dignitate.

Leisure with dignity.

Gentle and Resolute.

Suaviter in modo, fortiter in re.

Gentle in manner, resolute in deed.

This is the motto of Earl Newburgh.

Misery.

Res est sacra miser : noli mea tangere fata :
Sacrilegæ bustis abstinuere manus.

Respect is due to the sufferings of the wretched : do not add to my miserable fate : sacrilegious hands have always spared the tomb.

La Fontaine has imitated this idea with consummate skill :—

"On devient innocent quand on est malheureux."

To Know where you can Find a Thing.

Scire ubi aliquid invenire possis, ea demum maxima pars eruditionis est.

To know where you can find a thing is in reality the best part of learning.

WORDS AND LETTERS.

Vox audita perit, litera scripta manet.

The word, that is heard, passes away, the letter, that is written, remains.

TO BE HIS OWN MASTER.

Alterius non sit, qui suus esse potest.

Let no man be the servant of another who can be his own master.

TO LIVE WELL.

Sat vixit, bene qui vixit spatium brevis ævi :
Ignavi numerant tempore, laude boni.

He has lived long enough, who has lived well for the period of a short life; the slothful count by time, the good by deeds deserving praise.

JUSTICE.

Fiat justitia, ruat cœlum.

Let justice be done, though heaven fall.

LATIN INDEX.

2 T

F

ENGLISH INDEX.

3 A

EDWARD HOWELL, PRINTER, LIVERPOOL.

WORKS BY C. TAIT RAMAGE, LL.D.,

Author of "Beautiful Thoughts from Latin Authors."

I.

THE NOOKS AND BYEWAYS OF ITALY:
Wanderings in Search of its Ancient Remains and Modern Superstitions. Demy 8vo, cloth gilt, price 9s.

II.

BEAUTIFUL THOUGHTS FROM GREEK
AUTHORS: with English Translations and Index. Fcap. 8vo, half bound, price 4s. 6d.

III.

BEAUTIFUL THOUGHTS FROM GERMAN
AND SPANISH AUTHORS: with English Translations and Complete Indexes. Fcap. 8vo, half bound, price 6s.

IV.

BEAUTIFUL THOUGHTS FROM FRENCH
AND ITALIAN AUTHORS: with English Translations and Copious Indexes. Fcap. 8vo, half bound, price 6s.

EDWARD HOWELL, PUBLISHER, LIVERPOOL.